Beside the Troubled Waters

Beside the Troubled Waters

A Black Doctor Remembers Life, Medicine, and Civil Rights in an Alabama Town

Sonnie Wellington Hereford III
and Jack D. Ellis

THE UNIVERSITY OF ALABAMA PRESS
Tuscaloosa

The University of Alabama Press
Tuscaloosa, Alabama 35487-0380
uapress.ua.edu

Hardcover edition published 2011.
Paperback edition published 2014.
eBook edition published 2011.

Typeface: ACaslon

Manufactured in the United States of America
Cover photograph: Dr. Sonnie Wellington Hereford III and six-year-old Sonnie Hereford IV leave
Huntsville's Fifth Avenue Elementary School on September 6, 1963, minutes after being turned
away by state troopers dispatched by Gov. George Wallace. Taken by an anonymous photographer
who sent the print to Dr. Hereford several months after the 1963 integration.
Cover design: Erin Bradley Dangar / Dangar Design

∞
The paper on which this book is printed meets the minimum requirements of American
National Standard for Information Science–Permanence of Paper for Printed Library Materials,
ANSI Z39.48-1984.

Paperback ISBN: 978-0-8173-5789-4

A previous edition of this book has been catalogued by the Library of Congress as follows:
Library of Congress Cataloging-in-Publication Data
Hereford, Sonnie W.
  Beside the troubled waters : a black doctor remembers life, medicine, and civil rights in an
Alabama town / Sonnie Wellington Hereford III and Jack D. Ellis.
    p. : cm.
  Other title: Black doctor remembers life, medicine, and civil rights in an Alabama town
  Includes bibliographical references and index.
  ISBN 978-0-8173-1721-8 (cloth : alk. paper) — ISBN 978-0-8173-8506-4 (electronic)
1. Hereford, Sonnie W. 2. African American physicians—Alabama—Biography. I. Ellis, Jack D.
II. Title. III. Title: Black doctor remembers life, medicine, and civil rights in an Alabama town.
  [DNLM: 1. Hereford, Sonnie W. 2. Physicians—Alabama—Personal Narratives. 3. African
Americans—Alabama—Personal Narratives. 4. Prejudice—Alabama—Personal Narratives.
WZ 100]
R695.H47 2011
610.89'96073—dc22
[B]
                                                                    2010024098

For my wife, Martha Adams Hereford, and for all of my family
—Sonnie Wellington Hereford III

For Joy, Callie, Lyrissa, Nicholas, and Noah
—Jack D. Ellis

Contents

Acknowledgments

I am pleased to acknowledge the assistance of numerous individuals in the preparation of Dr. Hereford's autobiography.

Historian Waymon E. Burke at the Huntsville branch of Calhoun Community College in Decatur, Alabama, who played a key role in helping Hereford produce his 1999 documentary *A Civil Rights Journey,* read an early draft of the manuscript and made many useful suggestions, as did William H. Goodson Jr., a Vanderbilt medical school graduate whose career in psychiatry overlapped Hereford's years of practice in Huntsville and who was familiar with many of the people and events described in the book.

Several other local physicians were willing to share their memories of medical practice in Madison County during the 1950s and 1960s, particularly Richard L. Lester, Milton Booth Peeler, William A. Kates, and the late Virgil M. Howie. I am indebted as well to the late Geneva Drake Whatley, a Meharry nursing graduate of 1944 and widow of the local black physician Harold Fanning Drake (1922–1979), whom I interviewed at her Huntsville home in July 1999.

My former colleague at The University of Alabama in Huntsville (UAH), Andrew J. Dunar, author of several important studies in oral history, supported my application for sabbatical leave in 1997 in order to begin work on Alabama's African American physicians and as chair of the Department of History strongly encouraged my efforts over the years. The staff of UAH's Salmon Library provided constant assistance in my search for materials, including Gary Glover, Linda K. Vaughan, Elizabeth Rose, and Rose Bridgeforth.

My thanks also go to Ranee G. Pruitt, archivist in the Heritage Room of the Huntsville-Madison County Public Library, who helped me locate historic maps of Huntsville, and to Linda Bayer Allen, who served in the Planning Division of the city from 1976 to 2004 and shared her extensive knowledge of streets, historical structures, and locations of black neighborhoods before 1960. Mark H. Yokley, president of GW Jones & Sons, an engineering and land surveying firm that has been producing Huntsville city maps since the nineteenth century, provided computer scans and permission to use the map for 1948.

I especially want to thank Tim L. Pennycuff, assistant professor and university archivist at The University of Alabama at Birmingham (UAB), who from the start has been supportive of my efforts to preserve the oral histories of African American physicians in the state. The UAB Medical Archives and the Lister Hill Library were among the first places I worked as I began to document the largely forgotten role that black doctors have played in Alabama's history during the twentieth century. My thanks also go to A. J. Wright, associate professor and director of the Section on the History of Anesthesia in the Department of Anesthesiology Library of The University of Alabama at Birmingham, who for several years has been providing extensive Web-based documentation on Alabama's black doctors before World War I and who generously shared information with me.

Finally, I express my gratitude for the many excellent suggestions made by the readers who evaluated the manuscript for The University of Alabama Press and for the support and encouragement of the press's staff. As always, I owe a special debt to my wife, Diane M. Ellis, who read the manuscript and made valuable suggestions and whose knowledge of local historic preservation helped me provide an accurate historical context for Hereford's story.

Jack D. Ellis

Beside the Troubled Waters

Introduction

I first met Dr. Sonnie Wellington Hereford III in 1996 at a public screening of amateur film footage that he had made during Huntsville's civil rights demonstrations of the early 1960s. As I learned from the film, Hereford had played an active part in the local sit-in campaign of 1962, which had forced the city to integrate its lunch counters and, soon afterward, its parks and theaters. Next, he had led the drive to end discrimination at Huntsville Hospital, where black patients had previously been relegated to a small, poorly furnished section called the Annex, or Colored Wing.

Then, in September 1963, despite threats against his life, Hereford had held his six-year-old son's hand as they walked up the steps of the Fifth Avenue Elementary School on Governors Drive, where Sonnie Hereford IV became the first black child to integrate the public schools of Alabama. These early victories in the civil rights movement had happened without widespread violence, and they were achieved before President Lyndon B. Johnson had signed the Civil Rights Act of 1964 outlawing discrimination in public facilities.

The film that I watched was at that point a homemade production, but its images of black people marching in the downtown streets, some carrying posters that mocked America's claim to be the defender of freedom against the Soviet Union while denying freedom to its own citizens, were powerful and effective. The irony was especially appropriate for Huntsville, a city that was already forging a new conception of its past. It was one now focused on the exploits of Wernher von Braun and the team of German scientists who had once built rockets for the Third Reich and were now directing America's race to the moon at Marshall Space Flight Center. As this version was to evolve in the years after the moon landings of 1969, the racial discrimination that had once been a central feature of the town's history rated hardly a mention, and any role that black people had played in ending segregation peacefully and thus helping the city prosper as a center for investment and technology seemed largely forgotten.

When I met Hereford, I had only recently taken a position at The University of Alabama in Huntsville and was resuming research in the social history of medicine that I had started while at the University of Delaware. Broadly speaking, my interests focused on African American health care in the South, which in turn had grown out of my work on doctors and public health in pre-1914 France and from my efforts to identify comparative frameworks for illustrating the links between sickness and social inequality. A study of Alabama's black doctors, I believed, would shed light on a larger historical narrative detailing the struggle of African Americans to achieve physical health as well as social equality.

In July 1997, as part of a series of oral histories that I had subsequently begun with black physicians throughout the state, I held the first of many interviews with Hereford. He made himself freely available and had ample time to talk, having by then experienced a long series of problems with the Alabama Board of Medical Examiners that had brought his medical practice to an end. At the time, I knew none of the details of Hereford's troubles, but I indicated that I was willing to discuss them if he wished, especially in light of his belief that his treatment had been unjust and may have been linked to his earlier civil rights activities. It was still painful for him to talk about, however, and I did not press the matter. Eventually, as all hope of being restored to his profession faded, he decided to give his side of the story, which occurred in taped interviews I conducted with him in 2003 and 2004.

Because we lived in the same city, it was easy to schedule our meetings, which offered a rare opportunity for me to explore in depth the background, education, and career of a black doctor. As time went on, I began to see another story unfolding that showed the enormous diversity of the black experience in medicine. It was the story of a man who, against great odds, managed to achieve his childhood dream of becoming a doctor and along the way scored important victories in the struggle for racial justice, only to see his life collapse in ruin. Hereford's recounting of what happened thus provided an intensely personal and human dimension to the history of black doctors in the South.

As was evident in our conversations, Hereford's consciousness had been shaped by his early family life and by the code of hard work and discipline imposed by his parents. His father, one of 26,000 blacks from Alabama who had been drafted during World War I,[1] returned home from France and built his own church, where he served as pastor. North of the city, where the family lived as sharecroppers on a 160-acre plot known as the Buell place, he farmed mostly cotton, paying the absentee owner a fourth of the product. Meanwhile, he rented out his own forty-acre farm to another black sharecropping family, which paid him half the crop because he provided the seed, fertilizer, mules, and plows. That was the typical arrangement. Civil rights leader John Lewis has recalled that in Pike County down in the Wiregrass, where he grew up, "working on half" was the most common form of sharecropping.[2]

Landownership placed Reverend Hereford among a small elite of black farmers, of whom the vast majority lived under the tenant-sharecropping system described in Theodore Rosengarten's classic *All God's Dangers*.[3] That Hereford was an exception testified to his fiercely independent spirit and to his strategy of pooling family funds in order to buy up adjoining acreage over several years.[4] He devised numerous moneymaking schemes to supplement his cotton crop, including a sorghum mill, which he let others use for a portion of the syrup, and a portable hay baler, which could be drawn by a single mule to neighboring farms.[5] As cash dried up during the Depression, he put up his farm as collateral for loans, including one for $1,300 taken out under the New Deal's Emergency Farm Mortgage Act.[6]

Jannie Hereford shared her husband's belief in discipline and hard work and helped oversee the Buell place; among other things, she trimmed and salted the hams and shoulders of hogs killed in the late fall and cooked for the field hands hired during cotton season. Known affectionately as Big Mama, she kept a firm grip on management of the household, which, at the time of Dr. Hereford's birth, included his brother, Thomas, and two great-grandparents, Sonnie and Bettie Hereford, both born in Madison County during slavery times. Jannie Hereford also held the title of Mother of the Church, a term reserved for the most respected members of the congregation and that implied a center of power separate from that of the pastor.[7]

Dr. Hereford talked about his parents, cotton farming during the 1930s and 1940s, and how as a child he had witnessed the flight of black people out of the South. He described the powerful role the black churches had played in the life of the black community and how certain teachers in the city's all-black schools had encouraged him in his desire to learn. The schools themselves, he explained, operated under appalling conditions, plagued by chronic shortages of books and desks and offering little in the way of science education. Councill School, for example, named after the ex-slave who had founded Alabama Agricultural and Mechanical College, had only the barest of laboratory facilities to satisfy his growing curiosity about chemistry and biology.[8]

Among Hereford's most poignant recollections was the dawning of his racial consciousness and what it meant to be black in a white-dominated world. Reminders were everywhere, from segregated water fountains in the downtown stores to the occasional taunts he heard from white children in the nearby mill villages while walking to school. His awakening was one that other civil rights activists from John Lewis to Anne Moody to Melba Pattillo Beals have described.[9] Hereford's reflections enrich this literature of memory, and they help us understand the importance that he and other black children attached to black heroes like Joe Louis and Jesse Owens and especially the black first lieutenant who once visited his ninth-grade class at Councill School wearing the uniform of a Tuskegee airman.

From there, our discussions turned to Hereford's student days at Alabama A&M. The school was within walking distance of his house, and he and his brother, Thomas, would take turns plowing while the other attended class. Although it lacked an arts and sciences division, Alabama A&M offered courses in biology, physics, chemistry, and biochemistry, and Hereford was able to get a sufficient grounding in these to pass the Medical Profile Test and Graduate Record Examination. This earned him admission to Meharry Medical College in Nashville after two years at Alabama A&M. For part of his tuition, he was able to benefit from a 1948 agreement between Meharry and the southern governors, who, as a way of keeping their medical schools all white, had agreed to provide tuition subsidies to Meharry in return for its reserving a set number of places for black medical students from each participating state.[10]

Hereford recounted in detail his experiences at Meharry, which produced the vast majority of black physicians practicing in Alabama.[11] His oral account, supplemented by notes on his course and clinical work, provided insight into the education of an aspiring black doctor during the early 1950s. It told a larger story as well, which was how young people from schools long deprived of funding managed to prove themselves the equal of whites in the field of medicine. While failure rates for Meharry graduates on state licensure board examinations had averaged around 26 percent during the 1920s, that figure dropped as standards improved. By 1946, it stood at 7 percent, as compared with 9.9 percent for candidates from all approved medical schools in the United States and abroad.[12]

After a shaky start, Hereford soon settled in and began making progress, eventually finding work as a lab assistant. This, plus what he earned by helping his brother on the farm during summers, enabled him to finish on schedule at Meharry, where he graduated second in his class. After passing his board examinations, he interned at a small Catholic hospital in Hammond, Indiana, where he met his future wife, a nursing student named Martha Ann Adams, daughter of a Kentucky coal miner.

In 1956, the young doctor returned to Huntsville and opened a practice. As our discussions shifted to these years, he began to paint a richly textured portrait of what medical practice had been like for him in those days. His account of the unsanitary conditions that existed in the Colored Wing of Huntsville Hospital, for example, and the blatant racism that he witnessed on the part of some local doctors shed important light on the treatment of black people in the American health care system during that era.

When Hereford opened his practice, Madison County had a total of forty-three white physicians. They included a large number of young people, but there was also a small group of older practitioners, including eleven who had been born in the nineteenth century. Highly regarded in local social and civic circles, several of them occupied positions of power and influence within the Medical Association of the State of Alabama (known by its ironic acronym MASA) and on the staff of Huntsville Hospital.

On matters of race, the town's doctors exhibited a range of attitudes. By the late 1950s, a handful of the younger ones had begun integrating their waiting rooms; others would have been willing to admit black physicians to the Madison County Medical Society had it not been for the opposition of the more senior practitioners. The latter included a minority that could be described as militant in their segregationist attitudes. In several instances witnessed by Hereford, their conduct reflected a deep contempt for black people, the roots of which lay in a powerful strain of pseudoscientific racism that characterized the state's medical past.[13]

Hereford's exclusion from the all-white Madison County Medical Society denied him any chance to join the American Medical Association (AMA), which required membership in a local affiliate. Earlier in the century, black physicians in the larger cities of Mobile, Montgomery, and Birmingham had created their own organizations, and many black doctors in the state had been active in the National Medical Association (NMA) since its creation in 1895 as an alternative to the AMA. Nevertheless, these organizations did not provide the access to professional growth and opportunities that the white societies afforded.[14]

Adding to Hereford's isolation was the near absence of black colleagues with whom he could consult and who could fill in for him when he needed time off. In 1920, Alabama had just 106 licensed black physicians, which represented only 4.7 percent of all doctors in the state, though blacks constituted 38 percent of the population.[15] By 1950, the number had dropped to 73, reflecting medical flight to the North and the reluctance of newly trained black medical graduates to try their luck in Alabama. Those who did so were clustered in areas that had large numbers of black people, mainly Birmingham, Montgomery, Mobile, and some of the larger towns of the Black Belt counties. While the proportion of white physicians to the white population stood at 1 per 1,072 for the state, the ratio of black doctors to the black population was 1 per 13,605.

Huntsville itself had attracted relatively few black doctors over the years. Between 1879 and 1948 only eleven held degrees from a recognized medical school. The year that Hereford opened his office, there was just one other black physician serving Madison County, a Meharry graduate named Harold Fanning Drake, son of Alabama A&M's president. Yet by 1960 the county's black population stood at 22,000, about 19 percent of the total 117,000 inhabitants.

Hereford talked at length about the demands he faced in being one of only two black doctors in town, and he described in detail the grinding poverty he saw during house calls to black neighborhoods, where decrepit dwellings, overcrowding, lack of pure water, and ignorance of prevention often tested his skills. Some patients he treated for nothing, occasionally charging their medicine to his own pharmacy account. Others paid only minimal fees. His recall of places and events was remarkable and often corroborated by documents that he had saved from his first years of practice.

Although Huntsville's racial atmosphere struck many contemporaries as being less oppressive than elsewhere in the state, it was still a segregated community whose history had many dark chapters, including several lynchings. The presence of ten large cotton mills in the city, such as Lincoln Mills near Hereford's home, meant that thousands of poor whites were concentrated in company-owned villages surrounding the factories. The men, women, and children who worked the looms suffered their own forms of discrimination at the hands of respectable whites, which gave an ironic twist to the disdain and even hatred for blacks that often flourished in the mill villages and that Hereford and his brother experienced firsthand as children.[16]

Hereford's explanation of how he came to participate in a nonviolent campaign to end racial injustice is among the most compelling parts of his memoir. Although he had followed the Montgomery bus boycott while finishing his medical training in 1956 and admired the students conducting sit-in protests in Nashville and Greensboro in 1959 and 1960, his decision to become an activist grew out of his own private history—from his father's example and his own encounters with racism to the courage he witnessed early in his practice among several older blacks in town who were active in voter registration.

Starting with the sit-in campaign of January 1962, Hereford provided an eyewitness account of what was happening behind the scenes in Huntsville. Though events had been sparked by a young field agent from the Congress of Racial Equality (CORE), leaders of the black community quickly embraced the cause. In addition to his role in formulating strategy, Hereford served as the movement's physician, having volunteered for the task at one of the first mass rallies.[17] What was most striking in his account was the part played by ordinary people and the degree to which conditions at the local level, far more than any centralized civil rights leadership, determined the outcome of the struggle, a pattern seen in other places across the South.[18]

What happened next was harder for Hereford to talk about. While he remains convinced that the problems he began experiencing during the 1970s were linked to resentments against him because of his earlier civil rights activism, he conceded that these problems were compounded by excessive numbers of patients, poor record keeping, and the informal arrangements that he and the other black doctors in town had devised in order to cover for each other during absences.

The trouble began with Hereford's participation in Medicaid, a joint federal-state program that was implemented in Alabama in 1970 to provide medical assistance for the indigent. Like Medicare, Medicaid extended to health and welfare some of the victories of the civil rights era.[19] Though opposed by the AMA and the health care industry, both programs helped people who had long been deprived of care. At the same time, they contained hidden dangers for participating doctors, who had to cope with new medical bureaucracies and shifting political currents.

When Medicaid was finally put in place, great numbers of physicians, citing the program's restrictions, low fees, and excessive paperwork, refused to participate. A national survey of 3,482 doctors conducted in 1977 reported that 21.6 percent treated no Medicaid patients, while another 49.2 percent had practices in which Medicaid patients accounted for just 10 to 20 percent of their clientele. On average, Medicaid patients constituted just 13.3 percent of all caseloads. Large Medicaid providers, defined as those for whom patients in the program constituted 30 percent or more of their practices, represented just 15.8 percent of those surveyed.[20]

That the large Medicaid providers included many black physicians is not surprising. In 1969 Lloyd C. Elam, president of Meharry, estimated that 80 percent of the school's graduates practiced in poverty-stricken areas.[21] These, along with foreign-trained physicians in the inner cities, often bore the blame for driving up Medicaid costs through fraud, despite studies showing that the real cause was the growth in numbers of recipients, medical price increases, and soaring prices for nursing home care.[22]

In Alabama, a backlash against the social programs of the Great Society was visible on many fronts, starting with Governor George Wallace's resistance to the integration of state hospitals.[23] Politicians complained bitterly over Medicaid costs, even though Alabama, like many poor states, benefited from a federal matching rate that usually stood at three to one. By the late 1970s, the state began reducing medical services as well as fees paid to participating physicians, and there were calls for vigorous prosecution of any doctors suspected of defrauding the system. To this end, in 1978 the Medicaid Fraud Control Unit was placed in the Alabama attorney general's office.

The following year the fraud unit accused Hereford, by now one of the state's top Medicaid providers, of submitting claims for hospital patients whom he had not personally attended. His efforts to explain that he had not intentionally done anything wrong and that the claims in question were the result of agreements that he and his black colleagues had worked out to cover for each other during absences were to no avail. State investigators indicted him on forty-six counts—one for each patient for whom he had filed a claim. On his attorney's advice, and rather than face trial and the possibility of prison time, he chose to plead guilty to two counts, accepting a three-year probation and repayment of double the claims that he had been paid.

Although Huntsville's black community rallied to Hereford's support, the Medicaid charges were only the beginning of his difficulties, and soon a new cycle began. In 1985, the Alabama Board of Medical Examiners began querying him about his treatment practices, accusing him of prescribing pain medications without sufficient diagnosis. Then, in 1992, it filed a formal complaint against him, claiming to have discovered twenty-two instances in which the drugs that he had prescribed had endangered the health of patients. Hereford denied the accusations, insisting that the medications he had prescribed were only mild to moderate pain relievers and that he had always included proper diagnosis and referrals to specialists. Nevertheless, in February 1993, the board revoked his license to practice.

Hereford's account gives his version of these events and describes how the loss of his license proved financially and psychologically devastating. In an afterword, and for purposes of comparison, I address the issue of disciplinary actions taken against black doctors by state medical boards and provide a brief analysis of the numbers and percentages of black physicians in Alabama who have been disciplined in recent decades. In doing so, my aim was not to try to justify any mistakes that Hereford might have made during his years of practice but to place his problems in historical context and thereby shed light on the pitfalls that awaited black doctors who participated in the health and welfare programs of the 1960s.

The afterword also describes how in the years following the loss of his license Hereford set out to restore his sense of self-worth, from helping students prepare for careers in the medical field to educating younger generations about the civil rights movement. His latter efforts included frequent appearances in schools and churches to show his documentary film *A Civil Rights Journey,* which was a more polished version of the footage I had viewed during my first meeting with him and was produced in 1999 with the help of historian Waymon Burke of the Huntsville branch of Calhoun Community College in Decatur.

As noted earlier, my conversations with Hereford were part of a larger oral history project that eventually produced several dozen recorded interviews with African American doctors, the majority of whom practiced in Alabama. Each participant was asked to sign a Deed of Gift form that I had developed earlier with The University of Alabama at Birmingham whereby all tapes and transcripts would be donated to UAB's Medical Archives. The Hereford materials that form the basis of his autobiography include taped interviews and transcriptions, plus notes on follow-up conversations by telephone and in person. In reconstructing his story, we also drew on his private correspondence, medical daybooks, notes for community talks on health and hygiene, records of home deliveries, and newspaper articles. Finally, I conducted interviews with others who were familiar with the events that Hereford describes, including several local white physicians and the late Geneva Drake Whatley, Dr. Drake's widow.

Hereford's autobiography records the experiences of just one black doctor in a single southern community during the twentieth century. Nevertheless, it helps us better understand the lives and careers of other black doctors in the South, a topic that has attracted increased attention from scholars over the last few years.[24] While I have assisted him in getting his story on paper and in organizing and editing the material, it is told in his words and voice. I found him to be an engaging storyteller who spoke in measured terms and without exaggeration, even when describing events that affected him profoundly. His recollections were fresh and evocative and almost always borne out by external sources. Where appropriate, I have provided notes in the text citing relevant documents from his papers or excerpts from other interviews that I conducted during the course of my research. In places where his narrative touches on topics of general historical interest, I have also cited relevant secondary literature.

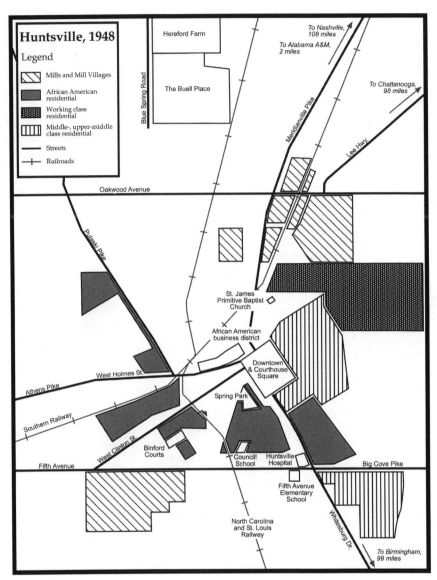

Huntsville, 1948

Legend

▨ Mills and Mill Villages

▩ African American residential

▦ Working class residential

▥ Middle-, upper-middle class residential

— Streets

┼ Railroads

Hereford Farm

The Buell Place

To Nashville, 108 miles

To Alabama A&M, 2 miles

To Chattanooga, 98 miles

Blue Spring Road

Meridianville Pike

Lee Hwy.

Oakwood Avenue

Pulaski Pike

St. James Primitive Baptist Church

African American business district

West Holmes St.

Athens Pike

Downtown & Courthouse Square

Spring Park

Southern Railway

West Clinton St.

Binford Courts

Fifth Avenue

Council School

Huntsville Hospital

Big Cove Pike

Fifth Avenue Elementary School

North Carolina and St. Louis Railway

Whitesburg Dr.

To Birmingham, 99 miles

City of Huntsville, Madison County, Alabama, 1948.

1
Through a Glass Darkly

I was born on the exact spot where the Dairy Queen stands, out on Max Luther Drive. That's where my house was, the exact spot. The place was in the country back then, north of the city limits, but you wouldn't think so now.

Across the road, right where the Dollar Store and the flea market sit, was my grandfather Tom's house, with a barn and a cornfield just beyond it. To the northwest, where red dirt outcroppings dropped off into good bottom land, and where you see a high rise and a cable TV company today, was a cotton field of fifteen acres, and a little farther on, another one of seven acres.

If you walked west, you'd run into a two-lane dirt road known as Blue Spring Road, which in the summer, as the trees alongside it grew out, became a one-lane dirt road. There was no Memorial Parkway back then, no trucks, no mini-marts—just our house and two others sitting out in the meadows.

Our place was a sharecropper's house of four rooms, without running water or electricity, no porch or stoop. Everything just opened onto a dirt yard. The house had a kitchen and a fireplace, a storage room, plus two small bedrooms, with me and my brother, Tom, sleeping in one, next to our parents, and my great-grandparents sleeping in the other. It was in this house that I was born, at the hands of a black doctor in town named Claxton Binford, and they tell me it happened in the year 1931, on the seventh day of January at seventeen minutes past 7:00 in the morning.

My daddy was the only child of Annie Hereford and Matt Stewart, who lived together for a time and then separated right after he was born. Matt was a fair-skinned man whose people later became one of Madison County's biggest landowning black families. Later on, he married a woman named Ollie, and they had seven or eight kids. Annie ended up marrying a fellow named Tom Johnson—he's the one whose house was across the road from where the Dairy Queen is—and they also had seven or eight children. This meant that Daddy had fifteen or sixteen half brothers and half sisters, though no full brothers or sisters of his own.[1]

I saw people from the Stewart side very little as a boy, and just a few stand out today—people like Aunt Mattie, a schoolteacher, and Aunt Muriel, an insurance writer, who'd go door to door in the black neighborhoods collecting payments for burial and life. Daddy would visit the Stewarts from time to time, but our families generally kept apart.

Daddy was what people called an "outside child," which means he'd been born out of wedlock and raised by his mother's folks. He was named after his maternal grandfather, Sonnie Hereford, the man he always looked on as *his* daddy. Sonnie Hereford Sr., as people called him, had been born in slavery, just like my great-grandmother Bettie.[2] The story I heard was that he belonged to one of the slaveholding Herefords out around Meridianville, but I don't know for sure. Back then, people didn't talk to us children about slavery because it stirred up such bitter memories.

Neither of my great-grandparents could read or write, of course, and had spent their lives working the land. They died a few months apart when I was eight or nine years old, first Grandpa Sonnie and then Grandma Bettie, so my memories of them are dim. I do recall one thing, and that was how Grandpa saved every receipt for every bill he'd ever paid, sticking them on a wire in a spindle attached to the wall. There must have been four or five hundred. The newer ones were white, but toward the middle they'd turned yellow and were brown at the back.

My mother was a Burwell, the daughter of Tom and Elizabeth Burwell of Madison County. Her name was Jannie, and, like Daddy, she was an only child, born before the turn of the century. Her mother, the one I always knew as Grandma Liz, was a Tillman, and Grandpa Tom, the man my brother was named after, was one of four children belonging to Wash and Mollie Burwell, both born in slavery times.

Mama's parents were good people, but they had a lot of problems owing to Tom Burwell's philandering, going off for days at a time. People did give him credit for being a good provider. He made sure his family had plenty of meal and lard and bacon in the house, for which the black community looked on him with more favor than would have been the case. But the marriage came close to falling apart. Once, Grandma Liz walked out on him and took my mother, who was just a teenage girl at the time, up to Memphis, where they worked as maids on a farm. The white owner tried to match up my mother with the lot boy, but Grandma Liz wouldn't allow it, and later on, she came home and made up with Grandpa.

Grandma Liz and Grandpa Tom lived near us, just over Davis Hill, but Grandpa passed when I was very young, so my memories of him are pretty faded. He passed in the fall of the year, and what happened was that he'd carried a bale of cotton to the gin and was on his way home, when he stopped by the Madison County Fair Grounds, out between Church Street and Pulaski Pike, to see the horse races. Black farmers would often do that—stop beside the road and stand in their wagons or look through the big wooden fence around the fairgrounds to see the races—and while Grandpa was watching he suffered some sort of pulmonary hemorrhage.

My brother was walking past the fairgrounds on his way home from school, and he saw the commotion and found that it was his own grandfather who had just died. This was very, very distressing to him, and he ran all the way home to tell everyone what had happened.

Grandma Liz moved in with us after that, and she and I became the best of friends. She was full of fun, and not much bigger than me, and the idea of discipline was usually the furthest thing from her mind. There were exceptions now and then, mostly from the fact that my brother, Tom, who was seven years older than me, had gotten his finger in her eye so bad [endeared himself to her] that she just thought he couldn't do any wrong. Once, he jumped on top of me, and when he heard Grandma Liz coming, he pulled me over on top of him, like I'd started it.

And in she came. For someone so small, she had a powerful right arm.

"Get off that boy!" *Whump!*

"I said, get off that boy!" *Whump!*

There I was, Tom working on me from below and Grandma Liz working on me from above, and I hadn't done a thing.

But most of the time, whatever I did was all right by her, and whatever she did was all right by me. And she loved to fish. We made our own hooks, we dug our own bait, and we'd go fishing two or three times a week. After she passed— I must have been seventeen or eighteen years old—I never felt like going fishing again.

My mother was a good woman, too, who'd gotten a ninth- or tenth-grade education at Oakwood Academy, which was a black Seventh-day Adventist school near her parents' house in the Indian Creek community and which sometimes allowed non-Adventist children to enroll. Mama was a strict Primitive Baptist all her life and served as a Mother of the Church. This was like a deaconess, you know, and you were supposed to be an example to the younger women, help with conferences, help with the foot washings, cook the unleavened bread, that sort of thing. Women could be seen everywhere in the work of the church when I was growing up, except in the pulpit. Not once in my life did I ever see a woman standing in a pulpit, not until the civil rights movement, when a lady from Chattanooga came down to speak in support of our sit-in campaign.

At some point, my mother had picked up the nickname Big Mama, and it sure did fit her. For one thing, she'd early on adopted the Bible's teaching about not sparing the rod. She'd say, "I'm gonna whup you for what you did, and when your daddy gets home, he's gonna whup you again."

Back then, even the neighbors would whup you if they caught you doing something really bad. They'd say, "Miss Jannie, I had to whup that boy for doing such and such," and nobody ever complained or said the neighbors had no right.

Now, Daddy was a very stern person, a disciplinarian, but he was all right as long as we did our chores and did our schoolwork. He had managed to get a tenth-grade education—I think from the laboratory school out at Alabama A&M—which, in those days, for a black person, was like having a master's degree. He'd tell us, "Make sure you learn, make sure you acquire a skill so you won't have to spend the rest of your lives working for Mr. Charlie." That's what he called the white man—Mr. Charlie.

Daddy had been drafted into the army during World War I and sent to France. Once in awhile, I'd hear him talking about it, about one thing or another that had happened over there, somebody hurt or killed by a shell, and how hard things had been in the trenches. One day, I heard him telling someone how if a black soldier was thinking of marrying a French girl, the officers would tell him that when the war was over, he'd have to divorce her, or else he'd have to stay in France. Bringing her home wasn't one of the choices.

As to how being a black person in the army had affected him, he never did say much of anything to me about it, but I know there were times when he was abused by some of the other people, you know, and he used to mention it to Mama, and I could hear them talking about it, though I never knew any of the details. I do remember that when my brother registered with the Selective Service during World War II, and we expected him to be drafted, Daddy kept saying, "I wish I could go in his place, because I've already been through the ropes, and I have the experience, and I'd know how to protect myself."

Before going into the army, Daddy had married a woman named Hattie Olvin, who was ten years older than he and had already been married twice. They were married for only about a year after he came home from the war, and then they divorced.

After that, Daddy set his sights on Miss Jannie Burwell, but he hesitated to press his case because he knew the old saying that no woman wants a second-hand man. When he did get around to asking Grandma Liz if she would give him her daughter's hand in marriage, she said, "Give you all I got?"

Daddy persisted, and Grandma finally gave in. The marriage took place at the Indian Creek Primitive Baptist Church, and Tom was born two years later and then Jimmy, but Jimmy died in infancy, of meningitis.

Meanwhile, Daddy and Grandpa Sonnie started buying land north of town, and by the late 1920s they had acquired a forty-acre farm out on Blue Spring branch at one hundred dollars an acre. But Daddy thought he needed more land to farm, so he put a sharecropper on the forty-acre place—I think it was one of our distant relatives—and then he moved us to a bigger farm, the place where I was born. It had 160 acres and was owned by a Mr. Buell of York Harbor, Maine. Mr. Buell came south only once a year, in November, just after harvest, in time to collect a fourth of what Daddy made, which was his due under our arrangement.

So by the time I was born, we were in the unusual position of being ourselves sharecroppers while having sharecroppers on our own place. The difference was that ours paid us half of what they made because we furnished the seed, the fertilizer, the implements, horses, and mules. That was the system. A tenant farmer paid the owner a fourth or a half of everything he made, depending on what had been furnished. Of course, our tenants were always black, because black landowners never had white tenants. White had white. White had black. And black had black. But black never had white, not that I knew of anyway.

It was the black tenants of white owners who usually got the short end of the stick because of the piling up of debts to the owner against next year's crop. The problem would start when the owner gave the tenant a furnishing check to be drawn from the owner's bank account should the tenant need a slab of bacon or a little lard or sugar or coffee. If differences arose-—if a white farm owner said you owed such-and-such an amount—you had to pay. About the only thing you could do was go to work for another owner, whose place was usually just down the road and where you'd sometimes have to wait until the present occupant had moved out, perhaps because of a quarrel he'd had with his owner.[3]

There was lots of moving around like this—people loading up their pots and pans, tying up their chickens, and throwing everything on the wagon. I had a cousin everybody called Kilbuck who'd moved so often people said, "Whenever the chickens see him coming, they lay down and cross their legs."

Besides farming, Daddy was a preacher, the pastor of St. James Primitive Baptist Church. He became a minister while he was in the army. He was not a chaplain, but he began preaching while he was in the army, and when he came back, he was ordained, and then he built St. James, literally and figuratively. He actually built it with his own hands. The church was located in town on Howe Street, and his congregation was something like 100 or 150 people. It was a nice frame building, with a steeple and vestibule, a choir room and a pastor's study, and a small parsonage, which Daddy rented out.

And he was a fine preacher. The words seemed spontaneous, but we knew his preparations had started on Saturday afternoon, when he'd leave the fields early and go to the house for his glasses and Bible. People would say, "There's only two good preachers in town. One is Reverend So-and-so, and the other is Reverend Hereford."

Daddy was good at farming, but by the time I was born, with the Depression going on, the price of cotton just kept falling. And cotton was always a risk. The Buell place had a mix of soils, from good bottomland to red clay that needed lots of expensive fertilizer. You started early in the spring by breaking up the biggest clods with a harrow, then you laid out the furrows and put down some fertilizer with potash and other ingredients.

In April came the planting. You could buy seed, or, if you'd saved seed from good healthy plants the previous year, you planted these. Daddy used a horse-drawn planter, and he was always careful to sow the seed thick to get a good stand, which would later be thinned out with a hoe. In May, June, and July you cultivated, and by the end of July, you'd lay by, which meant you didn't do anything for awhile except hope the wind and hail wouldn't hurt the bolls once they started opening.

By September it was time to pick, but since not all the cotton matured at once you'd usually have several pickings, right down to the last scrapping. To scrap was to take whatever was left, what some folks referred to as Christmas money or personal money that didn't show up anywhere on the books.

Because the Buell place was so large, Daddy would have to hire extra hands—first, to chop and thin the cotton plants, and later, to do the picking. He might hire ten or twelve people a day, all black, of course, women and children as well as men. He'd pick them up in the wagon early in the morning down in the poor sections of town, where they'd be standing out along Washington and Winston and Arnett streets, waiting for something to turn up.

Depending on the amount of rain you'd had, you might have to do several choppings to clear out the weeds and grass from around the plants, and what the people got for a full day's work doing this from sunup to sundown was seventy-five cents and find their own dinner, or they could take fifty cents and dinner, which is what we called the noon meal. Mama cooked the food, and the big garden and orchard out back of our house made it possible for her to vary the dinners so that the people never had to eat the same thing two days in a row.

For picking, the workers were paid by the pound, maybe a dollar per one hundred pounds. It took a long time to pick that much. When your sack was full, you'd drag it over to the wagon and have it weighed, and though you'd hear a lot of stories about people who picked three hundred or four hundred pounds in a day, I never saw it happen. I never saw anyone pick much over two hundred pounds in a single day. I was a pretty good picker myself by the time I was fifteen or sixteen, but I could never pick more than a hundred pounds in a day.

As a boy, my job was to carry water to the field hands from a well located along Blue Spring branch, about three-quarters of a mile away. I'd tote it in a bucket with a dipper, and the older people would try to convince me it was easier to carry two because it helps you balance. But I never wanted to carry more than one.

After the cotton was picked, you carried it to the gin, and though there were five or six to choose from, you had to be careful because some gins were better than others. You might pull up to one with 1,400 pounds of raw cotton and come away with only 490 pounds of lint. Another gin might be better at separating the seed from the lint, might give you 500 or better.

There was a set fee for ginning 500 pounds, maybe ten dollars or so, which you paid even if the yield was only 490 pounds. So if you were ten pounds under, that was throwing money away. The ginning fee was usually paid out of the seeds unless you wanted to pay it out of your own pocket, which you might want to do if you'd brought in good long-lint cotton from bottomland and you wanted to keep the seeds to use next year.

Daddy took our cotton to the Longview, a black-owned gin on Brown Street near the black cemetery. He owned a few shares of stock in this gin that brought him twenty-five or thirty dollars a year in dividends, and he and the other black shareholders would urge their friends to use it. Whites were rarely seen there or, for that matter, in most of the black businesses in town, though there were exceptions.

On North Jefferson Street was a blacksmith shop owned by Mr. Willie Fearn, whose brother was one of two black dentists in town. I was in his shop many times with my father, and I'd stare in fascination as Mr. Fearn worked over the coals—how he'd trim and measure the horse's hoof, mold the shoe with his hammer and anvil, then nail it on the hoof without injuring the quick. White people admired his skills as much as I did, as there always seemed to be more of them in there than us.

Hiring people to help pick the cotton meant less profit, and neighbors would use the expression, "You're just turning over dollars." By that they meant if you raised, say, twenty bales in a year, and if you got $100 for a 500-pound bale, that meant, in theory, you'd cleared $2,000. But suppose, as you went back over the books, you found that you'd paid out that amount in fertilizer and wages. You were just turning over dollars.

For many black people, hard times meant getting out of Alabama if they were able to. They'd be making, say, fifty or seventy-five cents a day, and they'd hear how some relative was making twenty-five dollars a week up North, and the only decision they needed to make was how to get money for a bus ticket. From time to time, I'd hear the adults talking about some friend or family member going up to Nashville or Chattanooga, maybe Chicago or Detroit. Most of them never came back except to visit, and then it was always at the front of the train or the back of the bus.[4]

For us, Daddy's preaching helped out, and we also had the rent money from the St. James parsonage in town. He never charged anybody for any wedding or for any funeral, and he never received a regular salary. Now, some ministers charged for weddings, and I understand a few even charged at funerals. But the ministers did not receive a salary. None of the black ministers to my knowledge received any salaries—just the Sunday contributions. I recall that on some Sundays we might raise ten, twelve, fourteen dollars as the total contribution of the membership. Eventually, though, Daddy had to take on a second church, the Indian Creek Primitive Baptist. He'd preach there on the first and third Sundays of the month, and at St. James on the second and fourth Sundays, and he might get eight or ten dollars from each offering.

Because he had some education, Daddy was also able to help black people with any forms that needed filling out—anybody that had any government forms or anything like that—and if they had problems understanding the forms, he was always available to help. He was able to get widows' pensions of servicemen who had been killed during the war or who'd been wounded and died later on and that sort of thing. He would help people fill out insurance forms for those who had lost loved ones or who had claims of illness or who'd suffered an injury of some sort.

Mostly, he did these things for free, though sometimes he received a small monetary consideration, like the time he became an overnight real estate agent. Now, I say real estate agent: he had no formal training in being a real estate agent or anything of that sort, but, when I was about nine or ten, Pearl Harbor happened. Then, the government decided to build Redstone Arsenal, and many families were displaced, and all those families had to find farmland somewhere else.

Both white and black farmers were displaced, but Daddy worked only with the black families to help find them new land, and for this he would get a small monetary consideration. I have no idea what percentage it was or if it was a flat rate or something of that sort, but I just know he spent a lot of time helping these people get placed. They could afford to pay Daddy a little more than other farmers because they owned good bottomland by the Tennessee River. And you'll still run into people in the black community who say the federal government cheated the black farmers out of the full value of their land when they decided to build Redstone.[5]

In the fall of 1937, Daddy enrolled me in Councill School, the only school for black children in the city. It had twelve grades, and, up until the sixth grade, there were usually two sections for each grade, and each section would have forty to fifty students. So in the first grade, you'd have about eighty or a hundred students total.

Every black citizen of the city who tried to get an education attended Councill at that time. Ask any black person around here who's sixty-five or seventy years of age where they went to school, and they'll tell you this was it. And it was a totally black school: black principals, black teachers, black students, and black janitors.

It was in September when I enrolled, the day after Labor Day, and Daddy took me himself, leading me around the halls to meet the teachers. The location of the St. James Primitive Baptist Church and parsonage on Howe Street, which was inside the city limits, allowed my brother and me to give that address as our home address and register at the city school. My brother and I and maybe five or six other kids living out in the county managed to slip in that way. Daddy had told us before we left home: "You just be sure you don't say you live at Route One, Box 280."

And it was a good thing, because however bad off the city black school might have been when compared to the white school, it was head and shoulders above the county black schools, which were a joke. The black county schools began in midsummer and closed in September for six to eight weeks so the children could help with the harvest. By the time they started up again, with bad weather setting in and no buses, the kids would have missed a lot of classes, and some didn't come back. Those who did often had no desks, no blackboards, no textbooks.

I remember one county school out on Stringfield Road that was little more than a shanty. Other classes were held in the black churches, where the children worked with slates. They baked in summer and froze in winter, with only a Franklin stove to warm them, and the wood and coal had to be brought in by the parents.

What you saw in most of the county black schools was usually one teacher to forty or fifty kids, mainly in the lower grades. At the higher end, you might have three kids in the sixth grade and one in the seventh, but the next year these might stop coming so that the highest grade taught could be the fourth or fifth. That's what you saw in those places, mostly children, maybe up to the sixth or seventh grade. The higher you got, the less kids there were.[6]

So Councill was a lot better-off, even though it sat right beside a dump, right where the Huntsville Public Library would later be built. And the dump curved around the school to a field across the road, which is where they later built the white First Baptist Church and its parking lot. Back then, it was all dump, or what I call the horseshoe phenomenon, since it curved in a horseshoe around the school. And to this day, I don't know which decision came first: to build the black school next to the dump or to build the dump next to the black school.

In front of the school was a dirt yard where we played, without swings or slides or anything of that sort. Our desks were doubles and triples, and what was called the library was just a room with a few dozen books contributed by some private citizens. We had no gym and no lunchroom, so most kids brought baloney or cheese sandwiches, or, if they had any money, they could walk down to Tuminello's, which sold candy and pop. Mr. Tuminello also sold cracklings [pork rinds], which he kept in a box on the counter and would scoop up with his hand into a paper bag.

Still, I thought I was pretty lucky to be going to Councill because the teachers were better in the city than in the county, though not nearly so well prepared as the teachers in the white schools. Most of my teachers had gotten their training at Alabama A&M, maybe about 50 percent. A few had gone to Alabama State. My chemistry teacher—he taught me chemistry and history and was also the football coach—went to Knoxville College.

For a good part of my school years, World War II was going on and then, a few years after that, the Korean War. So we had a number of teachers who had been drafted. And even before they were drafted—this is just off the top of my head—I believe that the teacher composition in most black schools in this area, in north Alabama, would have been like something like 75 percent female and about 25 percent male, and the principal was always male. After World War II started, the percentage probably dropped to something like 90 and 10, or about 10 percent male, and as a matter of fact, at one time the number of male teachers got so low that the school board finally gave in and decided to appoint two women to carry out the duties of principal.

Councill was about six miles from my house, so I was usually out of the house by around six, because it took an hour and a half or more to get there, depending on the weather. At some point, Daddy bought an automobile, which was unusual for a black person in those days, but he needed it for his church work. Because there were no buses for black kids, he'd sometimes pick us up after school during the winter months. Daddy's cars were always Chevrolets and always loud. During a fire drill one day at Councill, as we were standing outside, we heard an old car off in the distance just making all kinds of racket, and one of the girls in my class, who was two years older than I was because she had had to repeat the grade, said to my embarrassment, "Do y'all remember that car? It's the one Reverend Hereford used to have."

During my first months at Councill, it looked like my career as a scholar was over before it had even gotten started. The problem was a bad case of stuttering, which had developed early in my childhood and now threatened to do me in because of the amount of oral recitation required. But I soon discovered a secret: the more I knew about a subject, the less I stuttered.

This discovery led me to spend an unusual amount of time on my lessons, and I was lucky in having a first-grade teacher who understood my problem and helped me overcome it. Her name was Mrs. Helen Fearn, the wife of a black dentist named Henry Fearn, who had his office over on Church Street. She'd encourage me and write little notes to my parents telling them how well I was doing, and it made me try harder.

As my grades got better, other students started looking up to me and asking for my help. On the schoolyard, if they got into an argument about something, they'd say, "Let's go ask Sonnie." And they'd come up and ask me to settle a dispute. When did Columbus discover America? What did Vasco da Gama do? That sort of thing. Whatever I said, they usually accepted, and this was a thrill to me.

I was at Councill for only two years when I was transferred to a new school on the north side of town. It was called the Winston Street School, and it saved me about twenty-five minutes of walking. Here I finished the third and fourth grades and part of the fifth, then was sent back to Councill, returned to Winston for the sixth, and finally sent back to Councill for the seventh, where I stayed through my senior year. The official explanation for all this moving around was overcrowding at Winston, but the truth was, there was plenty of space, just not enough teachers and not enough desks.

Now about those desks—years later, I heard what had happened from one of the Winston teachers, who'd seen brand-new desks in our classrooms two days before the grand opening, where they stayed just long enough to satisfy inspectors that the federal dollars used in construction had been properly spent. No sooner had these inspectors left, she told me, then men in trucks came in and took the new desks over to one of the white schools. So the desk I sat in at Winston was one that would normally have been hauled off to the dump—a castaway, so to speak, carved up by the pocketknives of earlier students, who'd left behind a good supply of pierced hearts.

Winston's principal was a woman named Mrs. Myrtle Turner, whose father was one of Daddy's friends. She kept strict discipline, but she also tried to build up school spirit. For example, she created a Juvenile Court, which was meant to settle fights and disputes. You'd come before twelve jurors, all students, and you'd tell your side of the story and wait for a verdict.

One year, during the war, Mrs. Turner had the sixth-graders dress up in caps and gowns for their graduation ceremonies, the only time I ever heard of this happening at an elementary school. A third of us wore red gowns, a third white, and a third blue. She said it was meant as a tribute to the black men who'd gone off to war.

No one affected me at Winston quite like Mrs. Dorothy Langford Turner, the third-grade teacher who set aside time each Friday to read stories to the class. We looked forward to this with such anticipation that if we were misbehaving on a Monday or a Tuesday, just a hint that she might not read on Friday would usually do the trick. Mrs. Turner could also be more direct. Once, I was sitting in the front row with two of my friends, one of whom was Lawrence

Hundley, who became a dentist and lawyer. Hundley had a flair for telling jokes, and one day when Mrs. Turner was trying to explain something I laughed out loud at what he said and in an instant felt the smack of a yardstick against my forehead.

It was in Mrs. Turner's class that I heard about a man named Hitler and how he had attacked a country called Poland, and people started saying it was only a matter of time before we got in. I began to learn about the war and world geography by looking at newspaper maps, and I felt an incredible patriotism. In the fifth grade, I wrote a poem that I called "Roosevelt and Hitler," and in the poem Hitler is talking to Roosevelt on the telephone about how he can't break England or Russia. Roosevelt says, "Well, your business is just fine, but when you start at Uncle Sam, you'd better change your mind." And I thought, well, maybe the president of the United States needs to see this. So I mailed a copy to Mr. Roosevelt and later received a letter of thanks.

When I went back to Councill as a seventh-grader, I tried hard to stay focused on my studies, but by then I was old enough to work in the fields and had to miss a good many days picking cotton and doing other harvesting in the fall, plus plowing and preparing for planting in the spring. It was easy to lose interest.

One day, in Mrs. Bernice Penny's class—she was my homeroom teacher in the eighth grade—there were ten or fifteen boys who made airplanes and spitballs, and they kept disrupting her class, and I wanted to move to the back, where the action was. Mrs. Penny told me, she says, "Sonnie, you seem like a good student, you seem like a good person, and I know your father is a good person. I don't want you back there with those guys." She says, "Come up here to the front and sit with this gentleman named Jackson, because he's a good student, and he'll help you to be good."

Well, that's the last place I wanted to go, up there to the front. But I went up there, and the next day this guy Jackson, who had a chemistry set at his house, brought three test tubes and a medicine dropper to the class. And he said, "Let me show you something. You see this clear solution here? When I take this clear solution and put two or three drops in it, it's going to turn red."

I said, "Oh, I don't believe that's going to do that." So he puts these drops in, and here it turns red. He says, "Now, when I put them in this one over here, it's gonna turn blue." So he put the drops in the third tube, and it turned blue. Well, I'm thinking, this is interesting enough.

So then this guy Jackson was telling me he has this little Gilbert chemistry set. I said, "What's that cost?" He said, "It costs just $4.95." So I went and got a chemistry set, and then I think in about a year I got a $9.95 set, you know, getting real fancy. And I began to like chemistry. And I'd go to the movies and I'd see these guys with the white coats and the solutions bubbling and all that business, and I thought, gee whiz, doing research, this is really cool, now that's what I want to do.

But the science at Councill came solely out of a book. There was no physics lab or biology lab, and what passed for a chemistry lab had maybe seven or eight test tubes, two or three Bunsen burners and beakers, and half a dozen reagent bottles. Our teacher, Coach Kellam, did the best he could with what he had, but he had to do a lot with very little. And he was the chemistry teacher, the history teacher, the physical education instructor, the basketball coach, and the football coach.

So I began buying my own chemistry equipment and trying to learn at home, and the sets kept getting bigger and bigger. I paid for them with what we called a truck patch, which was a little plot where you'd grow extra vegetables to sell. I would peddle them from my bicycle along Adams and Franklin and Madison streets, and at home I made my own lab, just a few chemicals and test tubes in a lean-to against the barn, full of farm implements. I even started carrying my own reagents to school, and when we had experiments to do, we'd sometimes use my chemicals.

Mrs. Fearn, who'd been my first-grade teacher, taught me math in the seventh grade, and I loved math, and I loved to please her, and she was so supportive of me. When I got to the ninth grade, Mrs. Fearn also taught biology, and boy, that was really good, because she was good in biology, and I loved biology because I wanted to know how things lived by me being on the farm, you know. At home, I even rigged up an outdoor aquarium of sorts, with tadpoles and frogs and all that business, and I used to mount insects and leaves and things like that from trees and try to name the leaf according to the shape.

And I remember one thing that inspired me. We had a picture of George Washington Carver at the school, and I admired it so, and this Mrs. Fearn, she said, "Do you really, really like that picture?" I said yes. She said, "Why don't you take it home then?" So she let me take George Washington Carver's picture home.

Most of the Councill teachers would try to encourage you this way, though I do remember one exception. We'd been studying the famous painters and sculptors of the past, and one day, I said, "Well, maybe I'd like to be a painter or a sculptor." So one of my teachers sat me down and said, "Sonnie, let me tell you something. You're living in Alabama, and you're black, and you're gonna starve to death talking about being a painter or a sculptor."

I guess she was just being realistic. I was about fourteen, fifteen years old and living in Alabama, and this is about 1945 or 1946, and I'm talking about how I might want to be a painter or a sculptor, so she's saying, oh, this is crazy, you know. Nowadays, you might encourage somebody, tell them to stick with it, but she was giving me advice based on what she saw—how the only jobs the Councill kids could get were shining shoes or delivering groceries, how girls couldn't be bank tellers or receptionists, how the best you could hope for was to be somebody's janitor or maid.[7]

Some people thought I'd follow in Daddy's footsteps and become a preacher, but I never felt the call. At one point, he was made manager of the Primitive Baptist Publication Board, and I'd sometimes go with him to the meetings, which would take place in different towns. And I often attended the baptisms at the Big Spring downtown, which were widely advertised in the black community so people could make their plans. During the services at St. James Church, I'd see the outpourings of faith, I'd watch as people shouted and prayed, and I must have gone to the mourner's bench fifty times in hopes that God would touch me, that I'd start to sing and dance and feel God's presence. But it never happened.

By the time I was thirteen or fourteen, I was being drawn to things like the war in Europe and the Pacific, which made me want to know something about history, of which I knew almost nothing. I'd see the Confederate statue downtown in the square, would pass it by, but had absolutely no idea what it meant. And I knew very little about the history of black people, just a few facts I'd been taught about William Hooper Councill, the founder of A&M, and two or three others like Booker T. Washington and George Washington Carver.

I knew from Daddy's service that black people had fought for the country, and not far from my house was a place called Cavalry Hill, where Mama said she'd been told as a girl that black soldiers had camped during the war with Spain around the turn of the century. There was a man in town named Pettus—everyone called him Sergeant Pettus—who was looked up to by the black community because he'd fought in the war with Spain, though I never understood what it was he'd done. What impressed me most about him was that he was a sergeant, because you almost never saw black sergeants, and that he lived on a pension and didn't have to work, because I didn't know any black people who didn't have to work, no matter what their age.

As I got older, I learned about Jesse Owens, as well as Dorie Miller, the black sailor who'd saved his shipmates at Pearl Harbor. At the top of the list was Joe Louis—he was almost like a god in our eyes. We crowded around the radio to hear every fight, or we'd walk over to a neighbor's house or find someone who owned a car with a radio, and they'd turn it up full volume. There'd be twenty or thirty people standing around in somebody's front yard, listening to the fight. For years, people talked about Louis's revenge over the German fighter Schmeling. When Daddy would go into a café, he'd say, "I want a cup of coffee as strong as Joe Louis and a steak beat up as bad as Max Schmeling."

My first school knowledge of black history came in a ninth-grade course called Negro History, which was a half-year class taught by Mrs. Amanda Harper using a textbook called *The Black Man in White America*. I learned a lot in Mrs. Harper's class, but something else made an even deeper impression on me. Mrs. Harper's husband was a Tuskegee airman, and toward the end of the war he came home on furlough and visited her class. He stood there wearing an officer's uniform, and I shall never forget it. We'd seen mainly privates and corporals among black people, and now, standing in front of us, was a black first lieutenant of the United States Army Air Force.

What I really knew about black people was mostly just from my own experiences, what I'd seen in the black schools and churches and things like that. That's the way people back then identified themselves. They'd tell you where they lived, for example, by mentioning a particular congregation or maybe a fraternal order. They'd say, "I'm from the Indian Creek community," after the church there, or "I'm from Number 4 Hall," after a nearby Masonic hall, and people would know what they meant.

Down along Holmes Street, running west from Jefferson, was the black business district, the place where you'd find the stores and shops and cafés where people congregated and picked up the little things they needed. You'd sometimes hear it called "Nigger Main," an expression black people would use among themselves, in the same way young men used the word in talking to each other, and that stood as a reference point when you wanted to tell somebody where they could find you. There were some Caucasian-owned stores there, too, especially the Italian grocery stores, like Cicero's and Brocato's.

The black-owned establishments were also places of entertainment and socializing, like the barbershops. One that stands out in my mind was run by Mr. Nance, who gave my brother his first chance at barbering. When Tom was twelve or thirteen, Grandpa Sonnie bought him a pair of clippers so he could cut his hair, and soon Tom was cutting my hair and Daddy's, too—always the "skinny," as we called it—which would last a good six or seven weeks but gave him little chance for learning. So Tom needed some on-the-job training, and Mr. Nance gave it to him.

The barbershops always had lots of chairs, where black men spent hours talking and playing checkers and dominoes. They were like community centers, you see, at a time when black people had none. Of course, I saw them from a distance, because what was said in the barbershop wasn't meant for the ears of children. If you were a dropout and had a wife and job then you could mix with the boys but not before.

Daddy and Mama usually traded at black-owned stores, like Moore's Drug on Pulaski Pike and Donegan's at Church Street and Holmes. Donegan's was one of several stores owned by Lee Lowery, whose son Joseph later worked with Dr. King in founding the Southern Christian Leadership Conference. The older Mr. Lowery owned shine parlors, poolrooms, and residential property and was looked on as the richest black man in Madison County. A man named Harry Rhett was looked on as the richest white.

For us, the exception to buying at black-owned places was the grocery store. Some people said that the black grocers bought their produce from A&P and marked it up, and we were in the habit of referring to such places as grab-alls, since they would grab all your money. Mama didn't actually buy food often, but when she did she went to the A&P downtown, where things were cheap and she could buy a copy of *Women's Day* for two cents.

Only a few places were available to black kids for entertainment, and there was just one theater we could get into, the Princess, on Church Street. The movies they showed had already made the rounds at the white theaters, so if you really wanted to see a new movie, there was nothing to do but wait. What we saw was mainly what the white kids saw, like westerns and adventure films and cartoons, but sometimes we saw movies with the black bands and jazz musicians like Louis Jordan, or westerns with all-black casts and the singing cowboy Herb Jeffries. Admission was eleven cents, and for that, you had to put up with an awful lot, like the restrooms, which were covered in a good inch of grime and gave off a stench so bad you couldn't sit in the back rows of the theater.

Of the black people I knew, probably 80 percent were farmers. A few worked for some of the new and used car companies, a few on the Coca-Cola truck, a few on the furniture truck. A few were ministers and then some schoolteachers, but nobody had any real technical jobs, at least no black people I was acquainted with. Several worked in menial jobs in the textile mills. We had two big textile mills near us, and the few blacks who worked there had menial jobs, and if there were Caucasians with those same jobs, there was a different pay scale. If the black man had to take a sick day, and if he missed too many, he was told not to come back to work anymore. Or, if he went to work, he'd be met at the gate and told, well, no, we don't need you anymore.

As for white people, the first one I can distinctly remember seeing as a child was the Raleigh Man, who drove his truck through the black neighborhoods peddling liniments and hair preparations. And I especially remember the white photographer who came around to Councill one day to take our class picture, and how he collected half our money in advance. Back then, there were no black photographers that I'd ever heard about, and so they asked a white photographer to take our class picture.

Now, you would think almost anybody should be able to center his subjects in the camera frame, but the photographer who took our class picture got only half of my face in the picture, since I happened to be on the end. So on the day when we brought the other half of the fee to school, and I paid my quarter and got my copy, and when I saw that only half my face was showing, I was disappointed beyond words.

My awareness that the world I lived in was run by whites came on gradually, as I got older. Take the stores on the square, where the clerks would make you wait until all the whites had been served. You'd go into one, and maybe a clerk would be waiting on two or three Caucasian people, and you'd stand there and stand there, and then three or four more Caucasians would come in after you, and the clerk would finish up with every single one before turning to you.

Even in the places where you were treated with courtesy, you were always being reminded. A department store called Dunnavant's on North Washington used to place a large ad in the newspaper every December wishing everyone a merry Christmas, and the ad would be followed by a list of the store's employees and then a separate list with the heading "Colored Employees."

Worst of all was the segregation you ran up against every day—keep out of our restrooms, don't drink from our fountains, stay out of our waiting rooms at the bus station and the railroad depot, don't try to eat at the City Café. So they wouldn't allow us to use their restrooms, and if there was a drinking fountain in a store, it would say "White Only," or they might have one for whites and one for colored, but very few stores had colored fountains.

One day, I found a leaflet on the street that said, come visit such-and-such state park. I think it was over near Fort Payne, and it said the park was visited every year by tens of thousands of Alabamians and thousands of foreigners. And then, I saw at the bottom, in boldface, the words "White Only." So I'm thinking, the people from other countries can visit this park, and I live here, I'm from Alabama, and I can't go.

Everyone you saw in the magazines and newspapers was white, always somebody with blond hair and blue eyes, always white, even the mannequins in the department stores. One day, I passed by a photography studio down in the black business district, and I saw that the white owner had even segregated the sample photographs in the display window. On one side, propped up on holders, were pictures of white people and white families, and on the other side, separated by a cardboard fence, were pictures of black people.

When I was peddling vegetables downtown, I'd see the old mansions off the square, and I knew I wasn't supposed to be there. When I saw the Huntsville Armory being built near Daddy's church, I thought of it as just a place over there where the National Guard and the white guys in the reserve all met and drilled and had their activities—just a place I'm not supposed to go. Not once as a child did I visit a white school, or worship in a white church, or see a white face in a black church. As for hotels like the Russel Erskine, you got in only if you were a cook or a maid or a porter. There was a saying you'd hear among black people: if somebody wanted to do something and had absolutely no chance, they'd say, "You can do that sooner than a nigger can get into the Russel Erskine."

When I'd walk to school, we sometimes had to go in a roundabout way to get there, and the Caucasian kids always rode in the orange or yellow school bus, and whenever they passed by, when two or three or four of us black kids were walking, the only thing I remember about the school bus was that it blew dust in our face if it was going fast, and if it was going slow eggs and rotten tomatoes came from the windows of the school bus and hit us in the face.

Now I'm sure the driver must have known it, must have known that those kids were throwing those things, but nothing was ever done about it. At a younger age, some of the kids riding in the bus might have played with some of the kids walking, because it happened that there'd be a poor white family living near a black neighborhood, and the kids got along all right.

But the rules were already starting to form, because when they finished playing, the white kid could not invite the black kid to come to his table for a sandwich and Kool-Aid, though it was all right for the white kid to go to the black kid's house, and he'd call the black kid's mother Aunt so-and-so and say, this sure is a good sandwich, you know.

As I mentioned, there were several cotton mills in town, two not far from where I lived—the Lincoln Mills on Meridian Pike and the Dallas Mills on Halsey Street. A few blacks worked over there, like my cousin's father, whose house I was in and out of almost every day. But his house was not one of the mill village houses, you can rest assured of that. Oh, no, no such thing. There's no way they would have ever, ever ventured to put a black person in there. That would have caused a riot, and I mean it would have been the same day, not two or three weeks later. Even if the people had heard that they planned to put a black person in one of the mill village houses, there would have been a riot. No, if you were a black mill worker, you lived in your own house, in your own neighborhood, and you got to work the best way you could.

One day, when I was eight or nine years old, I was on my way to school, and I made the mistake of taking a route that brought me past the Lincoln School, a mill village school. There were about six or eight Caucasian boys out there in front of Lincoln School, and they grabbed my hat and wouldn't give it to me. And when I asked for it, you know, they just laughed, and there was nothing I could do because they were all larger, and them being eight of them to one of me, and them being white and me being black, you know. And there was nothing in the world I could do. So they just kept my hat, and I thought that was terrible.

Then there was the incident with the swimming hole. Okay, now, here we are, tenants living on Mr. Buell's farm, and Blue Spring Creek running through our farm, and two swimming holes there, no swimming pool at all in the city. The creek was clear and shallow with steep banks that flowed practically twelve months of the year, except for two or three weeks in the hottest part of August. Here, in a place where the sloping sides made it possible to get down to the water, we had two swimming holes. One we called Hi' Bank, and the other Blue Hole, and each one had good deep water that was accessible from the bank.

And so, here come the boys from these [mill] villages, the Lincoln village and the Dallas village, over to swim in our creek, and these guys decided which pool that they should swim in and which pool that we should swim in, and we were the tenants on the farm. The landlord wasn't going to do anything. He lived up in Maine and came to town only in the fall, and even if he'd been here, I doubt he'd have done anything about it.

Tom and I were always getting into trouble with the kids over there in the mill villages. Daddy would tell us to take our buckets and walk over to Lincoln or Dallas to get scraps from the garbage cans out back of the houses. This was to feed the pigs, and it was pretty serious business, because you slaughtered in the fall, and how much lard and bacon and ham you had to eat in the winter depended on how fat the pigs were. Poor people did it all the time, and some would actually bring wagons to haul the scraps away, which was known as "picking up slop."

So we'd grab our buckets and head over. The white people in the houses, the adults, they didn't seem to care, but if the kids spotted us, there was a good chance they'd throw rocks at us. They did it more than once, no doubt boasting to their friends that they'd "run the niggers out of here," feeling like they'd accomplished something for the day.

An even worse thing in my eyes was the banning of black people from the public library. This really hit me hard as I got older and began turning over in my mind the idea of becoming a scientist or a physician. So I got books wherever I could find them. If I wanted a particular book, I borrowed it or hoped some friend or relative had it or something similar to it, and sometimes we'd even pick books out of the trash. There was a small library for black people in town started up by a woman named Dulcina DeBerry, which was just a house with a few books where we could play checkers and Ping-Pong, but it didn't come close to the local Carnegie Library.

This library business really bothered me, as I had a thirst for knowledge and my family paid taxes, and still I couldn't use the library. I didn't worry much about not being able to go to the movies, because eventually the movie you wanted to see would come to our theater. It might be two years later, you know—some big movie and everybody raving about it—but eventually it trickled down to my theater. So that didn't worry me. But the library, that was different.

In the summer of '44, Daddy took to his bed and didn't get up. The problem was tuberculosis, or what people used to call "spots on the lung," which he probably contracted when he was in the trenches in France. Most of the time he kept it under control, but some of the things he did must have lowered his resistance. For instance, he used to preach 'til the sweat poured down, and he'd get overheated and cool down too fast, and Mama would beg him to put on a jacket.

So he took to his bed, and a white doctor came in and said he had typhoid and treated him for such, and another came and said he had malaria and treated him for such, and he got worse and worse until he passed in August, not having reached his fiftieth birthday. It's clear to me now that he'd suffered a relapse from the TB, but back then, people thought tuberculosis was a shameful thing and didn't even want it written down on the death certificate. So I think the official cause of death was listed as typhoid or some other disease.

Daddy passed just as we were getting ready for the harvest. The funeral fell on the third day of September, which was a Sunday. On the morning of the funeral, his body was brought to St. James Church, where he lay surrounded by more flowers than I'd ever seen in my life. After the service, as the hearse carried him to the cemetery, the line of old Chevrolets and Model A Fords seemed to stretch for miles.

Five months after Daddy passed, Tom was drafted and sent to Fort Benning, Georgia, then on to the Philippines. That left only Mama and me to work the farm, and the first thing she decided to do was to move off the Buell place and back to the farm we owned along Blue Spring Road, which was smaller and a lot easier to take care of.

Though I was only fourteen, I'd had a lot of experience planting and harvesting, and we also got a little help from a gentleman who had a farm near ours of about the same acreage and the same allotment of cotton and corn, and he and I worked in a fashion that farmers called "through and through." In other words, we would plow his field until the plowing was finished, then we'd plow our field until the plowing was finished. That way, Mama and I were able to raise ten or twelve acres of cotton and six or seven acres of corn. We also had a large truck patch, from which I continued peddling vegetables in the city. In the meantime, Tom started sending his paycheck home, and that, plus a small allotment from Daddy's pension, helped us survive.

My brother was in the army for seventeen months, and then, with the war over, they let him come home. Many tears had been shed when we put him on the bus, and many tears were shed when we picked him up at the station. They had discharged him at Fort Sam Houston in August, two years after Daddy had passed, and we now felt a little joy coming back into our lives. Tom was also engaged to be married, and he wanted to go to Alabama A&M under the GI Bill of Rights and become a teacher.

When Tom came home, I was just starting tenth grade, and I wanted to play football so bad I could taste it, but for most of my years at Councill there'd had been no organized sports, not until the male teachers who'd been drafted began coming back. When that happened, Coach Kellam got a team organized, but he had one small problem: no uniforms. So he went over to the white high school and asked if he could have their old equipment, and that's how we got our pads and helmets and a few old footballs. Councill's colors were blue and white. So the boys bought white sweatshirts to wear over the pads, and the girls in home economics sewed blue numbers on the shirts, so that the players had as many patterns of numbers on the field as the girls had styles of sewing.

Now, as I say, I wanted to play football, but Mama said no. She wouldn't let me play—I suppose because I was just 5'5" and 130 pounds. There was a big to-do about this, and it was only during my senior year, when I finally put my foot down, that I made it onto the field. Even then, I saw limited action, mostly kicking and punting. I like to think it was because the coach knew that I was thinking of becoming a doctor and just wanted to protect me. But I suspect it was because I was just too small.

Going to college and medical school had been at the back of my mind for some time, though I really didn't know much about black doctors. I do remember Dr. Robert Beard, a Meharry graduate, who had sewed up a gash in my ankle caused by an ax slipping out of my hands. By the time I was in the eleventh grade, a new black doctor had come to town, a man I really admired: Harold Fanning Drake. He was a Meharry man, had lived in New York City, and was the son of A&M's president. He was really something. I'd hear about the things he did, how people looked up to him and how he'd managed to bring Little Tommy Scruggs back from the point of death.[8] He had a beautiful wife and a beautiful automobile and a boat. He liked to go to the stock car races, and he would fly his model airplanes. And I'm thinking, if this is the kind of life a doctor leads, that's what I want to be.

So by my senior year, I'd just about decided I would go to medical school, and once the teachers found out that you wanted to make something of yourself, they would start to groom you a little, give you extra assignments, maybe counsel you on what colleges you could attend.

Finally, the day of graduation arrived, and all of us "forty-niners," as we called ourselves, looked forward to it with great anticipation. But my happiness on being told that my grades had brought me the honor of being class valedictorian vanished when I learned I'd have to make a speech. That's when my old fear of stuttering came back, except this time it would be in front of all the teachers, students, and parents. If I'd been expected to make a speech for just a few people, there wouldn't have been a problem. Or, if someone had just said, "Sonnie, get up there right now and talk," there wouldn't have been a problem. But three or four weeks of waiting—that was too much.

I finally told Mrs. Fearn I wouldn't be able to make the speech. So the honor went to a very smart young lady named Tometta Moore, the salutatorian. At the time, I felt like God had put a curse on me, but, as I think on it now, I know that my hurt feelings must have been small when compared to the kids who weren't graduating, who'd had to drop out.

In my first-grade class, there'd been probably ninety to one hundred kids. By the ninth, it was somewhere between sixty and seventy. By the end of my senior year, there were just seventeen, and only four of us men, including one who'd been drafted but was allowed to come home and march with us. Of the other three men, one became a research scientist with Douglas Aircraft in California, another a high school teacher, and the third went to California and to my knowledge has not been heard from since.

Shortly after graduation, and mostly out of curiosity, I wrote to The University of Alabama asking for an application, and when it came, there at the top of the page was a space asking me to put down my race. So I truthfully entered the word "Negro," filled everything out, and mailed it back to Tuscaloosa, and it was only a matter of days before I got a letter back telling me that I couldn't go to school there. The fact that I'd been valedictorian of my class made no difference to them. There was absolutely no place in the state of Alabama where a black person could go to get a medical degree, a dentist's degree, or a law degree.

So I set my sights on Tennessee State in Nashville, which had a program that let you take two years of premed courses and then start your regular studies at Meharry. If you fulfilled all of Meharry's requirements, you would then receive a bachelor's degree from Tennessee State and a medical degree from Meharry. Fisk had something similar, but I didn't want to go there because it was expensive and was looked on by a lot of my friends as a little uppity, by which I mean the students seemed to be mostly lawyers' and doctors' kids from up North. Tennessee State attracted kids like I'd been with at Councill, people I'd be comfortable with if my stuttering started up again.

One of those Councill kids was a bright young fellow named William Hyter, whose father delivered coal and ice in town. In science classes, Bill and I had often studied together, memorizing chemical formulae and the names of bones, and he said he'd like to go with me to Tennessee State and study to be a doctor, too. So that became our plan.

But that fall, the crops were poor, and the frost came early, and my mother and brother and I found it rough going, just barely able to meet expenses. I knew that if I wanted to stay in school I had no other choice than Alabama A&M, which was just a four-mile walk from the house. By now, Tom was already in his third year there, and one advantage of my going there would be that he could pass his books on to me. Thanks to the GI Bill, he could also get me all the supplies I needed free of charge—paper, erasers, pencils, everything.

My greatest fear was that A&M wouldn't let me take the courses I needed to get into Meharry. The school, which sat up on a hill north of town and had only a dozen or so red brick buildings, was mostly vocational, but it did have chemistry and biology courses, and I knew which ones I needed because during the summer I'd requested catalogues from Alabama, Auburn, and Tennessee State, just to get an idea of the requirements for medical school.

On the day of registration, Bill and I went out to campus and walked up to the desk where a man was advising new students. We told him our situation and what we wanted to do. Barely looking up, he told us that A&M had no arts and sciences division, no premed programs of any kind. He looked around and told his secretary, "Put 'em in secondary education."

Well, off we go to see the dean, and we told him what we wanted to do, that we just wanted to be doctors. The dean says, "We don't have an arts and science division, but we're just getting ready to create one. Why don't you fellows help me decide what courses should be in it?"

So we sort of helped the dean create this new curriculum because the way things were set up, we were going to be taking art and music and all this, which is fine, you know, but we wanted to be physicians, and we were thinking, should we be using our time taking these courses when we could be concentrating on the sciences? We wanted to do the same type of thing that Tennessee State and Fisk were doing so we could get into Meharry. So we started with the courses, and I can remember exactly what I had that first year: math, English, biology, social science, and general chemistry, which was a sophomore course.

Although A&M's chemistry lab was fairly well equipped, the biology lab had only a few specimens and display cases, plus three or four microscopes and some test tubes and petri dishes. The school managed to overcome some of its shortages with excellent instructors, like my biology teacher, Mary Chambers, who was my first teacher there and the best I ever had. The strongest personality on the faculty was the president's wife, Mrs. Ann Quick Drake, whose reputation for making students toe the line intimidated everyone. She taught French and German, and because I needed a foreign language to get into Meharry, I decided on German. I paid attention, too, because Mrs. Drake was famous for her rules: no talking, no whispering, no slouching, no gum chewing. No one knew what the penalty was for breaking the rules because no one ever had the courage to try.

Though a lot of the students were from Madison County, it was the kids from the big schools like Parker High in Birmingham who seemed to dominate campus life. Many arrived before the start of the term and got a jump on election of class officers and things like that. When graduation rolled around, it was the Parker High kids who seemed to stand out. None of this affected me because I was too busy with schoolwork and farm chores. Tom and I had worked out a deal where I'd take my classes in the morning while he plowed, and he'd take his classes during the afternoon while I plowed. He'd bring the mules in a little before noon, feed and water them, then head off to campus. By that time, I'd be home, and I'd take them back out.

Each month, Mama got a check for fifty-four dollars from the veteran's administration and would give me ten, which went into a savings account I had opened downtown. There was also a small scholarship of twenty-two dollars per quarter from the Masonic order, where Daddy had been an officer.

In my freshman year, I decided to pledge Omega Psi Phi, mainly because it was the one that many black doctors belonged to. But there was a price. Harassment by the brothers went on for a full year and included everything from paddling and hazing to walking into town late at night to buy hamburgers or shining shoes on command, some as big as boats (like Brother Rosser's from Birmingham, who wore size fourteen). Another trick was to blindfold five or six of us, then dump us on some country road after midnight.

But my grades were good that first year. I had just one B on my transcript. Then, in my sophomore year, I took advanced chemistry—quantitative analysis and qualitative analysis and organic chemistry. And I took physics and advanced biology, plus the English and math required of all students, and I didn't have a single B on my transcript.

At the start of my sophomore year, I applied to Meharry and was told that I should take the Graduate Record Examination and the Medical Profile Test as soon as possible. So I rode up to Fisk on the bus and sat for these exams with six hundred people from all over the country. On the basis of my performance, Meharry admitted me for the next fall term on the condition that I complete the courses I was taking at A&M—three quarters of general physics and two quarters of organic chemistry. I managed to do it all with a straight-A record.

During the time I was at A&M, only two incidents that I witnessed gave any hint of the civil rights activism that would appear on campus several years later. One was during my sophomore year when students started complaining about the cafeteria and curfew rules. Soon, they were talking about a strike, and a few announced that, as a protest, they wouldn't attend a certain lecture scheduled on campus by a very well-known scientist.

On the night of the lecture, a crowd began forming at the entrance to the hall, and rumors flew that they weren't going to let anyone go inside. Suddenly, President Drake appeared. He said that any students who refused to go inside would find themselves stripped of their scholarships and campus jobs by eight o'clock the next morning. Well, I've never seen such a mad rush to get into a door.

The other was when I was called to take my draft physical, also during my sophomore year. I got the notice to come downtown to the post office at six o'clock in the morning and was told that at six-thirty or seven we'd walk down to the Post Office Café and eat breakfast, then board the bus and be carried to Nashville for our pre-induction physicals.

So we all gathered—about fifteen blacks, several of them A&M students, and about thirty Caucasian young men. The director walked us down to the restaurant, and we stood outside while they were preparing for us. We could see through the curtains that the waiters were pouring coffee and orange juice and putting out tablecloths and silverware, and I thought, this is gonna be fine. Ice water on the tables and all that. In the country, you know, we didn't have refrigerators, and we weren't used to having ice water with our meals.

And just as soon as they opened the door and walked us in, the proprietor came and said, "You colored boys just follow me right on back here to the kitchen, and I'm gonna serve you back there." And he took us back to the kitchen, and he handed us our breakfast on a plate, which we were supposed to hold in our hand to eat. And the other guys were sitting at the tables and being waited on by the waiters, and I said, gee whiz.

And it was about then, thirty or forty seconds after the plates had been handed to us, and maybe one or two of the guys had taken a bite of toast, that I heard the first plate hit the floor, then another, and another, until everyone had dropped his plate.

One guy says, "They can put us in jail for this."

Another says, "Well, they can't put us in jail and send us to Korea at the same time."

Someone spotted a crate of oranges, and I think there were some apples, and we stuffed our pockets with oranges and apples to eat on the bus and walked out of the building and on down to the bus station. We never heard anymore about it. To this day, I don't know what they thought about the broken plates and bacon and eggs scattered all over the kitchen floor of the Post Office Café.

On the bus they separated us, but the minute we went through the gates of the pre-induction center, everything was equal. We undressed together, we had our examinations together, and they fed us together.[9] They finished, I think, at 4:30 or 5:00 in the afternoon, and they put us back on the bus, and when they put us back on the bus, that's when it started all over again. In the end, my acceptance into medical school got me a deferment.

Probably 98 percent of aspiring black doctors went to either Howard or Meharry. Meharry could not accept but sixty-five students, so Alabama's complement was about six students, and Tennessee five or six, Georgia maybe eight, and Mississippi eight, and so forth. After they filled those quotas, then I think maybe they had ten or twelve spaces left for all the other states besides the southern states. So I was fortunate enough to be one of the students from Alabama who got into that class.

That summer, Mama took in washing and ironing, and the little extra she earned went directly into my savings account. And because Tom had put in a crop during the spring, he and I agreed that I'd work for him until Meharry's classes started in September, and he'd pay me three dollars a day.

Then I heard from one of Daddy's half sisters living in Nashville, my Aunt Susie, who said I could come stay at her house, which was only twelve blocks from Meharry. She and her husband worked for a white dentist out in the country, and she said they'd be home only on weekends. Furthermore, she said I was welcome to cook and help myself to the icebox, and, except for my cousin Kilbuck, who'd given up farming and was now working construction, I would have the place to myself. This was like a gift from heaven, because at the time Meharry had no dormitory for men, and most students had to rent rooms at one of the boardinghouses.

Another piece of luck came from Tom's bragging around town that his brother was going to Meharry. One day he was playing cards at the American Legion Hut down on Gallatin, and at the table was a teacher named L. G. Fields, who later became postmaster at A&M. When Mr. Fields heard Tom say I was going to Meharry, he said he'd once been a student there himself until health problems forced him to drop out and that he still had all his textbooks, to which I was welcome. Some of those, like Gray's *Anatomy*, cost seventy-five or eighty dollars. When I went to see Mr. Fields, he told me he also had some dissecting equipment and other surgical supplies, plus a $299 microscope, one of the best you could buy, and that I could take it and use it as long as I needed it.

I even managed to get a little help from the state of Alabama, which provided scholarship money to any black person admitted to Meharry. It wasn't much—about forty or fifty dollars—which still left me short by about a hundred. So Tom went down to see Dr. John Cashin Sr., a black dentist in town whose son was then a dentistry student at Meharry, and Tom gets Dr. Cashin to loan me the one hundred dollars I needed by promising to pay it back with his first bale.[10]

Thanks to that loan, September came and I was off to Meharry. My trunk was packed with Mr. Fields's books and instruments and loaded into Tom's old Plymouth that he bought after getting out of the service, and the Plymouth was carrying me and the trunk and an old suitcase stuffed with a few clothes up to Nashville.

2
To Be a Doctor

Two weeks into my first term, I faced the worst crisis I experienced during the whole time I was at Meharry. Not since my early days as a stuttering first-grader at Councill had I felt the way I did now, sure that I'd bitten off more than I could chew. My feelings came not just from the fact that my classmates were all older—some were veterans or had already started their careers—but from their achievements. Two were pharmacists. One guy had been a jet pilot in Korea. Another had been a major in the army. A black major in the 1950s—now, you know he's got to be on the ball. Two had PhDs, and half already had master's degrees, and everyone but me had a bachelor of science degree.

Despite all the good teachers I'd had at Alabama A&M, my lack of self-confidence made me start wondering about the value of my premed courses, a feeling that only got stronger during our first class meeting, the get-acquainted meeting, when the fellows started talking about where they'd gone to school. This guy here was from Ohio University, and that guy was from the University of Illinois, and this one was from City College of New York. They were from Fisk and Morehouse and Howard, and they said, "Where are you from?" I said, "I'm from Alabama A&M," and they said, "Where in the world is that?"

Even worse was the situation at Aunt Susie's, where I was sharing the bedroom with my cousin Kilbuck. All night long he snored like a freight train—loud, rasping sounds that seemed to shake the foundations. The house was small; there was no nook or cranny I could escape to, no place to catch up on my reading and grab a few hours of sleep. I was a nervous wreck and was about to flunk out before getting started.

So I called home and told them what was happening, and before long Tom had driven all the way up from Alabama and was at the front door. Near tears, I told him how Kilbuck and his friends talked and played cards, how Kilbuck snored all night long, how I had a big box of bones sitting beside my bed whose names I still hadn't memorized, and he should just take me home, just let me be a schoolteacher.

Well, Tom drove over to the house where John Cashin Jr.[1] was living and talked to the lady there, and she said try the Omega House, over on Meharry Boulevard. At the Omega House, the fellow in charge said to Tom, yes, we've been saving a room for a guy who still hasn't shown up, and I could have it if I wanted it. So I took the room and finally got some peace and quiet. Soon, I'd settled in with nine other guys there and started trying to catch up, because the first quiz, in gross anatomy, was just days away.

The course was taught by the only full-time white professor on the faculty, a man named Miller—"Race Horse Miller," they called him because he talked in triple time. Taking notes was impossible, so I'd go back to my room and read over the textbook. I'd read for six or seven hours at a stretch, sometimes ten or twelve. After the exam, some of the guys were talking about how well they'd done, and I was sure I'd failed. The next day, Miller comes back and lays the papers on his desk, and he goes to the board and writes "Hughes, 96"—this was a fellow who'd taken the course before and was repeating the first year. Next, he writes "Jefferson, 83," "Jones, 82," and then—was I seeing things?—"Hereford, 81." It was as if I'd scored 1,000. This restored my confidence a little, especially after some of the other fellows started asking to study with me.

After that, the exams never let up—written and oral tests once a week, pop quizzes, lab exams. That first quarter was a blur of lectures and labs in biochemistry and anatomy, embryology, and histology. And the assignments seemed insane, especially for someone used to reading one or two chapters a week at A&M who was now being told to read three or four in one night.

That first year, the main courses were in gross anatomy, microscopic anatomy, developmental anatomy, physiology, and biochemistry. Those were the basic science courses, and if we had any other courses the first year, they were not nearly as important as these. The second year you had bacteriology, parasitology, and pharmacology, and you had physical diagnosis—those types of courses. They made sure that we got all of our basic science first.

And then the third year, you started on your clinical science. In fact, in the old days it was taboo for a basic science teacher to even mention anything to a class about any clinical work. So we were taught little clinical medicine during the first two years, mostly just the basic sciences, with anatomy at the top of the list.

For me, the most stressful part in the first year was gross anatomy lab, where eight or nine students were assigned one cadaver. All the cadavers were black people—I never once saw a Caucasian cadaver—and my impression was that they came from the ranks of the homeless, though families may have donated some. I recall one muscular male around 280 pounds who, it was said, had been shot and killed trying to escape from the state prison.

Professor Miller would move from table to table and instruct each group of students on what parts of the body to dissect, then retreat to his office. I found the work fascinating and would not normally have been bothered by it, except that my cadaver was an elderly woman who in size, color, and facial features looked exactly like Grandma Liz.

Physiology was almost as bad. It was a course that all medical, dental, and nursing students had to take, and it covered the subject in staggering detail. Lab started at ten o'clock and sometimes lasted until five, and unless people in your group could spell each other, you went without lunch because you might have a dog under anesthesia, testing its responses to various drugs. We also used frogs and rabbits, but it was mostly strays hauled in by Meharry's dogcatcher. Other than being told to treat the dogs humanely and overdose them mercifully at the end, we had no rules or guidelines, no one looking over our shoulders.

The physiology instructor was something of a legend at Meharry named Daniel T. Rolfe, who became dean shortly after my arrival.[2] Among themselves, the students referred to him as the Fat Man, an expression of respect, if not fear. He was well spoken and very cultured, and he talked a lot about the value of hard work and self-discipline and would lock the door once class began. As to how you survived his course, the word was, "Don't be conspicuously absent, and don't be conspicuously present."

One of Rolfe's tactics was to ask you a question and let you talk on, even after your ignorance became clear. And he knew who everyone was because he could match faces with names in his roll book. That roll book proved my undoing several times because my name stood out at the very top of page two. That meant that when he got tired of picking on Allen or Andrews, his eyes would wander over to the top of the second page, and there I was.

"Mr. Hereford, what did we talk about today?"

"We talked about red blood cells. We talked about white blood cells. And we talked about platelets."

"That was short but comprehensive," he said.

Another time, he asked me about "venous return," or what prevents blood entering the heart from the lower part of the body from flowing backward. I knew the answer because I'd read it in the text, but it was a little complicated, having to do with the muscles squeezing the blood through the veins and the downward pressures of the diaphragm. But as I struggled to put it all together, I heard myself saying that it was valves at the entrance to the heart that kept the blood from flowing backward, which was totally wrong. Rolfe pretended mock surprise. "Valves at the entrance to the heart, huh? Well, I'll be doggoned."

I finished my first year at Meharry ranked eleventh in my class, and after a summer spent working for Tom on the farm for next year's tuition, I returned in September. Meanwhile, my mother kept sending me a little money, and I did some babysitting for the children of a few faculty and married students, who would tell me to help myself to whatever was in the refrigerator.

There were a few Meharry students who didn't have any financial problems, who brought cars to campus, dated the girls from Fisk, and wore nice clothes. But most of the kids had to work, and they'd take their meals wherever they could, usually at one of the cafés or grocery stores around campus. One piece of luck I had was finding a box of clothes in the basement of the Omega House that had been left by a former student. They were a perfect fit and doubled my wardrobe.

By now, I'd become good friends with the brothers at the Omega House, but there was little chance to talk to people outside this group and not much time to do anything but study. I think I made just half a dozen trips downtown during my first two years, and I rarely went over to Tennessee State. There was some dating between the Meharry medical and nursing students, but there weren't very many nursing students at the time and no women medical students in my own class, though there were some in the class ahead of me. Two I especially remember, because they helped me with some diagnostic problems I had during my junior year. One was Clara Brawner, from Memphis, and the other was Marquenta Neblett, from Nashville, whose name always appeared on the dean's list. Marquenta was beautiful as well as smart, but she was also married, to the great disappointment of many Meharry men.

The pressures we were under made it tough on everybody, but things often seemed hardest for some of the older guys with families. Once, I was picking up my grades, and the man in front of me had just gotten his, and still he didn't move away from the window. Finally, he turned around, and there were tears in his eyes, and he said, "I'll kill the mother-fucker. He's messin' with my *life*."

Maybe 20 percent of our teachers were what the students called dollar-a-year men because they'd heard that these professors worked at Vanderbilt at their regular jobs and gave their services to Meharry for just a dollar a year. I remember one fellow in particular that I was extremely impressed with because he had written a neuroanatomy book that was used worldwide. His name was Dr. Lillard Clark, and naturally we used his book for neuroanatomy.[3] I didn't sense any resentment toward the white professors among the students because we wanted to learn and were thankful to the ones who gave their time. There was one exception I remember during my freshman year—this was a white instructor who was talking about the salivary glands and the ducts that carry saliva to the mouth. He said: "Colored people carry long knives and cut each other up on Saturday nights. So you better know how to repair these ducts, because there'll be many times when you face this problem alone in your home or office, and you won't be able to call on anyone for help."

One of the black teachers I developed a special bond with was Ralph Cazort, a professor of pharmacology and later dean of the School of Medicine.[4] He was a friend of Dr. Drake's and knew that I wanted to go back and practice with him. I got the impression that I was one of his favorite students, and at the end of my sophomore year, I applied for a job as his lab assistant. He agreed to take me on for the following fall term at fifty dollars a month.

At the close of my second year, I was ranked eighth in my class, still in the upper third. Back home that summer, I put on a hard hat and went to work for a dollar an hour in construction at Redstone Arsenal. That took care of the next year's tuition, and with my new job as Dr. Cazort's lab assistant, plus babysitting, I was now earning about one hundred dollars a month. On top of this, I had a free room at the Omega House after accepting the job of house manager.

Though my junior year at Meharry was the hardest, I loved it, doing the kinds of things I'd have to do in actual practice. We were taught how to read the language of the body, how to search out the most likely causes for pain and fever. We learned how to take a patient's history, how to do percussion and auscultation, or listening to the sounds inside the body, and palpation, or the art of touching. One of our instructors was a man named Robert Smith—we called him "Slick Robert"—who advised us to keep our hands and fingernails in good shape. He said he used sandpaper on his own hands because you sometimes make your diagnosis not by what you hear and see but by what you feel.

There was still a lot of didactic work, a lot of lectures and demonstrations, but the clinical part now took up 30 to 40 percent. Because juniors in the wards were at the bottom of the pecking order, you found yourself doing a lot of menial tasks, and someone was always looking over your shoulder, ordering you around. The clinical portion rose to maybe 60 percent during the senior year, and as you got closer to being a doctor, you noticed a change in the way people treated you. Even the cook we'd hired in our fraternity, an older woman we considered a sort of housemother, started showing us a little more respect.

George W. Hubbard Hospital was where the students did their clinical work. I thought the teachers were very good, and many of them had been pioneers. The head of the surgery department, for example, Dr. Matthew Walker, was in my opinion one of the greatest surgeons who ever lived.[5] He seemed to know everything. He knew biochemistry and physiology. He knew fluids and electrolytes, which some surgeons did not know. And he expected us to follow his example. If a student came up short or gave him an answer from out in left field, he'd say, "You're just trying to fool me because I'm old."

One of Dr. Walker's protégés was Dr. Dorothy Brown, who later was in the

Tennessee legislature.[6] She's known today as the first black female surgeon in the South, but at the time she was the only black female surgeon I'd ever heard of from any part of the country. She was very outspoken and a person of great talent. Dr. Walker made her chief resident in general surgery, despite grumbling from some of the men.

Hubbard Hospital was 100 percent black and 100 percent poor, and we saw just about every sort of disease you can imagine. We saw heart ailments and hypertension. We saw peptic ulcers and lower back problems caused by lifting, pushing, and having babies. We saw a lot of accidents. We saw syphilis. We saw metabolic diseases like diabetes and thyroid conditions, plus a good deal of gastroenteritis, especially during the colder months of winter when stomach viruses were most prevalent. We saw bronchitis and pneumonia and upper respiratory infections in children. We saw collagen diseases like rheumatism and lupus. I remember a young girl who had lupus, a very sad case. I will never forget that young lady.

And tuberculosis—well, most of the cases that came in were sent on to Memphis, and you wouldn't believe how many there were. Even before I went to Meharry, you would not believe how many young black women that I actually knew personally back home who had either died of TB or were severely infected with TB. After I got to Meharry and started studying some of the statistics, I found that Alabama had one of the highest rates of TB in the United States and the black race a higher rate than any other race, and females more than males, and teenagers more than adults. Some of the kids at home that I had participated in church functions with, like the Sunday school programs, had TB. I found out later that some of the choir members with visiting churches, mostly young, black females who sang for the congregation and greeted and hugged the members, had unknowingly carried the disease with them.[7]

Much of our training took place in Hubbard's outpatient clinics, where we were closely monitored. It worked like this: the class would be divided into four groups of sixteen or seventeen students, and each group would rotate for six to eight weeks in four areas: medicine, surgery, obstetrics, and pediatrics. Within each area, the students would be further divided into groups of two to assist with outpatient clinics, most of which took place in the mornings because we made rounds in the afternoon.

The outpatient clinics were known as clerkships, and they gave us a chance to work up the patient. We reviewed the charts, and we asked questions. When did the coughing start? What are you coughing up? Do you have chest pains or night sweats? Any trouble catching your breath?

You asked a lot of questions, because you knew that even if you missed on the diagnosis, you'd get credit for being thorough and logical in the way you went about it. You also knew that if you didn't probe deeply enough you'd be chewed out by the resident or the staff physician, though never in front of the patient. In the wards, the residents always addressed you as "doctor," no matter what. That's because they knew that no patient would be comfortable undressing for a physical exam in front of a mere beginner or even talking about the intimate details of his condition.

When all the questions were asked, you decided on lab work, which always included drawing blood. You followed up with a head-to-toe physical, and then you recorded your findings, positive and negative. One of the interns would wander in to look over what you'd done, then the resident, then the staff physician, all of them asking questions, poking and probing the patient a second time, then more questions. What's the treatment? Do we need a consultant? A mass in the abdomen? Then it's off to surgery. An ovarian cyst? Let's refer to gynecology.

If it was a simple case and you'd done your job, the staff physician would sign the prescription and okay the orders—when the patient could be dismissed, when he could go back to work, maybe a work excuse. Meanwhile, the patient put up with all this because that's what you had to do to get free care.

If an interesting case appeared in the wards—an adult with chicken pox, an unusual liver disease, a woman expecting triplets—the professors made sure that everyone had a chance to see it. Sometimes, the patient was wheeled into the amphitheater during the Clinical Pathological Conference, where we sat with the residents and interns. We'd be handed a sheet of paper listing the patient's symptoms and the lab findings, and our job was to arrive at a correct diagnosis. At a minimum, we were expected to deduce the proper classification of the disease—to be in the right church, so to speak, if not the right pew.

I found myself very much affected by the suffering of some of these patients and what was happening to their families. One episode that occurred right after I got to Meharry involved an eighteen-year-old boy who'd just come to Fisk on a football scholarship, and during the first week of practice he'd received a blow to the head and slipped into a coma. I was only two years older than he, and when I heard about the accident, I went by his room and saw in the bed a healthy-looking young man, six feet tall and 250 pounds, but he never woke up, and his parents were devastated.

In pediatrics, we'd have to rely on what the parents could tell us about what was wrong with the infants and young children they brought in. That's why our professors were always pushing us to improve our diagnostic skills. One of the most demanding was E. Perry Crump, a very talented clinician who intimidated some of my classmates.[8] If a student said that the patient's blood pressure was high and he had a temperature, Dr. Crump would answer that everybody had a temperature. "A corpse lying in the morgue has a temperature," he'd say.

I came to appreciate Dr. Crump on a personal level after he agreed to take a look at Tom's infant daughter Beverly, who was suffering from cerebral palsy. We never knew the cause of her affliction but thought it might have been the result of brain damage from the use of forceps by a Huntsville obstetrician. Dr. Crump gave the baby a thorough examination but couldn't give us an encouraging prognosis. My niece would later pass from this life at the age of fifteen having never walked or talked.

In clinical work, you soon realized the limits of what you could do for a patient. There was nothing really effective at combating mumps and measles, and Salk's vaccine for polio was just being introduced when I left Meharry. At that time, thousands of children were dying from polio or being kept alive in iron lungs, though I never saw a black child in an iron lung.[9]

I remember us being warned against performing abortions, and I heard about several black doctors in Nashville who'd gotten in trouble with the authorities over this. One day, one of the teachers told us that once we got into practice, we'd have people waving hundreds of dollars in our face to get us to perform an abortion, and he said, "Just open the door that leads to your waiting room and say in a loud voice, 'Hell, no, I don't do abortions,' and those people will clear out faster than Sherman through Atlanta."

One of the things I found out early was what I didn't want to do, and by that I mean surgery. I was assisting one of the residents with a gastrectomy, or removal of part of the patient's stomach and attachment of the esophagus to the small intestines. The operation began at 9:00 in the morning, and as noon rolled around, he was still at it. At 12:30, he called for orange juice, which a nurse gave to him through a straw. He didn't finish until 3:00 in the afternoon.

During my junior year, I had a chance to assist Dr. Dorothy Brown with a thyroidectomy, or removal of a diseased thyroid gland. Partway through the procedure, the bleeding got out of control. She called for help, and soon Dr. Walker was there helping to stop the bleeding and advising Dr. Brown on how to salvage the parathyroid glands, and to do so without severing the laryngeal nerve. All this just confirmed my earlier feelings that I didn't want to be a surgeon.

By the end of my junior year, I was ranked second in my class, and that summer, I got some valuable practical experience working in a black hospital in Fayetteville, Tennessee, a forty-minute drive from Huntsville. It was called the Donalson Hospital, named after its founder, Dr. Latha Donalson, and it was the only black hospital for eighty miles in any direction.[10]

Dr. Donalson was an old coon-hunting friend of Dr. Matthew Walker's, and I'd met him for the first time when I was home and decided to go up to Fayetteville with Dr. Drake to see one of his patients. Later, Dr. Donalson asked me if I'd like to work for him—he said he couldn't pay me an "extortious" salary, just twenty-five dollars a week. But I got to do a lot of patient histories and workups, and I also got to do half a dozen deliveries on my own, plus assist him in surgery. And every time I assisted him, he made sure he did two things first: he prayed, and he reread the technique. If he'd done the operation three hundred times, he still reread the technique.

I learned a lot from Dr. Donalson and admired the way he'd gone about building a practice. He often said that when he came to Fayetteville back in the 1930s, all he had was a ninety-eight-cent medical bag, a roll of tape, and a stethoscope.[11] As time passed, his clientele began to include whites as well as blacks. Once a few white patients came and found out that he helped them feel better and get well, I guess his reputation just grew. And then, a lot of times, if Mama and Daddy and Uncle came, the children would come.

But let me tell you, it was the funniest thing in the world. This is really strange now. You've got Granddaddy, you've got Grandma, you've got Mama and Daddy, and you've got the children. And when Mama gets pregnant again, she's got to go over there to another doctor, the white doctor, and to another hospital, the white hospital, and as soon as the baby is born, she brings him back over here to Dr. Donalson. He went along with the system, and the patients went along with the system. The other thing, too, were his fees. They were always lower than the white doctor's. He'd tell me that the secret of his success was "volume, volume, volume."

So at the start of my senior year, I kept working for Dr. Donalson on weekends. He'd give me money for the bus, and I'd leave Meharry a little early on Fridays and head down to Fayetteville.

I also had two brief externships. The first was at the Homer G. Phillips Hospital in St. Louis, which was an all-black hospital for the indigent. We left Nashville in the fall, about eight or nine Meharry seniors traveling in three or four cars, and we got to St. Louis and took rooms in the hospital, and over the next few weeks we tried to learn something about neurology and psychiatry.

Nothing I picked up at Homer G. Phillips made a deeper impression on me, a more troubling impression, than when I saw patients getting electroshock treatments. They used it for depression and schizophrenia, and it had a terrible effect, for when they pulled the switch, the patient's back would arch upward in the shape of a rainbow, and the whole body would start to convulse, without sedation or anesthesia.

From St. Louis, we rotated to the John Gaston Hospital in Memphis, where we roomed at the black YMCA. In the hospital, there was segregation everywhere you looked from the wards to the cafeterias. There were separate restrooms for black and white male staff, black and white female staff, black and white male patients, and black and white female patients. I thought, John Gaston seems to have more bathrooms than beds.

We were there to observe patients in the tuberculosis wards, but I noticed that some of the Meharry students who'd been so fired up in St. Louis that you couldn't keep them out of the patients' rooms now developed a certain reserve, afraid of being infected themselves. So the patients were twice isolated because they were victims of tuberculosis and because they were black.

My last year at Meharry gave me very little chance to relax. I might see a movie at the black theater near campus but never downtown, where you had to sit in the balcony. There was an occasional concert by the Fisk Jubilee Singers or maybe a play at Tennessee State, where I saw *Hamlet,* and I did agree to participate in a fund-raising project thought up by our class vice president, who organized an evening of songs and skits billed as "Comics of '53 by the Medics of '55."

Every three or four months, the Omega House would present Game Night, which was a way to raise money to pay our coal and electric bills. This was a wildly popular event that featured card games and dice and pulled in 150 people or more, including Tom, who'd drive up to get in on the fun. My role was hat-and-coat-check man, but we had to be careful because the police were notorious for raiding get-togethers like this if they thought liquor was being sold. So we made sure names were on each bottle. That way, we could tell the police, "Oh, no, sir, this is Brother Smith's bottle, and that one is Brother Townsend's bottle."

Most days, my roommates and I just said hello on our way to and from class or maybe talked a little at supper, then I'd go to my room and turn on the radio and read, finally falling into bed exhausted. I loved music, jazz and the big bands, and once, late at night, as I was reading and listening to the radio, the Arthur Murray School of Music started playing songs and offering free dance lessons to anyone who could call in and identify at least two numbers.

So I got on the phone and identified *every* song they played, and they congratulated me. But when I mentioned that I was black, because I thought this might be a problem, they said, ah, no, sorry, you can't come down here. No, no, they said, there's no way that you can take those free dancing lessons.

When I think about all the protests that happened in Nashville with the black students in the early 1960s, I'm amazed I saw so little hint of it. Or maybe I was just too busy. I'd heard about a civil rights leader named Alexander Looby and knew that some of my classmates had attended his talks, but I never met him.[12] I never saw a demonstration, never saw a protest rally. The most assertive thing I witnessed among black people was when I rode the Jefferson Street bus downtown and the black passengers sat anywhere they wanted.

With graduation coming up, I decided to do something about a little matter that had been eating at me for a long time. It was my lack of a bachelor's degree from Alabama A&M, which bothered me because if I'd done the two years I spent there at Fisk or Tennessee State and then completed Meharry's requirements, I'd be getting an undergraduate diploma as well as a medical degree.

It seemed really unfair now, because I was second in my class and had recently been one of only eight people inducted into Kappa Pi, the honor medical society. I'd also been invited to join the Society of the Upper Tenth, a physiology club that Dean Rolfe had created to recognize all the students in the top 10 percent of their class. It was a great honor and entitled you to attend a banquet that Dr. Rolfe and his wife hosted at their home.

So I wrote to A&M and sent them copies of the Fisk and Tennessee State arrangements, and there was a long exchange, but I seemed to be getting nowhere. Then, I received a phone call from the A&M registrar, who said, "We're having a graduation ceremony down here on May 30, and we'd like for you to come down and march with the class and receive your bachelor of science degree that day."

When Meharry posted the final grades, there was just one person whose average was higher than mine, though only slightly. So I ended up graduating second in my class. On the first Monday in June, a week after they had watched me graduate magna cum laude at A&M, my mother and Tom and his wife, Lytha, drove up to Nashville to see me march a second time.

The day after commencement, about two dozen of us Meharry grads were in a motorcade headed for Atlanta, where we intended to take the Georgia State Medical Board Examination. We chose Georgia because its exam was earlier than those in most of the other states—Alabama's wasn't until August—and because we had to report for our internships by the first of July. Because of reciprocity, a passing score in Georgia could be used to get a license in most other states, and we wanted to get it over with because we thought our medical knowledge was probably more comprehensive now than it would ever be. Also, none of us knew of any Meharry people who'd flunked the Georgia exam.

In Atlanta, a friend had made arrangements for us to room on the campus of Morehouse. The exam itself was given in the Georgia statehouse, right where the legislators met, and there must have been 40 or 50 black applicants and maybe 150 Caucasians, and the blacks sat on the right side of the aisle and the whites on the left, like Democrats and Republicans in Congress. It was a grueling, four-hour test, and I can recall only the anatomical portion, which required us to draw a cross-section of the thigh and list every bone, nerve, and artery. But I felt confident I'd passed it. Sure enough, two months later, the mailman delivered my certificate, rolled up in a cardboard cylinder.

With my boards out of the way, I got ready to start my internship, which was to be in a small Catholic hospital in Hammond, Indiana. It was called St. Margaret's, and how I chose it was purely a matter of economics. At the time, there were usually more internships than interns to fill them, which meant that when you submitted your top three choices to the agency that matched us up, chances were you'd get at least one. Hubbard Hospital was paying around $100 a month, and there was a hospital in North Carolina that was paying $200, and then this Catholic hospital up near Chicago, in the northwest corner of Indiana, was paying $300.

So I put them down in the order of their pay, thinking that this was a chance to make a little extra money while finishing my training. I never even considered the big hospitals up North. The rumor around Meharry was that you had to pay for the privilege of interning at places like Johns Hopkins.[13] As I'd hoped, St. Margaret's offered me the job. In fact, eight of the ten interns the hospital hired that year were from Meharry.

By the end of June of '55, I'd packed everything into my newly purchased Olds 98 and got ready to set off on my first trip north of the Mason-Dixon Line. I'd bought the car for the enormous sum of $2,000 from Mrs. Cashin, wife of the dentist who'd loaned me the final hundred to go to Meharry, with the understanding that my first car payment wouldn't come due until I started drawing a salary in Hammond. I was nervous about driving in Chicago traffic, so Tom, who was on summer break from his teaching job at Decatur Negro High School, said he'd go with me and visit with his wife's brothers and sisters in South Chicago and maybe make some money barbering there for a few weeks.

So the two of us drove north to Nashville and across western Kentucky and then through Terre Haute before finally rolling into Hammond. Only after we reached the outskirts of Hammond did I feel I was out of the South. Back then people viewed southern Indiana the way they viewed Cullman and Scottsboro here in Alabama—as places where black people weren't welcome. At Meharry, the interns used to tease one of the guys who was planning on opening a clinic in Marion, Indiana—told him he'd be better off in Mississippi. So Tom and I didn't try to eat at any of the diners along the way and didn't ask to use the restrooms at filling stations because you never knew whether the manager would say yes, no, or pull out a gun.

What I saw coming into Hammond was different from anything I'd ever seen before: a sprawl of steel mills and refineries and meatpacking plants, and lots of black people living in that area from South Chicago through East Chicago and the area called Indiana Harbor on Lake Michigan. Many had only recently come up from the South. It was like they'd decided to stop right there and go no farther so they'd be close to the road that took them back to Nashville or Huntsville.[14]

St. Margaret's was a five-story brick hospital with about two hundred beds, and all the interns were quartered in a first-floor dormitory, which was the first time I'd eaten, slept, and worked under one roof. The place was run by the Sisters of St. Francis, and though the Mother Superior was a fine nurse herself who kept a tight rein on hospital administration, there was no interference that I could see from her or anyone else on medical matters, though I did hear that she had revoked the privileges of one doctor who'd left his wife for his secretary.

Eight of the ten interns were black, and maybe eight of the twenty or so nursing students were black, and a few black registered nurses worked in the hospital. But we were in a pretty affluent area of town, and it was five or six weeks before I came across my first black patient. I'd estimate that just 2 to 3 percent of the patients were black, which was small in comparison to all the other ethnic groups we treated. Among local doctors who made up the staff, I met Italian doctors and Polish doctors and Jewish doctors, but only two black doctors—one of them was at least eighty years old.

As part of their control of hospital affairs, the Sisters had laid down the law regarding racial discrimination. They made it clear that St. Margaret's was to be a place of equality and tolerance. The white staff doctors were cordial and relaxed in our presence, and some invited us to drop by their offices in town to see how they practiced medicine. I saw few instances of racist behavior, although on one occasion I walked into the doctors' dressing room as some of the surgeons were scrubbing up, and they didn't know I was coming in and were telling Amos 'n' Andy jokes.

Of course, all the traditional rules regarding social relations between the races were still strictly applied. When one of the staff doctors found out that six of us were bachelors, he tried to be a matchmaker—I'm gonna match this intern with this nursing student, that sort of thing. And I thought it was funny that for every white intern he picked out a white nursing student and for every black intern a black one.

When I had a chance to go downtown, I found no barriers because of the color of my skin. I visited the library, I went to the movies, I walked in the parks. I liked walking in the parks, which I was forbidden to do back home. I liked to see the way people mingled, black and white, Hispanic, Asian, all having a good time.

In one of the music stores, I struck up a friendship with a white lady who was chief clerk. She saved me old or discounted recordings whose covers had been damaged, and I browsed there often, listening to Beethoven in one of the booths. I found out I could check out recordings from the Hammond library, and this fed my love for classical music, which I'd first learned about from Rev. Henry Bradford, Alabama A&M's chaplain.

Every three months, I rotated in the hospital's four main departments—medicine, surgery, obstetrics-gynecology, and pediatrics. I'd make rounds in the mornings and present my cases to the staff doctors. For the rest of the day, I'd do patient histories and physicals and enter my notations on the charts next to those of the staff doctor. Obstetrics-gynecology was the hardest because you were twenty-four hours on and twenty-four hours off, and you had to attend all deliveries.

Every ten days, we rotated through the ER in twenty-four-hour shifts. This took precedence over other duties, unless it was a slow day, which wasn't often. We saw victims of accidents in the steel mills and refineries, and lots of people who had been injured in car wrecks. Some of the black people coming up from the South on U.S. 41 drove much too fast, in a hurry, I guess, to leave Alabama and Mississippi behind because I saw more injuries and more mangled bodies from car wrecks than I care to remember.

St. Margaret's had no outpatient services, and this made my training at Hubbard and Donalson hospitals all the more helpful. I had done so many intravenous injections and phlebotomies, drawing blood and that sort of thing—all on black people—that when I got to St. Margaret's, where 98 percent of the people I treated were white, boy, it was just a breeze for me to get those veins because I could actually see some of the veins, whereas at Meharry you had to feel for them a lot of times.

So everything went smoothly at first. Then, about six months into my stay, the interns started complaining that some of the staff doctors were not doing enough teaching, and the staff doctors said some of the interns were lying down on the job. There was a meeting, and a lot of finger-pointing, before things got sorted out. During the meeting, one of the doctors said, "As far as I'm concerned, there's only one intern who's taking care of my patients, and that's Dr. Hereford." My face turned red, and I felt like a traitor to the other interns, whose side I had more or less taken.

As time passed, I started to fancy myself something of a teacher and would pass along a few gems of wisdom to the nursing students. One afternoon around two o'clock, when I was trying to get in a quick nap in my room, the phone rang and on the other end was a feminine voice telling me that a certain patient had pulled his IV out and could I come up and put it back in.

So I went up and got the IV started again. As I taped the patient up, I proceeded to explain the technique to the nursing student who'd called me, and when I'd finished, she said, "Thank you for teaching me how to do this. Is there anything else you'd like to teach me?"

Her name was Martha Ann Adams, and she was the daughter of a Kentucky coal miner named General Lee Adams. When she was a teenager, her family had moved to East Chicago, Indiana. Martha had graduated from Washington High School in East Chicago, then worked as a nurses' aid in a Catholic hospital. That's how she'd become interested in nursing and in the Catholic faith. She had begun her nursing studies at Saint Anne's Hospital in the city of Chicago, but because her family lived in East Chicago, Indiana, she had transferred to St. Margaret's in Hammond.

Martha and I began dating, and within a few weeks I'd met her parents. Martha had never been to Alabama, but she was troubled by what she'd heard. There were the newspaper stories of Mrs. Rosa Parks and the bus boycott in Montgomery, and there'd been the riots at the University of Alabama over the admission of a black woman named Autherine Lucy. In contrast to all that, Martha had good memories of East Chicago and Washington High, which had a fine curriculum with lots of choices for kids. She said she liked how people from all backgrounds and all nationalities seemed to get along. She told me how the schools and teachers were excellent as well as the facilities, and how a black person could become a lawyer or bank president or anything else.

And I thought about what she said, I thought about it a lot—about not going back to the South. Among my classmates at Meharry, probably a fifth ended up in California. Of the eight of us at St. Margaret's, there was one man, from St. Petersburg, Florida, who took a job at a mental hospital in California and later opened an office in Palo Alto. Another fellow, from Savannah, settled in East Chicago. Two from Louisiana—one from New Orleans and the other from Baton Rouge—moved to Louisville and Gary. Another, from British Guiana, opened a practice in Terre Haute.

Up North, a black doctor could make a decent living, maybe three or four times what he'd make in Alabama. Industry was booming, and in Hammond alone there must have been three or four big steel mills and factories where black workers held good jobs at places like Inland Steel and U.S. Steel. When you looked at a calendar, instead of seeing only the dates for Easter and Christmas highlighted in red, you saw the paydays of the various companies—Friday the fourteenth, payday at U.S. Steel, that sort of thing.

It was tempting. It was very tempting. Can you imagine trying to collect your fee from someone working for good money at a steel mill and trying to get your money from somebody back in Alabama chopping cotton for Mr. Charlie?

Still, Alabama was home, and Tom kept urging me to come to Decatur, which he said was "wide open" for a black doctor. Dr. Drake told me to come to Huntsville. He said, "You can come into my office, and we'll work together."

But Dr. Donalson said—these are his exact words—"You go to Huntsville, set up your practice by yourself even if you have to practice out of a chicken coop." He said, "If you go in with another doctor, I'll give you three or four weeks before you're gonna have a misunderstanding, and you're gonna have the biggest mess you've ever seen in your life. You can cover for each other on vacations and illness, if you need to go to the movies, a party, church, cover for each other, but don't go in the office together."

Back in those days, it was not routine for black doctors to have group practices. A few white doctors did. Many of them broke up, too, and had real hard feelings afterward. But not too many black doctors had group practices.

Anyway, there was no urgency about it because I was sure I was about to be drafted into the army, where I expected to be assigned as an officer to the Medical Corps. So I thought I'd go on back to Alabama. For one thing, I figured it'd be easier to get started in a place where I had family, where I was known. And I thought I was needed there. In Madison County we had one black doctor, Dr. Drake, to care for a very large black population.

So when my internship ended, I went home and then up to the Donalson Hospital, where I worked the rest of the summer waiting for my induction notice. Then Dr. Drake suggested that if I was going to open a practice in Huntsville, my draft board might consider it an essential occupation, seeing as how they needed more black doctors.

So I wrote to the head of the draft board and asked if I might qualify. Dr. Drake might have put in a good word on my behalf, and I know that Dr. McCalep, head of the Department of History and Government at Alabama A&M, wrote a letter to the board indicating that I was needed in the county.[15]

To my surprise, the draft board approved my request and gave me a deferment because my job in Madison County was declared essential. The county had just one black doctor and I guess about ten or twelve thousand black patients living in the city, and back in those days, black doctors took care of black patients, and white doctors took care of white patients and some black patients. Many of the white physicians didn't want black patients, or if they did see them, they'd push them off to the side in some small segregated waiting room. You'd just sit around until every white patient had been seen. One lady told me how she went to a white doctor's office in Huntsville at nine-thirty in the morning and by the time she got out it was dark.

And so I was declared essential for the area and didn't have to go into the army. With the draft no longer hanging over my head, I applied for an Alabama license through reciprocity with Georgia and was awarded my certificate in September of '56.

Finding an office was the first thing I needed to do, but not many owners would rent space to black people. I cruised around town looking for signs advertising suites of offices for rent, but when I'd go ask about the possibility of renting an office, I was told they didn't have anything. One of the drug salesmen told me there was a place right across from the hospital that had seven suites for physicians and dentists, two of which were available, but when I went to talk to the landlord, he said he couldn't rent it to me, said he'd lose all his white tenants, all the white doctors and dentists.

Dr. Drake had been through the same thing, and he'd thrown in the towel and bought residential property. That's the way many blacks practiced—out of a house. You'd buy the house and maybe put in one or two extra offices if there were other black doctors in town looking for a place to open their own practices.

I was finally able to get part of Dr. Beard's rental house on Church Street. He had passed a few years earlier, and his widow was willing to let me have it for fifty-five dollars a month. There wasn't a lot to the place, just two dilapidated rooms and a hallway that I used for a waiting room. I painted the hallways, hung a few pictures, and put out half a dozen chairs I'd picked up at a used furniture store. It worked fine as a waiting room except for the fact that Mrs. Beard's roomers were constantly coming and going through the room.

I had an examining table, a cabinet where I kept my equipment, a desk for the secretary, and a sterilizer. I also bought an old icebox because you had to keep two types of supplies on hand: injectibles and biologicals—your penicillin, vaccines, and so forth. Later on, a drug salesman bought me a small refrigerator. He wanted me to buy all my drugs from him and got a small refrigerator for the office as an incentive. But I started with that icebox.

The first thing you had to do when you were starting up was to let the black community know you were open for business. Dr. Drake helped by pointing some of his overflow in my direction. He'd been telling everyone how I was coming back and how we were going to work together and all, and he was very, very happy I was there because he'd been practicing alone. The poor guy was worked to death and hardly had any time off. If he wanted to have a short vacation or if he had to attend a funeral or something out of town, there were only one or two white physicians who would cover for him.

Another way to get the word out was to give your announcement to the pastors or the deacons. Ninety percent of the black people in North Alabama at that time attended some church. And even if they didn't go every Sunday, they'd get the word eventually. So you give it to the pastors, give it to the deacons. I learned this from Dr. Donalson and Dr. Drake, and that's what I did.

When I found out I wasn't going to be drafted, I called Martha and asked her to marry me. She'd been down for a few days' visit over the summer, her first trip to Alabama, and after that the depth of our feelings for each other had become obvious, and I'd run up a big long-distance bill to East Chicago. After thinking it over two or three days and talking it over with her parents, she said yes. That easily beat out graduation day at Meharry as the happiest day of my life.

The wedding was set for November 1, and Martha arrived on the last Sunday in October and moved in with Tom and Lytha, next door to my mother's. We were married in Tom's living room by the pastor of the Pine Grove Colored Methodist Episcopal Church. My mother was there, Tom and Lytha, my cousin Richard Hall and his wife, Marion, and Dr. Drake, who read poetry.

The next week, we left for Nashville on a two-day honeymoon, with a tin can tied to the back of the car. This was my idea, something I'd seen in the funny papers and movies and had looked forward to doing for years. Being black in the South usually meant nobody paid you any attention. Now, for a day, we were the star attraction, and nobody was going to get mad at a couple of black kids on their honeymoon because I figured everybody loves a bride and groom. But I tied on just one tin can because I didn't want to attract too much attention.

Shortly before we were married, Martha and I had our wedding pictures taken by Dr. Vivian Chambers, an entomologist at Alabama A&M and a very fine photographer who had a studio on the campus. I'd never seen anything in our local newspaper about a black person's wedding, and I thought that the medical skills Martha and I were bringing to the community would be of public interest. So I wrote up a story about her background and chose one of her pictures and dropped it all off with the Society Page editor at the *Huntsville Times*.

We were married on a Thursday, and by the following Monday nothing had appeared in the paper. So I drove down to the newspaper's offices and found the Society Page editor, who told me her boss had said they couldn't publish the photograph. I said I'd like to talk with her boss, and she led me into the office of the editor. I asked him if he knew about my wife's photograph, and he said, yes, he knew about it, but he wasn't going to publish it. I asked him why.

Sitting in an easy chair behind his desk, the editor was all politeness. "Dr. Hereford," he said, "do you realize what you're asking me to do? You're asking me to destroy the Society Page of the *Huntsville Times*."

"What do you mean?" I asked.

"Why, if I put your bride's picture in the paper—or that of any other Nigra woman—no white bride would ever bring me a picture in the future."

"Well," I said, "I love my wife just like anyone else, and besides, they do it in other cities."

"No, they don't."

"Yes, they do."

"Dr. Hereford," he said, "I'll tell you what I'll do. If you can bring me any newspaper with a picture of a colored bride—Atlanta, Birmingham, Memphis, even New York City—if you can just bring me one, I'll print your wife's picture."

I walked out feeling certain I could prove this editor wrong. The next day and for weeks after I went to the newsstand and looked through newspapers in search of a black bride. But I couldn't find one to save my life. I bought papers from all over the country, but I never found one picture of a black bride. I was never able to call his hand.

3
Medical Practice under Segregation

The daybook I kept when I started my practice shows that the very first day I was open for business, I had four patients and made eleven dollars. The second day, I had seven patients and made fifteen dollars. By the end of the month, I was seeing twenty to twenty-five patients a day and bringing in between forty and fifty dollars. By the end of my second year, I was seeing fifty to sixty patients a day, sometimes more.[1]

Most mornings, I'd be awakened by the phone at five, five-thirty, or six o'clock—so-and-so is sick, can you come by and see her before you go to your office? Or maybe two calls, and then, after I got hospital privileges, which was about sixty days after I had opened, I'd make rounds in the morning, and frequently I didn't get to the office until eleven-thirty or twelve. Then I'd work for two or three hours and take a lunch break, which sometimes was two-thirty or three, and then come back in thirty or forty minutes, and work till five or six.

Now, you have to remember that a good part of a doctor's practice in those days took place outside the office. The office was used mostly for histories and physicals, injections, minor lab work, blood samples, and urine samples to check for sugar and protein. The rest of my time was spent making house calls. You could always count on three, four, five, even a half-dozen house calls after you closed your office. You'd take your medical bag filled with your stethoscope, blood pressure cuff, thermometer, catheter, and syringes, and you'd also carry gauze and sponges, a tourniquet, some type of antibiotic, an emesis basin to catch the vomit, cortisone, female hormones for bleeding, headache tablets, and sleeping pills.

Over the course of my career, I did thousands of house calls. I would go to some of the poorest black neighborhoods in the city, like Cavalry Hill, and downtown, near Big Spring Park, and along Adams and Franklin streets and near Councill School. Some of the places I visited were nothing more than shacks, and the first thing you'd notice is that there would be six, seven, maybe nine people living in a place with just two bedrooms. The roofs would leak, and many places had outhouses—no indoor plumbing whatsoever, just a single faucet connected to city water out in the front yard. If there was interior plumbing, it was often not working. I remember many times not having a place to wash my hands.

I've made house calls until well after midnight, I sure have. I remember one night I made nine or ten house calls, some of them in outlying areas like Gurley, fifteen miles east of town, and Harvest, about ten miles north. And it was strange, if you had a house call to go to Harvest, you almost never got one in nearby Toney also. They'd almost always be at opposite ends of the county. You'd get one in Harvest, then you'd get one out in Madison west of town, half an hour's drive from Harvest. Or you'd get one in Chase out to the northeast, and then you'd get one out on Indian Creek Road to the northwest.

That's the way I spent a lot of that first year, doing house calls. Of course, most of the doctors didn't like doing them, though there was no danger of being attacked, like today. Nobody was lurking in your automobile.

We'd go to the patient's house, leave our cars unlocked, and go in there and treat the patient. If we were in a housing project or something, almost everyone in town knew the doctor's car, and sometimes when I'd come out of a house call, there were people standing by my car to ask me to come see Aunt Suzy or to go two blocks down and see Grandmother.

So if you went to a community and you parked your car, you would get one or two additional house calls right in that same community. Ninety percent of the time, they'd pay you right then. At the office, they might say they'd pay in two weeks and then never pay.

That first year, Martha was at the office every morning. She was the office nurse and did much of the paperwork. She knew how to give injections and take blood and urine samples, and she helped me with home deliveries. She worked until the following June, about two months before the birth of our first child, Sonnie IV, when she left for Indiana Harbor. She wanted to be with her mother in the weeks before delivery, which was the custom.

Just before she came south to Alabama, Martha had said, "I'll resume my nurse training down there." But when she got here, there was nowhere for her to go. There were nursing schools, but there was nowhere for her to go. So after we had been married, our first child was born almost ten months to the day. She decided after the first baby was born that maybe she'd go back to school.

But before she could find a place to go to school, she got pregnant again. And after the second baby was born, she decided to go to Grady [Hospital School of Nursing] in Atlanta. I took her over there to Atlanta, she took the examination to enter the school, and then she changed her mind because it was so far away from us. So finally, I guess about five, six years after that, St. Vincent's in Birmingham opened up, and because she was Catholic she was able to enroll there. She went to school for a year there in Birmingham and then later completed her work here in Huntsville after Calhoun Community College integrated.

Sonnie IV wasn't born until August 1957, but Martha left in June for Indiana Harbor because it was considered dangerous to travel in the last months of pregnancy. The person who replaced her was a black practical nurse named Herman Dixie, who had worked at Huntsville Hospital. She was fifteen years older than I was and greatly respected within the black community. I paid her thirty dollars a week.

In those days, if you weren't a member of the county medical society, you couldn't have hospital privileges, couldn't be on the hospital staff. For the white doctors, this was usually a formality, and if anyone was ever turned down, I was not aware of it. There were only thirty-five or forty doctors in the whole city, so the guys were really glad to have someone come in and help take some of the patient load off them at the hospital.

But the county medical society wouldn't admit black physicians. To get around this, the doctors at the hospital had agreed to let Dr. Drake have a special arrangement whereby he could admit black patients to what was called the Colored Wing, though he was not to be a voting member of the staff. He could attend the hospital staff meetings as long as he didn't come during the social hour and during the meal—he was to ease into the meeting after the meal and after the girls had picked up the dishes. He was allowed to be in the business portion of the meeting only.

So Dr. Drake wrote a letter to the county medical society for me and got me to sign it—I asked to have the same privileges that Dr. Drake had. The night he took my letter into the staff meeting, the first Wednesday in November, he went in two or three minutes too soon and the waitress made a mistake and poured him a cup of coffee. The guys had finished eating, but they were still sipping their coffee. When she poured him a cup of coffee, three or four doctors got up and walked out. Everyone in the room understood what had happened and why the doctors walked out. So Dr. Carl Grote [Sr.], the hospital chief of staff, quietly told Dr. Drake not to present my letter that night. "Let's just wait," he said, though they continued with the meeting.[2]

Dr. Drake took my letter back in December, and they approved it. I heard about it when I called up one of the doctors, a man named J. Ellis Sparks,[3] to ask him if he'd admit one of my patients to the hospital who needed an IV. And Dr. Sparks said, "You can admit her yourself. You've been elected to the staff." That's how I found out.

My privileges applied only to the hospital's Colored Wing, which had a few black nurse's aides and orderlies, plus one or two licensed practical nurses and two black RNs working under white supervisors. These women worked very hard with little hope of being promoted, they worked under a lower pay scale than the white nurses and aides, and there was absolutely no place in the hospital for them to eat.

The Colored Wing had one large room that served as our emergency room, delivery room, and operating room—what we called the ER, DR, and OR. The hallways could accommodate another ten or twelve beds; the administration did not mind having people lying out in the hall as long as nobody tried to go over to the other side. Upstairs you had thirteen or fourteen rooms with two beds each, and I think there was one room of four beds for postpartum patients.

And conditions could get crowded with people bumping into each other—Miss Suzie needs gall bladder surgery, somebody here is in labor, and then they wheel in Mr. and Mrs. Jones, who've been in a car wreck. The place was clean but otherwise inferior, down to the lack of hot water. You did an examination, and you needed to wash your hands, and the water coming out of the hot water tap was so lukewarm you could hold them under the faucet without moving them. The administrator told me it was the same all over, but I knew it wasn't.[4]

Probably one in twenty black patients had insurance, the ones who could afford the fifty-dollar deposit, and as for the ones who couldn't, the hospital would pressure their families to pay after they had been admitted. Blacks accepted this situation and the conditions in the Colored Wing because they didn't have any choice. But they didn't like being there. Sometimes the Caucasian administrators and nurses wouldn't talk kindly to them—back then, you know, you were called "boy" until you were sixty or sixty-five years old, and then it was "Uncle" or "Auntie" for an older woman—and the black patients would be afraid the white staff might be neglectful or indifferent concerning the right medicine to give them and the right doses. The hospital wouldn't even type "Mr." or "Mrs." on the patients' bracelets. That's why so many black people preferred house calls.

So Dr. Drake and I had to do our work under severe restrictions. We were not permitted to eat at staff meetings. We were not permitted to dictate our records on the hospital Dictaphone. We were not permitted to administer anesthesia. We had to watch ourselves every step of the way. The rule was, be sure to get a consultation if you think you need one. Be polite when you write an order—"Please do a chest X-ray for Mr. Jones. Thank you." Always watch what you say and do, unlike some of the white doctors, who'd come in cursing and chewing out the nurses. Always watch what you say, because you have to be a perfect gentleman every minute, or they'll start to look at you. Like Arthur Ashe, he couldn't be abusive, couldn't lose his temper, or they'd say, "See, I told you black people shouldn't be in tennis." And especially don't try to vote in any staff meetings because they would have noticed that, though most of the time they acted like we weren't even there.

Most of all, remember to be invisible. I found this out the very first staff meeting I attended, about a month after I was admitted. Dr. Drake hadn't shown up yet—the only people there were just me and maybe half the doctors on the staff—and they were hearing a report from the Tissues Committee, five or six doctors on the committee who reviewed pathology reports to confirm that nothing taken out of a patient was normal because if the pathologist said that the tissue removed was normal, then the surgeon had to justify what he did. If he couldn't, he might face sanctions because you just couldn't go around taking things out of people for money.

So the committee was asking one of the physicians—this was a respected doctor, a grandfather, second or third oldest on the staff—why he had removed a woman's womb, or uterus. This was a black woman of childbearing age who'd been having excessive bleeding, and they were asking why he had done a hysterectomy on her since there were hormone pills and counseling and other things he could have done to stop the bleeding without having to remove the uterus.

They asked him questions for ten minutes or more, grilling him in the presence of all the other doctors, and he became madder and madder and wanted them to understand why he had done the operation without his having to say it. But then he said: "I just want to tell y'all something. All of y'all have practiced here in the South. This woman was an ignorant nigger woman, and you know it ain't no ignorant nigger woman gonna take her medicine and keep her appointments like you tell her to."[5]

That stopped the discussion and they went on to something else, and nothing more was ever said about it. It was devastating to me, as I thought first about the woman, and then about how invisible I seemed sitting there, nothing more than a table or chair in the room, just a table or chair sitting there, or a fly on the wall.

Though many white doctors by the 1950s were seeing patients only by appointment, almost 100 percent of mine were walk-ins. The patients just walked in and waited until you could get around to them. Now, some people might call first and ask if they could come right down, but trying to schedule a patient, say, for eleven o'clock, had its risks and might upset him because he might have to wait an hour or more if you were tied up with a walk-in.

You just never knew what your day was going to be like. We found that there was usually a big influx just before noon, when we closed for lunch, and again just before five, when people started getting off work. Very few black people in those days could leave their jobs for a visit to the doctor's office.

If you treated the grandmother or the grandfather, and the patient was satisfied, the rest of the family was likely to start coming in because there was a lot of respect for the opinions of older people. Or maybe someone would remember that I had treated their grandmother in the emergency room, and they'd start giving my name as their family doctor. So you'd treat one person, and if that person was satisfied, you'd soon be seeing the whole family.

Often, patients brought their whole families with them because the mothers had no place to leave their children and because it was cheaper. I always gave some sort of discount if a man brought his whole family, and I wouldn't charge them what they would have been charged if they'd come individually. So if I doctored on three or more family members together, I gave a discount, because it was an efficient use of my time and often helped out the poorest families. It was the same thing on house calls. I remember going out to Senator John Sparkman's farm when we were having a flu epidemic in November or December of '57 to see his tenants. It was a gentleman and his wife and nine children, and practically everyone there had the flu. If they didn't have the flu they had bronchitis or a sore throat and were developing the flu.

I examined every single person in that family on a house call and gave them all injections and what I used to call a family bottle of medicine. I charged them twenty-five dollars. Not twenty-five dollars apiece, twenty-five dollars for the whole thing, and this up Pulaski Pike, eight or ten miles from town.

In the office, treating the whole family at a discount meant that you often had to have three or four chairs for every patient, which was a problem. In my next office, after the Beard place, I shared the waiting room with a dentist. It was less cramped there but still crowded and noisy, usually full of sick mothers with kids running back and forth, disturbing other patients and howling in pain after receiving a little parental discipline. I was generally tolerant because I was trying to build up my clientele and didn't want to get a reputation as a mean doctor.

I tried to be fair with my fees. When I opened my office, I knew practically all the black people in Huntsville—I knew their occupations, and I knew their salaries. I had a policy for an office visit that I would never charge people more than they could make in one day. It might be less, but it would not be more.

Maids were making three dollars a day. Janitors were making three dollars a day. The guys who worked for the car dealers made three, four dollars a day, and we didn't have any high-tech workers. There were people working on Redstone, but of the twenty thousand people out there, just a hundred and fifty or so were black people, all working in menial capacities and making five, six, seven dollars a day.

I used that as a rule of thumb—I never charged anybody more than they could make in one day. An office visit was usually three dollars, and a lot of times I didn't charge extra for urine tests or injections and if I did it would be one dollar, just one dollar extra.

I charged four dollars for a house call, plus one dollar a mile. We didn't say a dollar for a mile out and a dollar for a mile back, it was just one dollar. Then, you could always adjust that. For instance, if you went eight miles, you were gonna charge four dollars for the call and then eight additional dollars. So you might say, well, just make it ten dollars.

In the emergency room, for patients with lacerations and things like that, we'd charge a dollar a stitch. For a delivery, whether at home or at the hospital, the fee was fifty dollars. But you always adjusted the fee downward—the poorer the patient, the lower the fee.

And approximately 95 percent of my patients could be considered poor. At the beginning, 100 percent were black. This meant that many people who came to my office ended up paying nothing. And many were unable to buy medicines after they had received their examinations and prescriptions, so I would often furnish these patients with sample medications if they were available, or I'd just purchase medicine for them on my drugstore account.[6]

I'd say about 40 percent of my practice were patients who could pay in full, 40 percent could pay part of their bill, and 20 percent could not pay at all. If the patient had no cash, and if he didn't have Blue Cross—and only maybe 5 percent had Blue Cross—there was no way you were gonna be paid.

In early '57, a lady and her husband hired me to deliver their baby at home. The mother went into labor around daybreak, and I was at her house all day. The baby was born at three-thirty, maybe four o'clock in the afternoon, and I didn't get paid. The child grew up, joined the Marines, was discharged from the Marines, came home, and paid his own delivery bill.[7]

When I was deciding how much to charge a patient, I remembered something Dr. Donalson used to say, which was that you always treat the pastor free of charge—never charge the pastor one red cent. He said if a guy is pastoring a church, he's got influence. He'll send you hundreds of patients. And that was important, he said, that was the key to a successful practice.

You also had the matter of relatives. Should you treat them, and if you treated them, should they be charged? As a rule, doctors didn't work on members of their own family, but they often treated uncles and cousins and people outside their immediate family circle, distant relatives, and you soon discovered you had more distant relatives than you knew you had. It brought me trouble sometimes because some of them didn't pay their bills, and they referred people to me who also didn't pay their bills.

That first year cost me a lot more than I was able to make, starting with my medical supplies (over two hundred dollars' worth), then rent, office supplies, telephone, janitorial services, and gas and oil for the car. Gasoline was thirty-something cents a gallon, and counting the driving I'd done in Indiana, I put over seventeen thousand miles on the Oldsmobile, much of that in house calls.

My books show that from October, when I opened my practice, until the end of December—and this is counting my intern's salary—I took in $2,440 and paid out $1,936. That left me with $504 profit. It got a little better the next year. I had gross receipts of over $20,000 and after expenses made about $7,800. But none of this reflected the time I put in with patients who couldn't afford to pay and those I didn't expect to pay.[8]

Vocational Rehabilitation Services, a state agency that tried to get people placed in jobs, would pay the doctor five dollars for a complete examination on a patient to see whether the patient would be eligible to be in the rehabilitation program. The Department of Pensions and Security, I believe, would pay four or five dollars to see if the patient was completely disabled. I did a number of insurance physicals, and the reason why was that I had office hours Thursday nights. A lot of people in town were working people and they didn't want to take time off, or the boss wouldn't let 'em take time off, to get an insurance examination. But I had Thursday night hours till nine o'clock, and then Saturday hours, and this allowed me to get a good bit of insurance business.

But, as I say, most of my patients were black and poor. Many were living down where the public library is now on Pelham Street and where the L. R. Patton Housing Project is, except they called it Binford Court back then. Black people were also concentrated in the area around Huntsville Hospital down on Adams, Madison, and Franklin, as I mentioned. Where the Elks Club is on Pulaski, there are houses back there, the Pulaski-Cavalry Hill area, and it had a high percentage of black people living there, maybe 20 percent of all blacks in town. They were also out in the rural areas in Hazel Green and Tony and Harvest, in New Market, Madison, and Triana, farmers and tenants and their families out in the county.

Martha and I lived with my mother when I first opened my practice, and then when our daughter was born in November of '59 we moved onto Madison Street, near Huntsville Hospital, where the Colonial Bank is now. I bought that property there, and it was a residential house. The previous owner moved out because it needed to be renovated, and because it was zoned for commercial use, the city wouldn't allow him to do it. But because I was a doctor, and said that I was gonna use part of it for my office, I was able to renovate it. So where I lived wasn't far from many of my patients.

Binford Court, where I saw lots of patients, had been put up in 1941 or 1942 for servicemen and federal workers when they were building Redstone Arsenal. These were black servicemen and workers coming from out of town, people they needed to work construction, to be porters and janitors. So the government built this low-rent housing project. It was at a low elevation and flooded often, and it was all black, about 200 or 250 men, women, and children, living with the roaches, mice, and rats. I'd go on house calls there and see the roaches just run across the floor. Dr. Drake and I were physicians for probably 90 percent of the people who lived there.

We had many patients who were totally ignorant of prevention, who didn't trust doctors or who wouldn't take their medicine. I spent a good deal of time trying to educate them. I'd go around to the black churches and schools and other places where black people gathered, and I had a little fifteen-minute talk I'd been giving since medical school about the importance of health and hygiene. I spoke against smoking, and this was long before the surgeon general's report. I spoke against guns and about the need for gun control. I talked about diabetes and sickle cell and occasionally donated my services to the Huntsville chapter of Delta Sigma Theta Sorority when it was setting up sickle-cell clinics.

You also had to try to build good relations with the pharmacists, all of whom were white. A few didn't treat black customers very well, and, of course, none would let blacks eat at their lunch counters. At the time, about half the pharmacies had lunch counters. Others seemed to get along fine with their black customers, and most of my patients had a preference, based usually on convenience and proximity, since so few owned automobiles. Liggett-Rexall in the Heart of Huntsville Shopping Center was one that blacks favored because it was close to Binford Court and Hall Street and other black neighborhoods. It and Walgreen's also had injectible supplies like penicillin and cortisones and antihistamines. I kept accounts there, and if a patient could not afford a medicine he desperately needed, I'd have the pharmacists just put it on my account.

In my office and on my house calls I saw a lot of TB, a lot of syphilis, a lot of pneumonia, a lot of bronchitis, and, in kids, all kinds of upper respiratory things, like otitis, or ear infections, and bronchitis and rhinitis. I also saw a lot of gastroenteritis, given the amount of diarrhea in youngsters, especially in the winter. Some children actually died due to dehydration because their parents would wait too long before bringing them to the doctor. They'd try all kinds of home remedies, and by the time you'd see the child, he was completely dehydrated and his electrolyte balance all messed up. Before you could straighten the situation out, you might lose the child. Also, if they did a lot of vomiting, they would lose a lot of chloride; if they have diarrhea, they can lose potassium, you know, and those electrolytes can really mess 'em up.

So we had cases like that. When it comes to metabolic diseases, we had thyroid conditions, a lot of diabetes—a whole lot of diabetes. As far as the cardiovascular system, hypertension was just rampant. Of course, if you use a textbook definition of hypertension, 50, 60 percent of my patients had hypertension because black people have higher blood pressure than other races do, as well as a lot of heart trouble.[9]

I've had people come in with fibroid tumors as large as a cantaloupe, and I know the patient must have felt pressure and pain. Some women would bleed severely with their monthly periods and just let it go untreated. And then headaches—these sometimes would go on and on, taking an aspirin here and a Bufferin there, and no Tylenol back then, and then end up with a brain tumor or something like that until it had progressed so far you couldn't do a thing about it. Coughs that were attributed to cigarettes might be a pulmonary tumor or lung cancer.

And, as I say, people would put off going to the doctor. If they had an abscess, what they used to call a *risin'*, they'd put fat meat on it—fat meat and goose grease. And there was something else that bothered me, and I used to go to the churches and the schools and try to tell 'em about it. If somebody got cut and they were bleeding and they couldn't get to the hospital right away, they'd pack it with soot and ashes.

I saw many problems—so many different diseases. I saw collagen diseases like rheumatism and arthritis and lupus—I had a number of cases in that category. I saw heart disease and syphilis. We used to do a lot of blood tests for syphilis. Premarital tests were required then and were an important part of the practice. We must have had at least one couple come in every other day, usually about two weeks before the wedding. We would draw the blood and mail it off to the state health lab in Decatur, and the lab would mail its report to the local health department, which would then send it on to the physician.

If the test was positive, the marriage was delayed, and they'd have to have injections and what have you. It was sort of awkward, too, to discuss it with the couples because it was a delicate business. I tried to be as tactful as I could, and I sort of learned as I went along.

Now, the test didn't have to go through the state lab if you had money and could afford to pay a private lab, which would leave it up to you whether you contacted the health department or not. This avoided embarrassment because once you put a name into the system, they started to hound the individual, wanting him to give a name to be interviewed and all his contacts. So many of the doctors would just handle it themselves.

The public health physician here in town was a man named Otis Gay,[10] and I sometimes asked his advice on these matters. Once, after a patient of mine had tested positive for syphilis, he said to me, "Dr. Hereford, if I were you, I'd just give him a shot of penicillin and a pat on the back."

For gonorrhea, two small doses would usually do the trick, but syphilis was a little more tricky. You needed a longer-lasting drug, and the patient needed to be rechecked. I saw far more gonorrhea than anything else. Sometimes, if I examined sixty patients in one day, I might see two or three men with the disease. It was harder to diagnose among women, though most people on the street knew the symptoms, and some would go directly to the drugstore and try to sweet-talk the pharmacist to get antibiotics.

Where venereal disease is concerned, I'd sometimes see a white man sitting out in the waiting room, maybe a bank president, even a deacon, too embarrassed to go to his own doctor, who might be a member of the same church. They'd want medicine for the women as well as themselves. One white attorney asked me for oral penicillin, some for himself and some to slip into his wife's coffee.

Occasionally, there'd be a white person looking for drugs. This happened several times. Drug addicts would have their own little network of informants, and they might hear that "Dr. so-and-so is writing" and drive two or three hundred miles if they thought they had a chance.

A Caucasian lady came into my office one day and wanted diet pills, though she was thin as a rail. Of course I refused. One of my black patients later told me that there'd been a strange car parked outside my office that day, which might have been a state car, some state official or other trying to find out whether I would write an order for illegal drugs, trying to see if they could entrap me.

You had other problems like this—shopping around for diet pills, for instance. A person would go to Dr. Jones on Monday, Dr. Smith on Wednesday, and then show up at my office on Friday, trying to get a prescription filled, and I was often in communication with both Dr. Donalson and Dr. Hiram Moore,[11] a black physician over in South Pittsburg, Tennessee, about these kinds of patients.

I had one patient who used white out to change a legitimate prescription I wrote and write his own. I had two break-ins at my office in which prescription blanks were stolen. Once, someone started calling the pharmacies claiming to be a member of my staff, and I had to send out a letter to local pharmacists asking them to accept call-ins from me only.

Many of the patients I saw were suffering from injuries, major and minor. Some were work related, and we'd have a heck of a time trying to get employers to take responsibility when black people were injured on the job. Many companies, if they had a contingent of black employees, didn't have workman's compensation or accident insurance at all.

Dr. Drake's practice was maybe 90 percent black. I think something that may have contributed to the white patients he had was that he would go around to the hobby shops and the sporting goods places, and he'd buy golf clubs and fishing tackle and hobby paraphernalia, and he'd converse with a lot of the Caucasian people. Somehow or another he built up a white clientele like that. A lot of people also knew his father, who was president of the university.

I had my very first Caucasian patient about two years after I opened, and I think I had started to pick up a few others from the charity work I was doing at the hospital. If you were a member of the hospital staff, you were required to do a certain amount of charity work, which seemed strange to me because I was already doing it in my practice.

So I chose obstetrics. Each doctor would stay on the charity service for one month, and by treating charity patients, both black and white, I think my name came to be known in the white community. So some whites started coming to me who were friends of the patients whose babies I had delivered and treated afterward. Later, I worked in the prenatal clinic at the county Health Department, and I met a number of Caucasian patients like that. But I never had more than 5 percent white patients during the first years of my practice.

I would estimate that at least 40 percent of my total practice was obstetrics, if you include all the time I spent in prenatal and postnatal care, as well as the deliveries themselves.[12] In the thirty-seven years I was in practice, I delivered a total of 2,200 babies, half by lamplight and one on a Trailways bus. That was the woman who went up to Chattanooga to see her mother, though she had to disguise her condition; bus drivers wouldn't let a pregnant woman get on because they were scared to death she might go into labor during the trip. Sure enough, halfway back she went into labor. She told the driver I was her doctor, and he stopped and called me. I met them at the station, and the baby was born six or seven minutes after the bus pulled in.

So I did a lot of deliveries. There weren't many specialists in the field around here at the time, and not many black people could have paid their fees anyway. Besides, white obstetricians made no effort to attract a clientele among black women, which in their eyes meant complications and problems, plus the matter of collections. They just weren't thrilled at the idea of delivering black babies.

When I started, I'd estimate that for every 500 black babies born in Madison County, around 150 would be delivered by white doctors. Drake and I would account for another 200 between us, either at home or in the hospital, and the rest were done by black midwives. Midwives were still fairly active at the time, though their popularity dropped off later as more and more black women chose to have their babies in the hospital.[13]

By the late 1950s, we had, I think, about two dozen midwives in the county. And there probably were three or four dozen other people who were actually delivering babies, older women usually, some of them self-proclaimed midwives or relatives who might have assisted at a birth or two earlier, which they thought made them authentic midwives. The real midwives, the ones I worked with, were licensed and fairly well trained, though I encountered them only if they were having a problem and they'd call for help.

And I would go, because I'd made a solemn promise to always respond. If the midwife had everything under control, and I felt it was okay for her to continue, I'd go on to another call. If the mother was having difficulties, I might have to stay, and if there was a really serious problem, I'd call for an ambulance to take the mother to the hospital where there were obstetricians I could call on.

Most of my deliveries those first years were home deliveries because, among other reasons, expectant mothers didn't like being over in the Colored Wing. With most of them, you would have already done some prenatal care, checking their blood pressure and weight and urine, counseling them on what they should do and not do. Both Dr. Drake and I would go around to the black churches and clubs and talk about the importance of prenatal care, which was included in my delivery fee. If they couldn't afford it, I didn't charge for the prenatal fee, which increased its popularity. It also included circumcision, if the mothers wanted it, which many did because they'd heard some doctor had circumcised someone else's baby, and they'd say, "I just don't want him to suffer when he grows up."

For home deliveries, you carried a different bag, what we called our delivery bag, because you never knew what to expect. You knew that you were going to have to be the physician, the circulating nurse, and the instruments nurse all by yourself. In the bag would be your forceps, medications, and injections to stop bleeding, a fetoscope to listen to the baby's heartbeat, gauze, string to tie the cord, mineral oil to clean the baby, and always silver nitrate to put in the baby's eyes. You put that silver nitrate in for gonorrhea because if you don't, that baby can develop an infection within forty-eight hours and go blind.

At the house, the first thing I'd do was check to see who was there, see whether a midwife was already there or maybe an aunt or a grandmother who could help. Then I'd check out the sanitary conditions and make sure the mother wasn't lying on a dirty sheet. There was almost always someone to help out, some relative or neighbor to get things in order and clean up the bedclothes after the baby was delivered. If the mother was married, the husband would almost always be there. I never had one interfere, not once, though all of us had heard tales about husbands grabbing a gun if things went bad.

So here you are, with your delivery bag, a sterile glove on your hand, and maybe getting offers of support from onlookers, and your first job is to try to get an idea of how much dilation there is.

Sometimes I could see that the labor was going to be a long one and I might go get something to eat, or they might feed me something there. You'd try to judge how long it was going to be because if it's two in the morning, and you're scheduled to assist somebody in gall bladder surgery at eight, you need to let them know if you aren't coming. I'd estimate that 50 percent of all my deliveries were between midnight and dawn. I once closed up my office at five o'clock, went to a patient's house, and delivered her at four o'clock the next morning.

The hardest trials were those of the young mothers, the ones who hadn't been through it. The youngest I would admit to the hospital, some of them fourteen or fifteen years old, so that the majority of those I delivered at home were older women, most with three or four children already, some with eleven or twelve.

Back then men didn't want to use prophylactics. Birth control pills were just becoming available [in 1960], and there were no spermicidal jellies or anything of that sort. Women often heard bad things about birth control pills—

that they caused bleeding between periods, blood clots in the legs, ovarian cancer or breast cancer, and so on. And I think some of the big companies pushing the pills had no idea what their side effects might be.

A doctor had to be very careful about giving any pain medication to the mother because all the drugs we had at the time would cross the placental barrier. That means that whatever the mother took, in just a few seconds the baby would be taking it too, and you don't want a baby coming into this world having trouble breathing. The mothers understood, or they seemed to understand. Many had been brought up on the Bible and looked at birth and pain as two things that went together.

Now, you could run into some bad problems out there late at night in the rural areas. There were degrees of difficulty, but what I'd call the *very* difficult cases, say, 10 percent of the total, could be scary. And you had to keep calm, keep your cool, because you can imagine how the onlookers would react if they saw the doctor going to pieces.

One of the worst problems was when the placenta, the afterbirth, would get over the mouth of the womb, in front of the baby, and the blood vessels would break and the bleeding would get out of control. Or if the placenta ripped away too early, you'd get bleeding in the womb, very bad bleeding. If there was a prolapsed cord, or the cord in front of the head, every push of the mother would cut off the baby's circulation.

Or you might face a breech delivery, where the baby's feet appear first. There's also the problem of the baby with a large head and the mother with a small pelvis, which can mean eight to fourteen hours of painful labor, draining the mother of the strength she'll need when the moment of birth finally comes.

Out in Madison one time I saw a mother who had eclampsia just after her baby was born. With eclampsia, the mother starts convulsing, the blood pressure keeps going up, and the kidneys start getting into bad shape—what you often see in women who've had no prenatal care.

Most of my deliveries happened without incident, but there were a few exceptions. I lost a twin out on Moore's Mill Road—the mother later became Governor Wallace's cook—because I couldn't get the baby to start breathing after birth. During the flu epidemic of '57, there was a woman who'd had eleven or twelve children, and she was about five and a half months pregnant again when she started coughing, just coughing every breath, and went into early labor. But her cervix, the mouth of the womb, wasn't ready to dilate, though the baby needed to come out, and I got her into the hospital, and the obstetrician came to help, and we tried everything, but she kept on coughing, and the uterus ruptured through the bladder.

One of my worst memories—this was two or three years after I started practicing—involves a pregnant woman I'd already admitted to the hospital, and it looked like it was going to be long labor. I got a call from a family down in Farley, way down Whitesburg, a half an hour away, saying the grandfather was having an asthmatic attack and near dying, and could I come right away.

Well, you have to make a choice. They were saying that the grandfather is bad off, and your patient is already in the hospital, surrounded by nurses, and other physicians are there, and it looks like it's going to be a long labor.

So I went and attended the grandfather, and when I got back, the obstetrician was in the woman's room, and she had already delivered. The cord was wrapped around the baby's neck. It was a terrible thing, and I think the family blamed me. But I made the best decision I could at the time.

If a pregnancy threatened the mother's life, or if it had resulted from rape or incest, I had absolutely no problem recommending an abortion, though you had to get approval from a special committee at the hospital. It was called something like the Therapeutic Abortion Committee, and it met every other Friday. You had to present the case, so to speak, and they'd vote up or down and give you their answer in three or four days.

But doing an abortion just because the baby wasn't wanted, that was a problem for me and not just because it was illegal. This was years before *Roe v. Wade* and before doctors started performing abortions left and right. Still, people got abortions, black and white alike. What I mean is, certain physicians were willing to perform them, and there were special clinics here and there, over in Georgia, for instance,[14] where people would go to get them done, would carry their daughters over and bring back sealed records. Some of the parents would ask me to hold onto these because they thought some physician ought to at least have a record of what had happened. Many years later, when I had to close down my practice and was burning all my patient files, I put some of these envelopes, still sealed up, into the fire.

Now, there are a couple of things I want to say about the white doctors who were in practice in Huntsville when I opened my office. There were some white physicians who wouldn't hesitate at all to treat black patients, right down to house calls. As a boy, I remember one of them, Dr. Frank Jordan, coming out to the house to visit Grandpa Sonnie—the doctor had a nice car and a wife about half his age—and Dr. John Lary, who took care of Grandma Bettie and even complimented me once on my homemade chemistry lab.[15]

Most of the white doctors in town were willing to help if you ran into a medical problem, to consult with you and give you advice. That's one thing I have to give credit to almost every doctor in Huntsville. If a person seemed to be in distress or was having a problem, they would almost always help, at least until the civil rights movement, when a few of them stopped accepting referrals from me.

There were limits, of course. I recall an ear-eye-nose-and-throat doctor that Dr. Drake referred most of his patients to, and I did the same for about a year. Then, one Saturday night, I was in the ER and having a problem, and I called him up. I could hear music and the tinkling of glasses in the background, and he said, "I have people here from out of town and we're having a party, and I can't come." That ended our relationship because I thought he should have put the patient first.

I also knew several white specialists who did a good deal of pro bono work—surgeons like Milton Whitley, Charles Selah, and Thomas Wright, all of whom I assisted on numerous operations.[16] I was always grateful to Dr. Wright, because he started taking my referrals after another surgeon stopped doing so because of my involvement in the civil rights movement.

I could also mention obstetricians like William B. Cameron, who delivered our twins, as well as Horace Bramm, Ed Rice, and Alfred Owen.[17] There was also Ephraim Camp, the only radiologist in northeast Alabama, who used to do X-rays for Dr. Donalson and never charged him one red cent because he knew what Dr. Donalson was doing for poor people and said he wanted to help.[18]

These were excellent doctors who never got upset over how little money they made from these patients, and they stood out from some of the others, who'd say things to let you know they didn't appreciate your pointing poor people in their direction, or you could tell it by their attitude and body language, down to the poor level of care they would provide. The pure greed of some was astounding, like the ones who would keep their own patients in the hospital much longer than they needed to be there. They'd be making maybe ten dollars a day per patient, and there was that big mortgage to be paid, you know. One of them said to me one day, "You don't have anybody in the hospital right now? I always keep two or three. You have to buy flour and bacon and eggs."

I remember an incident involving one of the older doctors in town, one of those who'd led the exodus the time Dr. Drake came into the hospital staff meeting too soon and the waitress had made the mistake of pouring him a cup of coffee. One night in the winter of '57 or '58 I got a call at home from a woman asking me to come over and take a look at her mother, who was in bed with the flu. I knew her mother; she was in her seventies, and pneumonia was dangerous for a person her age. So I drove over to her house on Hall Street, over by the black cemetery, and examined her by the light of a kerosene lamp. I listened to her chest. I took her blood pressure and temperature, which was elevated, and I decided she needed a shot of penicillin.

The lamp was on the far side of her bed, so I walked over to the fireplace for a better light, to be sure I got the right cc's, and when I did, I noticed a milky substance splattered on the bricks, something milky and dried up on the fireplace bricks, like it had been shot out under pressure. I asked the woman's daughter what it was.

"It's penicillin," she said.

"How'd it get there?"

"Well," she said, mentioning the older physician who'd walked out of the meeting that time, "the doctor was here about two hours ago, and he said my mother needed a shot. But as he was getting it ready over by the fire, he asked how I was going to pay for it, and when I said we didn't have any money, he just squirted the penicillin on the fireplace and closed up his bag and left."

A black doctor could maintain friendly relations with most of the white doctors as long as everything was strictly professional. Back in '55, when I was home from Meharry and helping out Dr. Drake so he could take a little vacation, he told me if I had any problems to call a physician named Robert C. Bibb.[19] This was the man Dr. Drake was working alongside when he revived little Tommy Scruggs by massaging his heart. Dr. Bibb and I developed a good relationship, and I called on him two or three times when I was having complications in deliveries.

I also had a good relationship with Dr. J. Ellis Sparks, who was always courteous and fair, and probably did a few things behind the scenes early on to make things easier for Dr. Drake and me. Dr. Sparks did my physical when I signed up with Metropolitan Insurance, though Drake was the personal physician for me and my family, as I was for his. Dr. Drake delivered our second child and was supposed to deliver the third, but the baby came too quickly, and I had to do it myself. Later on, when there were complications with the birth of our twins, Dr. Cameron did a C-section, and a fine job, too, or they wouldn't have survived.

Still, despite my cordial relations with many of them, almost all the white doctors upheld the system of segregation, starting with their offices and waiting rooms. I knew of one who'd make his black patients wait for hours until he'd seen every white person out in his white waiting room, and even then, he'd sometimes wander over for a nap at the Russel Erskine Hotel, where he was house doctor. One day, I saw this same doctor at the hospital using a textbook to bring his patients' charts up-to-date. You were supposed to do the diagnosis yourself, get the symptoms from the patient, but if he thought he knew what the problem was, he'd sit and use a textbook and write down on the patient's chart whatever the textbook said. If he suspected gallstones, he'd write "yellowish in color, pain under the right shoulder" or something like that, right out of the book.

One night—this was in the early '60s—a black man was brought into the ER who'd been shot in the face. The bullet was close to his brain, and they said he'd been shot in the face while breaking into an insurance company not far from the hospital. And so this doctor, a very respectable doctor, a nice man, is there working on him, and he's talking about how it's just a shame black people go around doing things like this, breaking and entering and getting themselves shot.

As it turned out, the black man had just been picking up his girlfriend, who was a cleaning lady at the insurance company, and the white manager there had been having an affair with the woman, and when her boyfriend came by, there was a big argument and the manager had shot him, then had broken a window and called the police and said this black man was trying to break in.

So this doctor in the ER, he says it's just a shame how black people do these things, which shows you how he accepted a story like that at face value and could never imagine a white insurance company manager having sexual relations with a black maid, though the police said all the broken glass was on the outside of the building. But it wasn't shame on the black man. It was shame on the white man, double shame, because he shot the black man out of jealousy and was trying to hide his affair from the community.

Even doctors with the best intentions who were liberal on the matter of race would start to change once they'd been in the system long enough. They'd go to the white clubs and parties, they'd sit around the doctors' lounge talking about their stocks or the boat they owned over on Lake Guntersville, and pretty soon they'd get to thinking like everyone else.

So however cordial things might appear, Dr. Drake and I were still outsiders. Many of the doctors had gone to school together, belonged to the same church, or were in Rotary and Kiwanis. A few had group practices where they could give each other support. But Dr. Drake and I were limited to the Colored Wing of the hospital and could only make social calls in the white wards. Though we would work late at night delivering babies, suturing lacerations, setting bones, and what have you, we could not eat at the restaurant across the street. As the only two black doctors at Huntsville Hospital, we always had to make sure we didn't offend anybody or make any mistakes on the forms. I remember getting up some mornings wishing that all I had to worry about during the day was how to get my patients well.

Once, when I was living near the hospital, I'd just come back to the house from the hospital at about 2:30 in the morning, and I got a call from the ER orderly—there were no ER physicians then, just people on call. The orderly said there was a lady who had been traveling and was having abdominal pains, and could I order a shot for her, something for her pain so she could go on up to Nashville to her regular doctor.

I asked who was on call, and he said it was Dr. so-and-so, but the orderly was afraid to wake him up. So I told him, I can't order anything without examining her, and he said, "But she's white." And I told him, well, if she's too good for me to examine, she's too good for me to order medications for, and I hung up.

So I never spent a whole lot of time at the hospital because I was too busy doing house calls and home deliveries, and because in the contacts I did have with the hospital staff, there always seemed to be something to remind me to stay in my place or that left me feeling bad.

There was one doctor at the hospital who did what I thought was a very dirty thing to me. This was later on in my career, and the doctor had just come to town. He was working in the emergency room; by then they had a physician on duty—not a regular ER physician but one of those private doctors who would contract to work in the ER, and if you were white and your private practice was not good, you could always get hired there.

So there was a black family that brought their mother in after hours, and she was terminal. They brought her in, and this white ER physician gave her an examination. And I think she probably lived only ten, fifteen minutes after she arrived at the emergency room. The family asked this ER physician what he thought was the cause of death, and apparently he had no idea what the cause of death was. He started asking them about what diseases she'd had in the past, and then he asked them to bring all of her medications to him.

So they went home, and they came back with this sack full of medications, I'd say roughly eighteen or twenty bottles from about four different physicians, maybe five. And there were two bottles that had my name on it. One was a kidney medicine that I'd given her about two months earlier, an atropine, just something to sort of relax the muscles, that's all it is, and you'd have to take a barrel of it to do any harm to you, and pyridium, a kidney medicine that makes your urine turn red, a sort of antiseptic that kills germs only in the urine. I'd given her this pill that had some atropine in it and the germ-killing complement that's fairly innocuous.

And they were asking him, why did she die? And he picked up that bottle with my name on it, and he said, this is probably what killed her. He had no idea what had killed her, but that particular bottle had *my* name on it, and he said that that was probably what killed her.

I just wonder, why did he do that? You can imagine how that made the family feel toward me. Later, I sat down and explained it to them, and I think they changed their minds, but you can imagine how they must have felt, and how I felt.

About four years into my practice, I began to give some thought to leaving Alabama. It wasn't a lack of success that was bothering me. By now, my waiting room was always full, and my income, though never great, was starting to improve.

But I could never get used to the situation at the hospital, and being barred from hotels in Alabama and other places in the South where medical conferences and refresher courses were held made me fear that I was in danger of falling behind. Even if I could have found some other place to stay during the meetings, I still was not allowed to enter the hotels.

I worried that when it came to some new technique or therapy, I was being left out in the cold. There'd be a seminar or a reception for new doctors at the Russel Erskine or the Huntsville Country Club, and black doctors were never, never included, unless they were sent an invitation by mistake. I got one of these once, but I knew it was a mistake and chose not to go.

To join the American Medical Association meant that I first had to belong to the state organization, which in Alabama was the Medical Association of the State of Alabama. But to get into *it*, you had to be a member of the county medical society. Yet, four years after opening my office, I was still excluded. I think some of the people in the local society would have been willing to let us join, but there was a group that opposed it, wouldn't open the door. One of the doctors said to me one day in the hospital lounge, "I know you and Dr. Drake have been wanting to get into the medical society. You will probably get in shortly. We only need several well-attended funerals."

I could have joined the National Medical Association (NMA), which was for black doctors, and which I did join later on, sometime around 1959. But at the time I felt so isolated, I didn't know what benefit the NMA would be to me down here in Alabama, or maybe I just wasn't able to see that it was something necessary.

As a doctor, I had fairly good relations with whites in town and was seen as being a little bit above the hoodlum on the street, so to speak. The loan officers and the bank presidents might treat you with a little more respect. Their racism might be a little more sophisticated. If I were looking at new automobiles, I sometimes felt that the salesman would show me a little more courtesy than he would some of the other black customers. And I suspect the same was true for Dr. Drake whenever he went to buy his golf clubs. But neither of us would have been allowed to use the restroom at the dealership.

Several of my friends had run-ins with the police. One of them was John Cashin Jr., a dentist in Huntsville. He was badly beaten by a policeman near Fayetteville, and then they carried him to the hospital and threatened to shoot him. One of the nurses told me that she believed that they would have shot him if she had not stepped between the policemen and the doctor.[20] I never had any personal experience with that sort of thing, just the problems all black people had—for example, taking a trip: where to sleep, where to eat, worrying that if you have to stop on the side of the road to answer nature's call, the state troopers would arrest you.

So we didn't do too much traveling in Alabama. We did drive to Florida once, and on the way back we had a little incident at a Pure Oil service station. We'd already purchased our gasoline, and the owner wouldn't allow us to use his restroom. We had a verbal confrontation, and when I got back home, I wrote him a letter and told him I was sending a copy to his home office. I didn't expect to hear from him, but he wrote me back, and he said that the majority of his customers were local people and that if they'd seen me using his restroom, they would boycott his business.

Here in north Alabama, we were hoping things would get better with the space program, that the technical people coming to Redstone and NASA would force some changes. We found that a few of the white newcomers did have some convictions and feelings on racial inequality in the beginning, but as soon as they started to encounter problems, they became acclimatized and went along with the program.

About this same time, I started having problems with some of the insurance companies, who said some of the claims my patients were filing weren't legitimate. They'd say, "You wrote in your report that her leg was fractured, not broken. If you had written broken, we would have paid."

I knew what was going on. They were thinking, here's a black doctor: we can bluff him, and we won't have to pay the claim. And a few times they threatened me that I was gonna lose my medical license. And you start to feel vulnerable. Now add all this up, plus I've got a growing family, and you can understand why I would consider leaving.

My first child, Sonnie IV, was born August 30, 1957. Almost two years and three months later, our second child was born, a girl, whom we named Kimela. Approximately two and a half years later, the third child, who was also a girl, Lee Valerie, was born. Years later came the twins, Linda and Brenda, and then our last child, whom we named after Martha.

Sometime in early 1960, I got a chance to go to Paris for a week, which was really exciting for a guy who'd never been much farther than Atlanta and Chicago. The purpose was to attend a workshop to study hypnosis and its potential in medical practice. I'd first heard about it from the doctor in East Chicago who had delivered Sonnie IV and told me that he had successfully used hypnotic trances for natural childbirth. I thought it was worth looking into because of the dangers in giving too much anesthesia to the mother.

So Martha and I flew to New York and then to Brussels and Paris. We stayed at the Claridge Hotel on the Champs Elysées, we visited the Louvre and the Eiffel Tower and the Arc de Triomphe, and for one of the few times in my life I felt free as a bird. We toured some of the hospitals, including the American Hospital in Paris, and everywhere we went, the people treated us with courtesy. We could go into any restaurant, any café or theater, and I never worried that if

I accidentally bumped into someone they'd hang me from the highest tree. For one week, I didn't see a single policeman carrying a gun.

In the workshop itself were mostly American physicians and dentists, twenty-five or thirty in all, of which I was the only black. The workshop mostly involved teaching us how to hypnotize a person—how to get the patient to listen, to relax, to accept suggestion. I even volunteered to be hypnotized. They said, "You'll feel pressure but no pain," and when I opened my eyes, I saw a needle sticking in my hand.

All this was fascinating, of course, and I tried it when I got back to Alabama, but I never used the technique for more than a dozen or so deliveries. For one thing, many black patients were suspicious of hypnosis, which was something outside their experience. And then, to succeed, you needed to spend a lot of time with the patient. Meanwhile, your waiting room is filling up with people who have headaches and bellyaches and tonsillitis, and you just can't afford to spend an hour and a half on one person.

The year I went to France, I applied for and received reciprocity in California, which meant that my medical license was recognized there and that I could move there and start a practice anytime I wished. I knew several doctors who had settled in the Los Angeles and San Francisco areas, where the pay for doctors and nurses was far higher than in Alabama, where there were fewer house calls, and where there was greater personal freedom.

Not long after, I signed up with a University of Southern California (USC) group to attend a seminar in Hawaii, which was offering sessions with leading cardiologists, obstetricians, surgeons, and neurologists. There were about twenty professors and a hundred students, and I attended mostly workshops dealing with upper respiratory diseases, pediatrics, and maternal care. For the first time in five years, I was able to update my knowledge of diagnosis and treatment.

That particular trip was a revelation in other ways, too. Prior to leaving, I went to the Cain-Sloan Department Store in Nashville and paid ninety-nine dollars for a Kodak eight millimeter, hand-held camera, plus a screen, projector, and three rolls of film. That's the camera I would use later on to document the civil rights movement here in Huntsville.

Next, I planned out our route to California. I had a very good friend who lived in Dallas, Texas, and who had worked at Oakwood College, and I was his doctor while he was here before he moved to Dallas. So we decided our first stop would be at his house. He had mentioned that we could probably stop in El Paso because there was a black motel there called La Luz.

So we called the motel and made a reservation, but when we drove up to the motel—I guess it was about maybe ten or ten-thirty in the evening—we found cars stacked two and three deep in front of every room. And when we finally got a chance to talk to the proprietor, we found out that he had given our room away, and he said he had to give it away or else they were gonna shoot him because he had so many people out there waiting to get rooms.

We were in a convertible, and although we had the top up, it was still a convertible. So we parked there because there was no way we were going to get into any other hotel. We asked the manager if there was another hotel in El Paso we could go to, and he said no. He told us we could sit and wait in our car until someone checked out of their room, about four-thirty or five o'clock in the morning. So we sat out there, and we endured the mosquito bites until about five o'clock, and then we were able to get into a room. We slept three, maybe four hours, and then started traveling again.

In Los Angeles, we caught the flight to Hawaii, and the first thing I noticed when we got off the plane were the brown mannequins in the stores. I was thirty years old, and I had never seen a brown mannequin in my life. I looked and I looked and I thought, and all of a sudden it occurred to me, there's something different here. First of all, they were brown, and second, they were small. In other words, they were my size. Everything else I saw seemed exotic, unlike anything I'd ever seen in Alabama.

The seminar's organizer was Dr. Phil Manning, dean at USC's medical school, and he had an instructor on his team named McNulty, a well-known gynecologist in Los Angeles, whose brother was the singer Dennis Day and who was married to the actress Ann Blyth. So there we were, Martha and me, sitting at a Hawaiian luau across from a famous Hollywood gynecologist and his wife, Ann Blyth. Connie Stevens was also in town filming ABC's *Hawaiian Eye,* and she came to one of the parties.

Back in Los Angeles, for two or three days we stayed with the man who was president of my graduating class at Meharry. He took us to a restaurant not far from his house, and we sat in a booth across from Barbara Stanwyck. I thought, this sure beats Huntsville.

On our way back to Alabama, Martha and I drove all day on the first day and made it to Arizona. We stopped at a little hole in the wall and asked for a hamburger, but they wouldn't serve us. The guy said, "If you're gonna take it with you, maybe I could wrap it, but otherwise I can't serve you because we don't feed 'em here." Those were his exact words: "We don't feed 'em here."

So we refused the hamburger and ate Tom's Peanut Butter Sandwiches we got from a vending machine. We rode on and on, and when we got back to El Paso, once again La Luz was all filled up. We went to get gasoline, and there was a young Mexican boy, eighteen or nineteen years old, who filled our car, and we asked him about facilities. He said there was nowhere in El Paso that we could get a hotel room.

And I said, can *you* get a hotel room? He said, yes, I can get a hotel room here. I said, well, if we were to cross the border, could we get a hotel room? And these were his words: "Señor, if you have the money, you can live any-where in Mexico." And you can imagine how that made me feel. If I have the money, I can live *anywhere* in Mexico, but in my own country, I could not get a hotel room.

So we slept in the car again. This was mid-August 1961, and there we were, in the car trying to sleep, and I thought, I have in my briefcase a certificate from the dean of USC saying that I have completed this postgraduate course. I'm a well-read doctor and have all my credentials in order and my degree from Ala-bama A&M signed by the governor of the sovereign state of Alabama, but I still can't eat that hamburger or get into that motel.

By the time we got home I was thinking hard about California. But then you get to thinking about other things as well, like your family, your friends, and your patients, all asking you to stay. And you think about what brought you back to Alabama to start with, which was the need, and suddenly, you realize there's more to leaving than leaving.

And I did seem to be winning the confidence of the black community. The president of Oakwood College, for example, had earlier asked me to serve as clinic physician, which I had accepted at a salary of $120 a month. Then, in 1961, Dean R. A. Carter of Alabama A&M offered me a part-time position teaching histology and physiology at a salary of $225 a month. The next year, Alabama A&M asked me to serve as their clinic physician and their team doc-tor, and my salary was raised to $500 per month.

Added to this was the presence of a new black physician to help relieve the pressure on Dr. Drake and me. His name was James Major Belle Jr., also known as "Sonny," a Meharry man, class of 1961, whose father had worked at A&M and who opened an office on Church Street. The three of us were able to cover for each other, and by Dr. Belle being here, that helped out a lot.

In the end, what made me stay in Alabama was my belief, and Martha's be-lief, that change was possible and that our kids and other kids might be able to attend good schools, get good jobs, and be free from the denial of opportunity that black people had always faced.

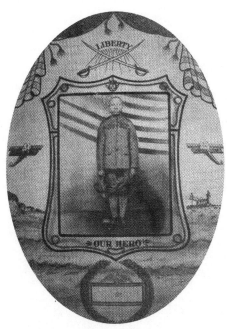

Hereford's father, Sonnie Hereford Jr., in a photograph commemorating his service with the American Expeditionary Forces in France in 1918–19. He was among 25,874 African Americans from Alabama who served in the army during World War I. Hereford family collection.

Jannie Burwell, daughter of Tom and Elizabeth Burwell of Madison County, Alabama, around 1917. Hereford family collection.

Known affectionately by family members as Big Mama, Jannie Hereford appears in this 1938 photograph with her husband, Rev. Sonnie Hereford Jr. Hereford family collection.

Sonnie Wellington Hereford III at age six. Hereford family collection.

Hereford as a student at Alabama A&M in Huntsville, Alabama, 1949. Hereford family collection.

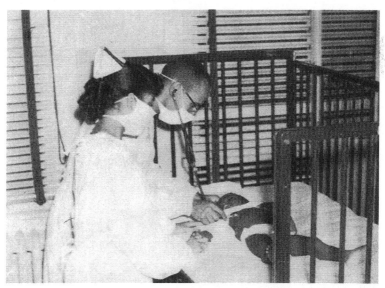

Young Hereford examining an infant at George W. Hubbard Hospital, teaching hospital of Meharry Medical College in Nashville, 1954. Hereford family collection.

Wedding announcement photograph of nursing student Martha Ann Hereford, née Adams, of East Chicago, Indiana, in 1956. The editor of the *Huntsville Times* refused to publish the photograph on the grounds that it would destroy the newspaper's Society Page. Hereford family collection.

Hereford wedding in November 1956. *Left to right:* Dr. Hereford; Martha Ann Hereford; Thomas Hereford; Rev. Thomas Pratt, pastor of Pine Grove CME Church, Huntsville. Hereford family collection.

Dr. Hereford and Sonnie IV during a civil rights rally at First Missionary Baptist Church in Huntsville, 1962. Hereford family collection.

Dr. Sonnie Wellington Hereford III and six-year-old Sonnie Hereford IV leave Huntsville's Fifth Avenue Elementary School on September 6, 1963, minutes after being turned away by state troopers dispatched by Gov. George Wallace. The photograph was sent to Dr. Hereford anonymously several months after the 1963 integration. Hereford family collection.

Sonnie Hereford IV smiles up at the photographer in his first-grade class at Fifth Avenue Elementary School. This is the child the Huntsville Board of Education had warned earlier in federal court would tear the school system to pieces. Courtesy of Fifth Avenue School, Huntsville, Alabama, school photo.

Dr. Hereford and family shortly before a testimonial dinner organized by leaders of Huntsville's black community during his Medicaid troubles. *Left to right, top row:* daughters Linda and Lee Valerie; Dr. Hereford; daughter Kimela; Sonnie IV and wife Donna. *Bottom row, left to right:* granddaughter Beth Joy; Martha Ann Hereford; daughter Martha Jacqueline; Mrs. Jannie Hereford; granddaughter Catherine; and daughter Brenda. Hereford family collection.

Hereford speaks during the 2004 dedication of a marker commemorating the 1963 integration of Huntsville's Fifth Avenue Elementary School, which had been torn down a year earlier. Martha and Sonnie Hereford IV are at Dr. Hereford's left. Hereford family collection.

4
Bringing Freedom to the Rocket City

I first heard about the sit-in from an old classmate named James Fields, who called me at my office. He told me that Rev. Ezekiel Bell, the pastor of a new Presbyterian church on Meridian Street who had just moved from Memphis, was inviting everyone to a mass meeting in support of students from Alabama A&M and Councill High. He said the students had just started a sit-in campaign at some of the downtown lunch counters and wanted to know if I would attend the meeting, and I said I would.

The meeting was to take place at the [black] First Baptist Church downtown, which was one of the few places that could hold large numbers of people. The pastor was not a civil rights militant, but the fact that he was allowing his church to be used was significant. As best as I can recall, the plans for the meeting were made either on the day the sit-ins started, which was the first Wednesday of January of '62, or the next morning. On both of those days, the students had gone into Woolworth's and Sears in the Heart of Huntsville Shopping Center and occupied the lunch counter stools for fifteen or twenty minutes.

The black community quickly mobilized in the students' support, and how they did it says a lot about how black people back then were able to communicate and make decisions. They would get on the phone, and one person would then call another until everyone knew what was happening. Mr. Charles Ray—Charlie, we called him—had a van with a loudspeaker on top, and he would drive through the black neighborhoods telling people what was going on and that a meeting was going to be held and where it would be held, and that's what he did after the students started their sit-ins.

Mr. Ray was a cab company owner and a club owner, a man who'd mastered the art of making money and knew his way around the back streets. He was also a man who wanted to be free. He'd meet you on the street and tell you so. And he spoke from the street person's viewpoint. I heard him get up at one of our mass meetings later on—this was after several speakers had been describing the effects of segregation in very lofty language—and he says, "When I go downtown, and I'm trying on a one-hundred-dollar suit of clothes, and I happen to be taking a laxative, if the laxative kicks in while I'm trying on the suit, there's nowhere for me to go. I can't walk. I have to run."

So the people were itching to show their support for the students, and I agreed to attend the mass meeting with no hesitation whatsoever. When I had come back to Huntsville, I had wanted to get along with everyone, just like Dr. Donalson and Dr. Drake. I had tried to accommodate myself to the system, and my only political act had been registering to vote, which I did in September of '56, just before I opened my practice. Henry Slaughter, one of my longtime friends, had gone with me to register and take the test. As I recall, there were questions about the Constitution and citizenship. But they couldn't have been anything like what a friend of mine told me they had in Tuskegee, where people with master's and doctoral degrees were failing the test.[1]

There was a man in town named Mr. R. C. Adams, a Normandy veteran and house builder, who'd been conducting his own voter registration campaign for years. He was doing it almost every day, and he was doing it all by himself. He'd get in his car and go downtown, grab somebody by the arm and throw him in, take him over to the registration place, help him prepare for the test, and then vouch for him, which was required. And he'd sit there while the guy took the test. Whether you passed or failed depended on the examiner, and even if you passed, you still had to pay your poll tax, which many black people could not afford. As a result, there were just four or five hundred blacks in the county who were registered to vote.

So that's the first political thing I did: I registered to vote. Then, in 1961, came that trip to Hawaii and the humiliating acts of discrimination Martha and I faced driving to and from California. If I had never had any other problems, that would have been enough in itself. But there were lots more. Just to give you a small example: There was the time I decided that I was destined to write a song. I used to write poetry, and now I wanted to write a song, but I knew I needed to read music and learn to play an instrument. I chose the violin, and I found out that there was a fine teacher in town who was also the conductor of the Huntsville Symphony Orchestra. He agreed to be my teacher, and he told me that he had a friend in Philadelphia who made excellent violins. He wrote to him and asked him to send me down two to choose from, one new and one used. I tried them both and chose the new one. It cost me $500, which was a lot of money.

So I bought the violin and started the lessons, and one day, when I was finishing up, my teacher told me there was a gentleman who had just moved from St. Louis to work on Redstone, and his trunks still hadn't arrived, and because this man was an accomplished violinist he wanted to feature him at a concert they were having that night at Huntsville High School. But the man did not have access to an instrument worthy of his playing, and so my teacher asked if he could borrow mine, and I said sure. So I left my violin there, and on the way home from my office that night, it just hit me like a ton of bricks: My violin can attend the concert, but I can't.

Now, one day, when my son was four or five years old, we decided to go get something to eat. As we are driving up Memorial Parkway, he sees Shoney's Big Boy Restaurant, and sees that little kid in the checkered pants and the suspenders standing out there holding a hamburger. And as we drive by, my son says, "Daddy, this is where we go to eat, isn't it?"

I said, "Well . . . ah . . . no, no, not really."

He says, "Well, why is that guy standing out there holding that hamburger?" He is thinking, if this is not where we go to eat, what's he standing there holding that hamburger for?

As my daughter Kimela got older, I'd want to take her and Sonnie out to the park, or take them skating, or go watch people skate, or go to a ballgame, but we could never go.

So that sort of thing, little things like that caused me to think. I wasn't allowed to sit at the lunch counters downtown. That bothered me. There were no black policemen, no black mailmen, no black clerks in the stores. That bothered me. Even the black veterans of World War II, the ones who were promised an education through the GI Bill—if they'd only gone, say, to the eighth or ninth grade and needed to finish high school, then they had to go over to Councill, to the black school, and be taught only by black teachers. That bothered me.

And if you were a black doctor or a black dentist or a black lawyer, the poverty of black people affected you. If your patient didn't have a job, he couldn't pay you. Yet, black people had little chance to get a good job.

We saw how the federal government was pumping money into the city and how the city was calling itself the Space Capital of the Universe. We saw the money going to Redstone Arsenal and NASA, where Wernher von Braun and the German scientists were working to get us to the moon. But little of that money seemed to come our way. We heard they had 20,000 people working for the government at Redstone Arsenal, but there were just a few blacks working there, probably not more than 150, and almost all of them in menial jobs.

As for the German scientists, they didn't seem to be of much help to us. And when you really think about it, about Von Braun—here's a guy who helped build the V-1, the V-2. Most of the leaders of the Nazi Party had been executed or they'd been sentenced to life in prison, and now, all of a sudden, he gets a chance to come to the greatest country in the world and to do something he likes and to be paid for it—I mean, *well* paid for it. Now, can you imagine this guy coming over here and rocking the boat?

There were others in town who'd been outside the South and wanted to change things. One was the dentist John Cashin, and I'd known him during my student days when I'd sometimes catch rides with him to Meharry, where he finished ahead of me. Afterward, he went into the army and rose to the rank of captain and was stationed for a time in France. His wife, Joan, was a Fisk graduate, and she'd met John while she was on a student trip to Paris. The story I heard was that he had proposed the next day on the condition that they live in Alabama and try to make it a better place, and she had agreed. She was not real outspoken. She was quiet and reserved around strangers. But she was never intimidated.

The same goes for Reverend Bell, who was a recent arrival and who became our version of Dr. Martin Luther King Jr. He'd been an activist in Memphis and was a very well-educated man who knew how to inspire people. Even before the sit-ins started, he and a few other black ministers had started talking to local whites and meeting in private homes to drink coffee and discuss race relations. Dr. Cashin and his wife went to these meetings, and there was a white pediatrician named Virgil Howie and his wife, Evelyn, who also went.[2]

So there were people in town who wanted to get the ball rolling. It seems like they were all just waiting for something to happen. And that's when a young man named Hank Thomas showed up. He was a student at Howard University and a field agent for the Congress of Racial Equality, or CORE, and he'd been one of the Freedom Riders on the Greyhound bus that a white mob had firebombed outside Anniston. Hank Thomas just rolled in one day and got some of the kids at A&M and Councill to go downtown with him and start sitting-in at the lunch counters. That's what started it.[3]

So I went to the meeting that Reverend Bell had called. There's no way I would have missed it. I did not make a speech. I made a five-dollar contribution, but I didn't make a speech that night, which was one of the few times I didn't make a speech because all my old fears of stuttering were gone. I just sat in the back and watched the church fill up, maybe four hundred people, including the teenagers who'd been arrested that day at the Parkway City [shopping center] and were out on bail. The people sang hymns and said prayers, and the students told about their experiences at the lunch counters. And you could tell that the people were all waiting for something to happen.

The next day, the *Huntsville Times* ran an editorial with the title "Let's Keep Our Heads."[4] But more and more students started coming out and going to the lunch counters at other places, like Liggett-Rexall Drug, in the Heart of Huntsville Shopping Center, and G. C. Murphy's, a variety store at Parkway

City. The police would arrest them based on an old law called "trespass after a warning." The way it worked was that if any merchant or any landowner had someone on his property and didn't want him there, for whatever reason, he could just call the police, who would arrest him and take him off his property.

See, they couldn't arrest you for *asking* for the hamburger, but they could arrest you for staying on the premises after being told to move on. And the penalty could be pretty severe: a $100 fine and 180 days of hard labor.

So even though the black leaders in town hadn't even known that the sit-ins were being planned, the arrests just seemed to galvanize everybody. At that first meeting, we chose a committee to go talk to the mayor. The mayor at that time was R. B. Searcy—Spec Searcy—and everyone was hoping that he might be willing to try to convince the merchants to integrate their lunch counters.

Among the people named to our delegation were Reverend Bell, Dr. Cashin, Mr. Ray, Reverend Binford, and Rev. M. C. Barrett, pastor of the Lakeside United Methodist Church. Reverend Barrett knew practically everybody in town, and though he was not a civil rights militant, he supported what we were doing. Mr. J. E. Harris, manager of Atlanta Life, one of the largest black insurance companies in town, was also named, as was Rev. Earl S. McDonald, who'd been manager of the company before Mr. Harris.

The delegation met with the mayor on Friday, and on Monday night they came back and told us what he'd said. And what he said was, there are no problems in Huntsville. The mayor said the Negroes and the white people had always gotten along well together. They stand in the same line at the bank, they go to work, they come home, and they should be law-abiding citizens. So there're no problems; there's nothing else for us to talk about.

That night, I remember, at the second meeting at the [black] First Baptist Church, there was another overflow crowd. The students who'd been arrested during the day were cheered, and we decided to form a committee. We said, we'll call this the CSC, the Community Service Committee, and they said, we'll need a president, and a first vice president, and a second vice president, and Reverend Bell was elected unanimously to be the president.

So then they said we're gonna have to have subcommittees. We're gonna have to have a subcommittee on education, a subcommittee on negotiations, a subcommittee on finance. And we're gonna have to have a subcommittee on public facilities, and one on jobs and employment. And they made me chairman of the subcommittee on education, which was only reasonable since my son was soon going to be eligible to enter school.

Then Dr. Cashin says, "We need a subcommittee for psychological warfare." He had been in the military, which is where I guess he got the idea, and he said, we need to try to outsmart the opposition because they'll do one thing and then another, try to pull something over on us, and we need to be able to throw up a smokescreen now and then, make it appear like we're gonna do one thing when we're really gonna do another, and that's why we need this subcommittee.

And I thought having this subcommittee was a good idea because we were a small force and didn't have much money, and we knew the city controlled everything—the police, the merchants—and could hurt us in all sorts of ways. We agreed to create a subcommittee on psychological warfare, and we made Dr. Cashin the chairman. So we established the CSC, and it started functioning and started raising money. We had to raise a good bit of money to get started, and we ended up raising close to $10,000.

The mayor's first answer to our request had made us realize how much the city hated the idea of sitting down to talk, and that only made us more determined to force them to the bargaining table. So more and more students started showing up at the lunch counters, and soon the newspaper ran another piece accusing us of hurting the city's image.[5]

By the second week of January, several dozen students had been arrested and thrown in jail, and what funds we'd managed to raise would have been exhausted had not several people been willing to post bail money, just so the kids could go back and get arrested again.

To post a real estate bond, you had to own property worth a certain amount—I don't remember how much but something like $30,000 or in that range—and you had to be able to prove it by your last tax statement. This allowed you to put up $5,000 for each person arrested. I signed a lot of these bonds, plus a few more for black leaders like Reverend McDonald. Dr. Cashin and Mr. Ray probably signed more than anyone. Of the local whites, Dr. Howie and his wife were also willing to sign the bonds.[6]

Dr. Howie paid a price for his actions, and that's because one of the places pediatricians get their referrals is from obstetricians. In other words, the man who delivers the baby has some influence over who the mother picks to take care of it because the obstetrician can't take care of the baby. And so Dr. Howie had a confrontation—one of the white obstetricians told him one day in the dressing room at the hospital, "Hey, you're gonna be signing all these bonds for these niggers, I'm not gonna send you any more patients."

And Dr. Howie says, "Well, you know, I guess I'll survive if you don't." The man who threatened him wasn't the only obstetrician in town, but there were only about four, five at the most. And some of them had group practices, so if A doesn't send you anything, B and C won't send you anything either.

Dr. Howie came back and told us, but he says, "I'm not gonna stop signing the bonds." Still, it really hit him in the pocketbook when some of the obstetricians stopped referring patients, though Dr. Drake and I were able to send him some, and we did a lot of deliveries.[7]

Now, the CSC, the Community Service Committee, had started holding mass meetings at least once a week, usually on Monday nights, and at the second or third of these, I had stood up and said that if anyone got sick or injured while participating in the sit-ins, they might have a hospital bill, but they would never have a doctor's bill.

I mentioned that our movement had started the first Wednesday in January of '62, and I mentioned the black person who was conducting the sit-ins at Parkway City, the black fellow from CORE who was in charge, Hank Thomas. So Mr. Thomas was conducting a sit-in there, and he had students from Councill School and from A&M and three or four adults. And somehow or another, the other people found out which car was his. And they put oil of mustard on his seat, and he was not aware of this, and he went and got in the car and sat on the seat.

See, we don't know until today whether some of the policemen may have been the persons who were able to unlock that car. We know that they do have methods of unlocking cars. But he never dreamed that anybody would single out his car, and so, when he got in the car and sat on the seat, he started burning. And it got so bad he had to go to the emergency room.

So this gentleman, Hank Thomas, was taken to the emergency room of Huntsville Hospital, and he asked them to call me. I came down, and he was hurting so bad I had to treat him with morphine and admit him to the hospital. It was oil of mustard, and that is a caustic and very, very irritating chemical—maybe not anything that would be life threatening, but, see, we didn't know it at the time. We had no idea what it was. I admitted him to the hospital, and we started applying various soothing substances to his skin and keeping him under heavy sedation because he was almost delirious and wanting to climb over the side rail he was in so much misery.

The newspaper got word of it, and they wanted to write a story. The hospital administrator said, well, I'd like for you to write a story, but I want you to get the straight of it, and you could come down and interview Mr. Thomas and his doctor, but better still, let us assign two hospital doctors, two doctors from the Huntsville Hospital staff, to check this guy, too, so that you won't get a biased report.

So they got the pathologist and one of their surgeons to examine him with me. They came over, and they saw that we had applied the soothing medications to the skin, and there were fairly thick layers on the skin. And they wrote up their report, which I'll paraphrase: This gentleman claims that he sat in some irritating chemical in his car while conducting a sit-in at Parkway City. We don't know whether this happened or not. Nevertheless, he says he did, and we came to examine him today, and he's lying comfortably in his bed, and he has some sort of white paste on his skin, and we are hesitant to remove this paste to examine the skin. That was their report.[8] But the patient was lying comfortably because the nurse was giving him a quarter-grain of morphine every four hours. I was his doctor, and it was my job to try to keep him comfortable.

So they turned this report in to the newspaper without my knowledge. I didn't even know anything about the hospital administrator getting their report and sending it to the newspaper, and the newspaper wrote that story up. We had two or three technicians from Redstone come and run tests to try to determine what this chemical was, and they could not reach any conclusion.

Then, about five, six, seven days later, there was a Caucasian gentleman who was participating in the sit-ins along with all these black students. He was an adult who, as I recall, was hired on Redstone, and he lived on the outskirts of Huntsville, near a wooded area. Well, somehow or another, somebody found out where he lived. So that night, three Caucasian gentlemen went to his house and knocked on the door under the pretense that they were having car trouble. And when he unlocked the screen, they threw a .45 automatic in his face and said, come with us. Well, what else could he do? So he went with them and they carried him out into the woods, deep into the woods, made him strip, and doused his body with the same chemical, oil of mustard.

When they brought the second gentleman to the emergency room, I started working with him, and the first thing I did was to give him something to quiet him down. Then I got on the telephone, and I called every single one of those people who were responsible for putting that report in the newspaper—the hospital administrator, the pathologist, and the surgeon—and had them come down. Although it was 1:30 in the morning, I insisted that they come and see this man while he was still in misery.

Then we got in touch with the Redstone technicians, and they came down, and when they saw this case, they were able to determine that it was oil of mustard. They wrote up their report. And the people at the hospital apologized for their negative comments concerning the other gentleman, Mr. Thomas, the CORE activist. They apologized to me, but nothing ever came out in the paper about anything. I heard that the captain who wrote the report about what the chemical was, who was on Redstone, was ostracized by all of the other officers. Shortly afterward he was transferred to another base. The gentleman who had participated in the sit-ins, the Caucasian gentleman, resigned from his job and left Huntsville.[9]

We were now about a month into our sit-in campaign, and I had already developed a routine that allowed me to participate in the work of the CSC without neglecting my duties. Mornings were spent in hospital rounds, afternoons and early evenings in seeing patients at my office or making house calls, plus the time I spent with students at Oakwood College and A&M.

Unless I was called away by a delivery or other medical emergency, I attended all the strategy sessions of the CSC, which were held in the [black] First Baptist Church or the Cumberland Presbyterian, occasionally in Mr. Harris's office at Atlanta Life. We met at least once a week, sometimes, two, three, or four times, depending on the urgency of the situation. All meetings were opened with prayer and closed with prayer, and there was always spirited discussion. In the end, we voted, and whatever the majority agreed upon is what we did. I've been in clubs and fraternities all my life, but I've never been in any organization whose members were closer than we were.

When the movement started, I decided to take the eight-millimeter camera I'd bought for the trip to Hawaii and go downtown and start filming what was happening. At the time, I just wanted to get some footage of the students and be able to document what was happening because sometimes whites would deliberately bump into the students or shove them off the stools, and we were always alert to the possibility of being beaten. I'd shoot a reel, throw it in a shoebox, and put in a new one. So I was usually down there with the students filming the sit-ins and the rallies. Whenever I wasn't in the operating room or the delivery room, I was on the street. In this way, I became the photographer of the movement.

At some point, the CSC had come up with the idea of creating a biracial committee to examine our complaints. Our thinking was that cities that had established biracial committees during times of trouble usually achieved desegregation faster and more smoothly than others.[10] So we went back to see the mayor, who by now could see that we were in earnest, and this time, he says, "Well, maybe you do have a problem. But I don't know what I'm gonna do about it."

We said, "Can't you appoint a biracial committee and let 'em look into it?"

He said, "Well, no, I don't think so, because even though you might get some Negroes to serve on it, I don't know of any white people who would serve on it."

So we stepped up the poster walks and the picketing. All those downtown businesses on Washington and Jefferson, the department stores, the five-and-dime stores, wherever they had lunch counters and water fountains, these were the places we targeted. By now, we must have had three hundred students picketing the downtown stores and meeting on the courthouse steps to sing and pray.

About that same time, Sears in the Heart of Huntsville Shopping Center was just opening. And we found out that they didn't hire a single black. At the grand opening, we took a crowd down there and surrounded the place. And guess what we discovered? There were some white people, potential customers, who refused to cross the picket line.

We stepped up the prayer marches, too. We had a prayer march almost every Saturday to the courthouse, and sometimes we'd have three hundred, four hundred, five hundred people marching to the courthouse. During one of our rallies, I'd seen a man furiously snapping photographs of the marchers. Someone came up to me and said, "Do you realize what he's doing? He's trying to get pictures of the people with the CORE caps on, so he can get as many faces attached to CORE as possible." Well, the state of Alabama then banned CORE, like it had banned the NAACP a few years earlier.

About the same time, we heard that Governor [John] Patterson had fired Dr. Drake as A&M president. I wasn't surprised because word was out that the governor had called him earlier and said, "Hey, you know, you're gonna have to keep the kids straightened out up there." That was Drake's offense. He wasn't controlling the students, dozens of whom had been arrested by now.

We had no black lawyers in town to defend the students, so we got help from a black firm in Birmingham that had three men—Orzelle Billingsley, Peter A. Hall, and J. Mason Davis—who had lots of experience pleading civil rights cases. They agreed to come up and do what they could. They'd leave Birmingham at four or five in the morning in order to get here in time for the city cases, which were usually heard at 7:30 or 8:00. Sometimes only one of them showed up, sometimes all three, and in all the cases they worked on, I'll bet you we never paid them more than fifteen hundred dollars. They just worked on case after case after case. I'll bet you they didn't even get reimbursed for their gas expenses.

In court, it was most often Billingsley who appeared, and he knew more about civil rights than almost anyone I'd ever met. Mainly, he would argue that the students had been sitting at the lunch counters on the store's invitation to the general public and that their arrest violated the First and Fourteenth amendments. This always failed to convince the judge who usually heard the cases, who would always find the defendants guilty. He'd say something like, "It just gets my goat to see adults misleading teenagers like this." To us, he was just another of the good old boys who drank beer and played golf together and knew when he left home in the morning how he was going to rule.

Within the CSC, there was debate over what tactics to use in answering the mayor's refusal to appoint a biracial committee. We were very fortunate because we had a gentleman on our committee named Randolph Blackwell,[11] who later became an advisor to Dr. King. He had come to A&M as a political science professor, but he had been trained to be an attorney, though I don't think he had done any practicing. But Mr. Blackwell had participated in the Greensboro, North Carolina, movement and was able to tell us about the things they'd run into in Greensboro and ways to avoid legal problems with the city.

For example, the Alabama legislature had passed a law that said you could be arrested not only for boycotting but for *advocating* boycotting. So, when we saw black people shopping in the stores downtown, we knew that it was against the law to walk up to them and say, "Don't shop here." Mr. Blackwell said we should just have some cards printed up the size of a business card with a question that said, "Are you shopping for freedom or buying segregation?" Just a question, you know.

And the people would look at that card, and they would think, and they would walk out of that store. It worked time and time again.

Mr. Blackwell also told us, "Make these posters. Make them as large as you want to." He says, "Walk up and down the street with them—it's freedom of speech, they're not gonna arrest you for that. I guarantee you, if they arrest you for that, we'll have every labor union in the United States backing you."

The posters we carried were mostly simple statements about freedom, usually with a little sarcasm mixed in: "I ordered a hamburger and they served me a warrant" or "Khrushchev can eat here but I can't." This was meant to show how contradictory it was for the country to be fighting for freedom overseas while black people here in Alabama couldn't eat at the lunch counters.

Another said, "This Is Rocket City U.S.A. Let Freedom Begin Here." Another one, which I penned, said, "Worried about freedom in Laos and Berlin? We want freedom here!"

Once, when Reverend Bell and I had been trying to get in to see the mayor, we were directed to the assistant city attorney, who asked us whom we were representing. We said we were representing the black community. He asked if we were lawyers, and when we said no, he told us that we could be arrested for impersonating lawyers. It scared us to death, and we got out as soon as possible because while we didn't mind being arrested, we didn't want to be arrested for that. I'm sure it gave him and his lawyer friends a good laugh for a day or two.

Probably 80 percent of the people doing the sitting-in were Councill students or A&M students, and we made certain that the kids who went into the stores knew the techniques for nonviolence. We sure didn't want to get people we couldn't control. We didn't want people to go down there burning cars and knocking out windows. We had a few that didn't like the methods of nonviolence, and we had to weed them out.

We knew about Gandhi, we knew about Dr. King, we knew what was happening in other cities. Reverend Bell and a few others went up and talked to people in Chattanooga, and I went along with a group to Memphis. I met some of the same lawyers who had helped get out the vote for John F. Kennedy during the presidential campaign of 1960, and they told us what kinds of nonviolent methods they were using in Memphis.

I also went to Nashville and talked with a Meharry graduate who had formerly practiced medicine in Decatur named Edward Caldwell. I'd met him in 1951 when I went to Boy Scout gatherings at Camp Drake near Rogersville, and he'd showed me how to do first aid and physical examinations. In Nashville, he told me about some of the techniques they had used there in 1959 and 1960, and how the student demonstrators had been so well disciplined that they were able to keep their place at a counter stool when people came up and spit on them and sometimes even put lighted cigarettes against their arms.

Reverend Bell would have people like that come down to Huntsville, usually for a whole day. In the afternoon, they would talk to the executive committee of the CSC and do workshops for the demonstrators. One of them was Rev. James Lawson of Nashville,[12] a light-skinned man who had studied Gandhi's methods and did workshops on nonviolence for the Southern Christian Leadership Conference. He came to Huntsville, and he taught the kids a lot of techniques, like how to protect your head with your hands and arms, how to keep from taking a blow to the skull.

There were other peaceful techniques, like doing the snake hip, which is when you're standing in line at a movie theater and trying to get admitted, and when white customers start trying to get around you, you can sorta swing your hips out with the others who are standing in line and keep the white customers from getting up to the ticket booth.

So our young people knew the techniques, knew not to carry weapons of any kind, not even a fingernail file, no alcohol, no narcotics, nothing like that. And none of our people ever resisted. No, when they said, we're gonna arrest you, they just went ahead and let them arrest them because we felt that on appeal, the cases would be reversed.

We learned some other things, too. For example, whenever you get the other side to the bargaining table, and you start negotiating, one of the first things that you want to get clear is, there'll be no cooling-off period because once you have a cooling-off period, you're gonna start to lose ground.

Number two, they're gonna have to drop all the charges, and the attorneys had informed us that the mayor had the authority to drop cases anytime he wanted to. All he had to do was sign on the dotted line. Mr. Blackwell said, "I know the mayor can do it, because I've had some of the professors from the college arrested for DWI, and I went into the mayor's office, and with the stroke of a pen, the case was completely wiped out."

The kids doing the sit-ins were the real heroes. One who stands out was an A&M student, Miss Frances Sims, who had been recruited by Hank Thomas and was arrested five or six times, and her sister, Mrs. Edna Dailey, at the time a fifteen- or sixteen-year-old Councill student and one of the youngest we had out on the streets. She had more courage than any young person I'd ever seen. Two other sisters, Lucille Jones Mixon and Ada Jones Phipps, both of them Councill students whose father owned a big farm north of town, were arrested several times. A young man named Dwight Crawford was arrested five or six times.

An A&M student named William Pearson showed special courage considering how badly he'd been hassled by the police in Birmingham, where he grew up. As a teenager, he'd gotten a job in a bowling alley, but to get to work he had to walk through a white neighborhood. One night, a policeman stopped him and told him not to be walking through there again, and he had to give up his job. Pearson was arrested more times than anyone.

Another I remember was Harold Dickerson, whose grandfather had started the first black taxicab company in town. He had a fine voice, and during the demonstrations, he used to sing protest songs in the style of the old Negro spirituals, except he would change the words to suit the occasion.[13]

By now, many people had been arrested, but they always said, we're going again tomorrow. There were about 400 arrests, but that was not 400 individuals; it was about 250 individuals. Some people were arrested twice and some five or six times. Sure enough, they went back, and back, and back.[14]

Some of the demonstrators who had jobs were threatened. At the hospital, the supervisor of nurses found out that one of her orderlies had been sitting-in with us. She told him point blank that if he associated with me and participated in this movement one more time, just once, he'd lose his job. He came and told me about it. And the guy was in school and depending on that job as an orderly to pay his way through school. Well, you have to be realistic. He wanted to be a physician, and he's an orderly, and he's in A&M, and this is the only way in the world he can pay his way through school. His parents were separated and not able to help him, and so he stopped participating.

But most of the kids couldn't get jobs anyway, and there was nowhere they could go to eat, nowhere to go for entertainment. In the meantime, Grandmother is getting her pension check, and she has food on the table, she's not gonna let you starve. So why don't you just come on and sit-in and try to change things?

One day, one of my patients came by my office, and she wanted to tell me about her nephew. She said, "I heard that so-and-so has been marching with you. I haven't been able to catch up with him, but you tell him I said, he's gonna come up dead."

When I finally got to him and relayed the message from his aunt, he said, "Well, I don't know whether I'm gonna see her or not, but would you give her a message for me? Tell her I said that if you don't stand up for what you believe in, you're already dead."

Throughout February and March we kept up the pressure, and the police started arresting people again, probably six hundred before it was over, though, as I said, this included some individuals who were arrested more than once, until finally some of the store managers decided they would just try ignoring us. But that was all right, too, because if the students went to a lunch counter, and the management ignored them, they would sit there all day long occupying the stools, and if they're doing that, no one else can sit there. If the man has thirteen stools, and we send fifteen people down there, he's not going to have any business that day.

So the kids would ask to be served, and if they were not served they would sit and take up space that white customers would ordinarily take up. If the manager finally gave up and called the police, in jail they could always count on Mr. Howard Barley, who owned two black restaurants in town—the Sweet Shop and the Sugar Bowl. He would prepare food for the students and bring it right to the jail. Or he'd bring food outside the places where the kids were sitting-in, because sometimes they'd start at 8:30 in the morning and stay till dark, and some of them would almost fall off the stool they were so hungry.

Many times we had to select the target according to the number of students we had available. There were days when we might have twenty or thirty on the streets, but if it was exam time, this might drop off to three or four. But even with a few people, we could still do a lot.

For example, we could tie up one theater for the whole afternoon. The first student would walk up to the window and ask to buy a ticket, and when the ticket lady said no, I can't sell you a ticket, he'd just go to the end of the line. Then, the second would walk up and ask to buy a ticket, and she'd say no, and he'd go to the end of the line. And they'd just keep going back to the end of the line.

By now you have white families living down in southeast Huntsville, and they'd like to take their kids to the movies, but they'd say, I can't go up there with all those Negroes in front of the theater picketing and in the line.

Sometimes, we'd have 300, 400, or 500 people march to the courthouse from the Church Street area, and the newspaper would say, "Fifty or sixty Negroes marched to the courthouse, sang songs, and prayed prayers." That's it. Nothing about why they went up there, nothing about the results, or anything. And this would be on the fifth or sixth page of the paper.

The editor at that time, by the way, was still the man who wouldn't print my wife's picture. We got the impression—and I don't know this for a fact—that the powers that be had told the reporters that if they ignored this, it would go away. Let's not give them any publicity.[15]

The courthouse was a place you'd normally gravitate toward when you went downtown to demonstrate because if you had to relieve yourself, it was either go home or over there to the segregated restrooms. One day, Mrs. Joan Cashin was down there with my little daughter Kim, who needed to go to the restroom. And Joan just decided right there, I'm going to the white restroom. So they went in and used the facilities in the white ladies restroom, and nothing happened to them. No one said anything, no one did anything. After that, black people started going to the white restroom. That was actually one of our first victories, a small one, but still a victory.

And that's the way it went for a time. Anything in the world we could do that was within the law, or that wouldn't get us into too much trouble if it was outside the law, we would do, just to get them to the bargaining table. Of course, we knew that we had a few in our ranks who were reporting everything we did to the authorities.

Oh, yes, we had people who would carry information back to the police, and occasionally, the word would be whispered around among us, I think so-and-so is doing such a thing, and once it was suspected that a person was an informant, a stool pigeon, the leadership would give him an assignment, and if he didn't do it, we'd almost always know that he was, and if he did do it, it would embarrass him with the other side, and many of them would just quit. That was one of our ways of dealing with it.[16]

Only a handful of white residents ever expressed any support for what we were doing, and most of those who did, I think, had come to Redstone from up North. I don't remember seeing any local white clergymen in our marches. Among the black ministers, probably 80 percent were with us. And the others, the ones who weren't involved, with the exception of two or three, did not speak against us. You know, there's a black spiritual, "I'm on my way to Canaan, if you ain't going, don't hinder me." And we approached the ministers with that. Many of them, even if they were not avid civil rights workers, permitted their congregations to participate and to do what needed to be done.[17]

Besides the students and the ministers, we had a lot of the common people with us, the people on the street, the black laborers and cab drivers and delivery men, the people who felt they had been mistreated. Many of them were women—maids and cooks and so forth. Yes, I remember a lot of women, like a beautician named Mrs. Odell Pearson Booker—her daughter was one of the first to go into the schools—and Mrs. Mary Townsend, also a beautician, who was the one woman on the executive committee of the CSC. The beauticians always had Mondays off, like the barbers, and you could always count on the beauticians and the barbers to come and march with us on Monday.

We had a few in the black middle class who stood by us, but after the first couple of mass meetings, and especially after the arrests started, some of those sort of shied away. At the time, we had a good number of black businessmen in town. We had insurance men, a few entrepreneurs, some property developers, some financiers even, and morticians, as well as building contractors, because there were a lot of buildings going up. These, and some of the professors at A&M, were the most active people from the black middle class.

Some of the black businessmen had made their peace with the system. Others empathized with us, but they had to worry what their white customers would think. I'll give you an example—the man who ran the radio station. He wouldn't participate because most of his business was coming from advertisers, and most of the advertisers were white. And then a lot of the other people who had businesses were so busy running their businesses that they didn't have time to participate.

The black schoolteachers were at a great disadvantage—the city, county, and state schoolteachers—because they had been told in no uncertain terms that if they were seen participating, that would be it for them. Even if there was no reason to fire them, they'd be fired. Still, there were a number of teachers who participated. A few were still brave enough to get out there and march, like my brother, Tom. He taught in Decatur. First he taught shop, then they switched him to biology and chemistry. And he often marched with us. But most wouldn't get out on the streets.

And did I tell you about the lady we had who could change her voice? She was a teacher, and she could impersonate anybody. If we wanted to know something, she could find out for us. If there was an owner of a big department store, and we wanted to know exactly how he felt about opening his lunch counter or hiring blacks, she'd get on the phone and pretend to be Mrs. So-and-so, down in southeast Huntsville. And she'd say, I want to know, what do you think about all this rabble-rousing going on around here, and all this. And boy, he would just pour his heart out to her, and she'd come back and tell us everything. It was something. It was really something.

Throughout the spring of 1962, we did everything we could to keep the pressure on. But with so little to show for our efforts, discouragement began to grow. Our first rallies and prayer marches had brought out four or five hundred people, but as time went on, and we still weren't able to bring the other side to the table, the numbers began to drop.

To keep spirits up, we began bringing in veteran speakers of earlier struggles, including some of the ministers who'd been active up in Nashville—people like Rev. C. T. Vivian, Rev. Kelly Miller Smith,[18] and, as I mentioned, Rev. James M. Lawson. All were inspiring speakers, and all at one time or another had worked with Dr. Martin Luther King Jr.

Then, during one of our strategy sessions, someone said, why don't we bring in Dr. King himself? Everyone thought this was a fine idea, though we knew it would cost us money. We'd raised maybe five or six thousand dollars by now and were sure that we could raise more.

Most of what we'd spent, aside from the cost of speakers at the weekly rallies, was for appearance bonds, publicity, and transportation, even money to pay fines for people who had nothing to do with the sit-ins because the police had started setting up roadblocks and radar in the black neighborhoods as a way of depleting the funds we could use with the mess downtown. The police knew what they were doing. And they turned their backs a lot of times, to let things happen.

All the little activities we engaged in also cost money—money to buy flags and make phone calls and buy gasoline. So every time we had a mass meeting, we raised money. Some did it by selling dinners. Others made private contributions. I suspect that about 20 percent of those came from Dr. John Cashin Jr. because later on I became the CSC treasurer. I knew where the money came from, and he made a lot of contributions.

So we got in touch with Dr. King, and to our delight, he said he would come for expenses plus an honorarium—I think it was $1,500. We couldn't put him up in a hotel or motel, so citizens would have to put him and his entourage up in private homes. Then we began trying to figure out where he would speak. And somebody said, well, the [black] First Baptist Church. They said, no, no, for several reasons. Number one, if he spoke that night with the big rally at the First Baptist downtown, you're not gonna have enough room to hold the people. And second, you'll have a security problem downtown. They said, if we move it to Oakwood College and go to their gym, we'll have adequate space, and we'll have security because we'll use the Oakwood security.

And we were able to finally convince Oakwood that it was gonna be all right. You see, the Adventists have a policy—the reason why they didn't sit-in with us—that they were not supposed to commit any violence, and they were not supposed to provoke anybody else to commit violence. They thought that if the people downtown say they don't want you in their business, and you go down there and you sit-in their business, then you are provoking them.

When Dr. King arrived at the airport, about twenty-five people were there to greet him. We had several cars, and I had a yellow Cadillac convertible that was just two months old. And they asked Dr. King which car did he want to ride in, and he said he wanted to ride in my car.

So I put the top down, and he and his two lieutenants—Rev. Ralph D. Abernathy and Rev. Wyatt T. Walker—got in, and we drove slowly through town, though we couldn't exactly call it a parade. Then we went to the A&M campus, and we drove around so the kids could see him, and then we went to the Oakwood campus, and we drove around there so the kids could see him.

That afternoon Dr. King spoke to about three hundred people at the First Missionary Baptist Church and that night at Oakwood to more than two thousand. That first speech, he just spoke in general terms, but once he got to Oakwood, he came in with this speech about how segregation is on its deathbed and the only thing left to decide is how expensive a funeral they were going to give. And he used some of the same words and phrases that were in his "I have a dream" speech the next year at the Lincoln Memorial.

Dr. King came to Huntsville on March 19, 1962, and if you look at my films, you'll see that from the first marches that occurred after that, the crowds start getting bigger and bigger. Still, his visit didn't even make the front page of the paper, which hurt us in our ability to bring outside pressure on the city. We'd try to get UPI and the AP interested in what we were doing, and the first thing they'd ask us was, "Did your local paper carry the story?" And we'd say, "Well, no, not yet." And they'd say, "Well, there's your answer. If the local paper doesn't carry it, why should we?"

That's the reason we came up with our next idea. Well, it was actually John Cashin's idea in the psychological warfare subcommittee, which was to have my wife, Martha, who was expecting our daughter Lee Valerie and was about five and a half or six months pregnant but looked nine months, and Mrs. Cashin, who had a four-month-old daughter named Sheryll, sit-in at one of the lunch counters and get arrested.

We figured the *Huntsville Times* would have to print that—a doctor's wife who's pregnant and a dentist's wife with a baby in her arms getting arrested and thrown in jail. We were trying to drum up some support, trying to get some publicity, and trying to get the mayor to establish the biracial committee. All this time was being wasted, and you can't even get to the bargaining table.

When I brought up the idea with Martha, she immediately said yes—didn't hesitate a second. See, she was with me during that trip to California, and she knew about the segregated hospital facilities and the fact that I couldn't get proper staff privileges. She was born in Kentucky, you know, where they used to get the mutton sandwiches out of the side windows and all that.

So her decision didn't surprise me at all, any more than Mrs. Cashin's. During all the demonstrations, after I would have seen my patients and made my way to the site, Joan Cashin was already there, every day. If we had fifty people, she was there. If we had three people, she was there. I remember one evening, during a strategy session, when someone suggested we meet again the following night—we'd already met three or four times that week—Joan Cashin said, "Well, you know, I sure would like to have just one night at home so I could tuck my kids into bed."

So the two wives, plus Miss Frances Sims, went down to Walgreen's during the lunch hour. They go in and ask for a hamburger and a cup of coffee, and the waitress refuses, and then the manager asks them to leave, and when they won't leave, he calls the police and signs the affidavits, and they are arrested for trespassing after warning. They were taken to the city jail for fingerprinting and then on to the county jail, because if you were arrested by the city, after you'd had your arraignment, you'd be transferred to the county.

When the cases were heard, the ladies were fined $100 each plus 180 days in the county jail. The sheriff's deputies called the mayor, who said he would release the two women on their own recognizance, but when they heard he wouldn't do the same for Miss Frances Sims, they refused to leave. The sheriff was Mr. L. D. Wall, and it was an election year, and the deputies pleaded with the women to leave. The city just threw you on us, they said, but the women wouldn't leave.

So Martha and Joan Cashin stayed two nights in the jail until they figured the point had been made. Howard Barley, who owned the two black restaurants, brought them hot meals so they wouldn't have to eat jail food. And Joan Cashin's mother, who'd come down from Jersey City to take care of her grandchildren while Joan worked in the movement, took them blankets and sheets so they wouldn't have to sleep on the lice-infested mattresses.

We thought this would stir things up. That's all we were doing, just trying to get to the bargaining table. We felt that by having all these government installations here, if word got out to Washington what was going on, the city would probably lose some of the government contracts on Redstone. And we kept reminding the city fathers about this situation and what it might do to their contracts.

And boy, were we right, did they pay attention after the arrest of Martha Hereford and Joan Cashin. You talk about people rallying to the cause. Once the AP, UPI, *Jet* magazine, and others picked up the story, the local paper had to print it, was embarrassed not to print it—a doctor's wife, expecting, and a dentist's wife, with a baby in her arms, carried off to jail. Yes, this story did go out. Once the *Huntsville Times* printed it, it went out to the national press.[19]

After the arrests, we started picking up some publicity outside the South. I know because some of my former classmates at A&M and Meharry would write to me and send me clippings from their newspapers. They also sent them to the mayor because by this time we had a letter-writing campaign going, and I'd been writing to former classmates and others who had moved out of town, asking them to bombard the mayor's office with letters in support of a biracial committee to try to solve the problem.[20]

When I'd gone up to Nashville and talked with Dr. Edward Caldwell, he told me about something else they had done up there called Blue Jeans Sunday. Now, black people have two times of the year when they really, really shop: Christmas and Easter. And Christmas was the toys, and also clothing, but Easter was clothing. Almost every black person in town wants a new suit or a new dress for Easter. And what they did in Nashville was instead of buying $100 suits and $100 dresses, they decided to spend $5 on a pair of new blue jeans for Easter, and I brought that idea back to Huntsville.

The leaders of the CSC liked the idea. They thought, if there are twenty thousand black people in Madison County, and ten thousand of those in the city, and if there are even ten thousand black people failing to buy $90 or $100 Easter outfits, that's a lot of money in losses for the merchants downtown. It could cost them a million dollars or more.

Easter was on the third Sunday of April, and we had to keep our plans secret. See, you can't tell the Man in February or March that you're gonna have a boycott in April because then he wouldn't take out the bank loans and purchase all the things that he would ordinarily purchase for his stock. You have to slip up on him. You let him go and borrow the money he needs to purchase his stock. And then, after he shall have done that, you leave him there to look at the stock. And that makes an impression on him.

Rev. C. T. Vivian of Nashville, who had been a leader of the Nashville movement, came in and gave a workshop, telling us how they'd organized the boycott up there. So that's the way we did it. We didn't make a general announcement that we were going to have a boycott for Easter.

Then, a few days before Easter, we went to Oakwood and got their master plan. They had a plan whereby you could canvass the whole city of Huntsville in two days. They used it for telephone solicitation for religious literature, and, using Oakwood's plan, we passed out self-denial folders that said, now that the Easter season is here, we want you to fast and pray, etc., etc. This was to get around the anti-boycott law, you see.

Not everyone in the black community liked the idea. I remember at one of our CSC meetings, when we presented it, one of the ministers there stood up and said he didn't like it, he didn't think women should be wearing pants.

My wife belonged to a club, and some of them didn't like it either, maybe fifteen or twenty women who were mostly middle-class people. For her, the straw that broke the camel's back was the night I went to the club and made a presentation. I'd been filming the demonstrations, and I had about twenty-five minutes of film, and I showed them what we were doing and said I wished that they would join us and that they'd already had Blue Jeans Easter in Nashville.

Well, after I left, my wife told me that some of those ladies got up and threw cold water on the whole thing. You know—"I don't think we ought to get involved in that." Somebody said, "I was in Nashville, I don't remember seeing anybody wearing any blue jeans," and "Nothin's gonna come of this, just a lot of people out there rabble-rousin', and you're never gonna get your freedom that way," and so on.

But most people in the black community came through, probably 90 percent. The men didn't shop, and the women didn't shop, and some of the women bought denim cloth and made themselves denim skirts, and the men wore blue jeans, and some of the women wore blue jeans, though it wasn't fashionable in those days for women to wear pants.

But we didn't buy the blue jeans in Huntsville. We bought 'em in Fayetteville, we bought 'em in Athens, we bought 'em in Decatur. We didn't even want the local merchants to have the five dollars.

And the boycott was very effective. We had about five groups of people who weren't shopping, and some of those were unexpected. You had, first of all, the black people who were committed, they weren't gonna shop. You had white people who belonged to the labor unions and didn't cross our picket lines. You had white people who didn't go downtown to shop—most of the shopping was downtown then—because they didn't want to be in all that confusion down there. You had white people who came down there to encourage us. And you had white people who came down there to jeer us and taunt us. None of the people in those groups was shopping. Yes, even the taunters weren't shopping. They were out on the street taunting us.

Finally, Mayor Searcy gave in. In April, a few days after the arrests of Martha and Joan and after Blue Jeans Sunday, he agreed to establish a biracial committee.

But first he tried to handpick the black representatives, and he chose two men we all knew were Uncle Toms. I won't call their names, but we knew they were Uncle Toms because of their history. They'd been on committees before where they could have spoken up for black people, and we knew some of the things they had said. We knew after talking to them you could tell basically what their response was going to be. We wouldn't accept them. We told the mayor, "We don't want those men to represent us."

So the mayor allowed us to suggest two people. Now, you can't have Dr. Cashin and Dr. Hereford on the biracial committee, they're too radical. Oh, no, the other side would've loved to have had that. But we wanted somebody who was gonna stand up for us. So we chose Mr. J. E. Harris, the manager of the Atlanta Life Insurance Company, a very articulate person, very intelligent, settled with a family. And we chose the dean of Oakwood College. His name was Malcolm Dean—Dean Dean. He had spoken at one of our mass meetings and had said, "You shouldn't mind going through hell for a heavenly cause." That impressed me, him being a minister, and an Adventist minister, too.

But the mayor began dragging his feet again, making excuses, telling us he just couldn't find any whites who were willing to serve on any biracial committee. We thought, well, it's time to crank up the pressure again.

By now we were feeling we could win this thing. On Mother's Day, right after church, I got a call from Reverend Bell, who said a bunch of them were going to go try to integrate Big Spring Park downtown, and he wanted to know if I'd like to go along. He said he wanted me to take some film of the thing, just to stand outside the fence and look inside in case something happened, to be ready to film it.

I said, "Yeah, I'll go," and we all went down there, maybe five adults and five or six children, and they went into the park, and the kids started swinging and playing on the slides and the merry-go-round, and some of the other people there, the white people, stared, but nobody said anything, nobody did anything. Ever since that day, black citizens have been using that park.

Then we heard that George Wallace would be visiting Huntsville and that he would give a speech at the courthouse. There was a gubernatorial race going on, and he was seeking the Democratic nomination. At that time, if you wanted to be the governor of Alabama, all you had to do was win the Democratic nomination. Wallace said he'd gotten "out-niggered" in 1958, as he put it, and after John Patterson had won the election that year, Wallace had vowed he'd never be out-niggered again.

Governor Wallace's visit to Huntsville was on Armed Forces Day in May 1962. One of my friends from way back had this truck, and he said he wanted to get into the movement. He was an elderly fellow, and he'd had all kinds of discrimination against him. So he let us make signs and tack 'em on his truck, and then he drove us all around the courthouse on the day Wallace spoke, and we had patriotic music that one of the music professors at A&M had recorded for us on the organ, and we played the songs on a tape recorder from the back of the truck. We played "My Country 'Tis of Thee" and "Battle Hymn of the Republic" and "America the Beautiful," with our flags and Bibles and balloons and so forth.

Wallace was on the south side of the courthouse, and we were on the north side. I guess we drove around the courthouse eighteen or twenty times. And this was a gubernatorial race—I think they'd had the primary. He was going all over Alabama making speeches. I think he just ignored us.

I don't remember seeing a single word in the *Huntsville Times* about our rally. There were some black people who just stopped buying the paper—not exactly a boycott, but they didn't want to read it anymore, and there was a movement among many of the black people in town to cancel their subscriptions to the newspaper. This came up during one of our planning sessions. Someone said, you know, they don't ever give us any good press—usually they don't write anything about us, and when they do write something about us, either they downplay what we are doing or they write derogatory things about us. So let's just cancel our subscriptions.

Mr. R. C. Adams, the man who had long been leading voter registration, had a station wagon, and he started driving to Fayetteville to pick up bundles of the *Nashville Tennessean*. He went around throwing newspapers in yards. Can you imagine this one man trying to supply newspapers to all the black people in Huntsville?

But on that particular day in the courthouse square, we made sure people heard about us, because one of the last things we did, after the Wallace crowd had cleared out, was release some of the helium-filled balloons we had on the truck, each one with a message tied to it.

Here's an example: "This balloon was released by Negro students in the courthouse yard at Huntsville, Alabama, May 19, 1962. In this city millions of tax dollars are spent each day to build up Free World defenses, while city leaders, who benefit from these expenditures, oppose Free World policies."

We dropped some of these messages on the courthouse steps, too, so the mayor and the city councilmen would be sure to see them.

Well, by now, the mayor is telling us that he had finally been able to find two white people to serve on the biracial committee. One was Will Halsey, a wholesale grocery owner, and the other was Harry M. Rhett Jr., one of the old elites and very wealthy. The white members were very careful about not letting anybody know they were serving, and nobody was to know where or when these meetings were to be. So the black people who attended would come back and bring the CSC a report. They would take notes, and they had briefcases, but no secretary, no tape recorder. They talked at the utilities—the manager of the utilities complex allowed them to have space there—and that's where their meetings took place.

And they told us how when Mr. Rhett would get ready to come to a meeting, he'd put on his bowling shoes, and take his bowling ball, and tell his mother that he was going bowling. He even mentioned to the black members that he thought it would cause real problems if his mother knew he was coming to a meeting like that. So when our people reported this back to us, I made a little joke about it. I said, "Mr. Rhett came to the meeting tonight, but he told his mother that he was going bowling because he was afraid that she would disinherit him. Then he'd have only thirty million instead of forty million."

After the biracial committee was in place, city leaders began approaching the merchants, quietly asking them to consider serving black people at their lunch counters and getting rid of their segregated water fountains and restrooms. The city said, we're not gonna put you on the spot, but we're gonna have at least a half dozen of you desegregate at one time. But the merchants said no, we don't want any part of it.

So we decided to tighten the screws, and few things seemed to have a more dramatic effect than what we did next. It started on the day before George Wallace came to town, when Mrs. Cashin's parents and a half-dozen A&M graduates showed up outside the New York Stock Exchange. They stood there passing out handbills, which said, "To invest in Huntsville, Alabama is to invest in segregation" and "To bring new plants and businesses to Huntsville aids segregation and subjects additional employees to racism."

The handbills reported that great numbers of black people had been arrested since the sit-ins began and that city officials were still refusing to negotiate with the black community. The story was picked up by the AP and quickly got the attention of a city whose financial well-being depended on outside investment.

Then, one night in early June, Martha and I, Reverend Bell, and one of the A&M professors and his wife slipped out of town and drove to Chicago. We met two former Huntsville residents there, and the next morning we picketed in front of the Midwest Stock Exchange. That's on my film. We passed out leaflets that said, do not invest in companies that do business in Huntsville, Alabama. And we talked to anyone who would listen about the companies that had government contracts on Redstone Arsenal and in the space community, and now and then, we'd have someone shake our hands and say, thank you.

We finished our picketing about 2:00 P.M., and at 2:30 I was at the post office in Chicago, mailing the mayor copies of the handbills we had distributed. We came down the highway to Indianapolis. I stopped at the post office in Indianapolis and anonymously mailed the mayor some more handbills. We came down to Louisville, and I mailed some handbills. We came down to Nashville, and I mailed some handbills.

Not long afterward, city leaders decided that they would have a trial period of desegregation at lunch counters in Walgreen's, Liggett's, Woolworth's, and several other places in town, a total of eight, I believe. The biracial committee got together with the lunch-counter owners and agreed that the trial period would be in July, at which time one, two, or three blacks would go to each one of the lunch counters simultaneously and sit down and eat a meal or drink a cup of coffee. This was prearranged with the Huntsville Police Department, the owners of the establishments, and the mayor.

Now, the city had told us to keep the details a secret, especially the names of the restaurants to be integrated and the day and hour the integrations would occur. But we could announce that a trial integration was planned, and Mr. Ray got into his car with the loudspeakers on top and drove around the black neighborhoods to tell everyone about the meeting on Monday and that there would be a special announcement.

That night, Mr. Blackwell got up and introduced Rev. Mordecai Johnson, retired president of Howard University and one of the great black preachers of his time, and there followed one of the most powerful civil rights speeches I've ever heard. Then, Reverend Bell told the crowd that we would select some of the hard-core student demonstrators to go down and test the lunch counters. We decided who they would be the following Thursday. We didn't want any hotheads. We wanted people who would stand their ground, who were rooted in nonviolent techniques, and so we picked people to go to each of these eight lunch counters, well dressed, well groomed, no more than three per lunch counter.

The mayor cooperated by having some of his off-duty policemen come in plainclothes and stop at the magazine racks or the toy counters and look out of the corner of their eye to see what was happening over at the lunch counters.

We sent in groups of twos and threes to test the lunch counters. That was July 9, 10, and 11, and the first day we went at 10 A.M., the next day at 2 P.M., and the next day at 4 P.M. That was to throw the Ku Klux Klan off, because the newspaper had printed an article that said in the next few days, several lunch counters in Huntsville would have a trial desegregation, and if there were no problems, they would continue to serve. Well, isn't that a hell of a way to write the article? If there are no problems, they will probably continue?

So we decided if they were gonna write it up like that, we'd better change our testing hours. Everything was always well planned, and that was because of those three, four, five meetings a week where we had to sit down and plan because we didn't want it to fail. And there was not a single incident. Our people just eased into there, and the plainclothesmen were present, at least two at every establishment.

The mayor could have integrated the lunch counters much earlier. I never even saw a white person get up and leave, at least at the lunch counters I went to. My wife and I went to Liggett's, and nobody reported such a thing. We ordered hamburgers and Cokes, and everything went smoothly because the merchants had agreed to it. They'd said, we're not gonna do it unless everyone else does it at the same time, and all of the employees had been informed that they were to serve us and that the plainclothesmen would be on the premises.

So our movement had achieved its first big victory, and we'd managed to do it with almost no violence, without any deaths or serious injuries, as had happened in several other cities across the state. For that, I'd have to give most of the credit to the methods we used, plus the courage and restraint of the students. From the very start, the leaders of the CSC had adopted a practical, low-key approach, kept the lines of communication open, and carried out everything in stages. And throughout it all, we remained firm in our commitment to nonviolence.

I know that the mayor and other city leaders also wanted to prevent any violence from happening. Huntsville was becoming a high-tech town. So the city took special care to try to prevent any incidents, and though at first the city resisted our demands, once it saw that desegregation was coming, it tried to make things go as smoothly as possible. As a result, we had gained one of the most important civil rights victories in Alabama since the bus boycott in Montgomery.

5
Integrating the Hospital and the Schools

In the midst of our sit-in campaign, the leaders of the Community Services Committee elected me a committee of one to go and talk to the hospital administrator about integrating the hospital. The administrator's name was Mr. Larry Rigsby, and I had several meetings with him.

At the first one, Mr. Rigsby told me: "Dr. Hereford, I can see it coming. I know we're gonna have to do something. Let me just think this over for a day or two, and you come back, and we'll meet again, and I'll tell you what I've decided, and you can tell me whether you and your committee will be pleased with that."

So at our second meeting, Mr. Rigsby says: "I'll tell you what I've decided, and you tell me what you think about it. In about two, three weeks, I'll just quietly walk over one morning, and I'll tell the nurses in the newborn nursery to accept black babies. And then, another eight, ten days, we'll integrate the pediatric ward. And then, after that has soaked in, and they get used to that, we'll integrate labor and delivery, and the postpartum ward. And assuming that things are still going along fine, we'll do medicine. And then we'll do surgery."

And I brought that back to my committee, and my committee seemed satisfied with it, and we took it to the mass meeting. And everybody was quietly relieved, because the administrator didn't want demonstrations, and we didn't want to have to put on demonstrations. Mr. Rigsby did it just like he said he'd do. He walked over one morning, and he told the nurses running the newborn nursery, "We're gonna have all the babies born today and from now on, you accept them."

Sure enough, the pediatrics ward was integrated, and I don't know if Mr. Rigsby got the idea from some other hospital or if he came up with the idea himself, but it sure did seem like a wonderful plan to me because in the newborn and pediatrics wards, the kids didn't know they were not supposed to like each other anyway. And then the labor and delivery, when those women came in there in pain getting ready to have a baby, I don't think they cared about who was next door to them. So that seemed to work out just fine.

It took about twelve months for the hospital to complete its desegregation and for people to become acclimatized to it. In the meantime, Mr. Rigsby had started integrating the eating facilities. When I had started practicing, there'd been no eating facilities at all for the black doctors and black nurses, who would have to take brown bags with them. Back in the old days, the nursing shifts were twelve hours long, and you can imagine a person going to work as a nurse, a nurse's aide, or an orderly to work in a place for twelve hours and have no eating facilities whatsoever.

So the black nurses used to eat right there on the unit from their brown bags, in the Colored Wing. Later, some of them were assigned to duties on the white side, though never in administrative capacities. They also had black maids, orderlies, and nurse's aides working over there, but none could eat in the cafeteria.

Well, about 1960 or 1961, the hospital had set up one small room where black people had two tables. They could come through the line with their trays and pick up the food, but they knew they needed to go to the side room after they picked up the food. It was only after the hospital integrated that they actually integrated the cafeteria.

For the first few days, when I went to the cafeteria to eat, you could cut the tension with a knife. But it gradually got better and better, and in eight or ten days, you could tell it was just a little bit different, and in another two or three months, there were black nurses and white nurses sitting at the same table, laughing and talking. We're all working together on a unit at the same time, lunch break at the same time, walk back to the unit.

When we started our sit-ins and marches, and once integration came, I became extremely unpopular among some of the white physicians in town. I recall one surgeon, a man I'd gotten along with just fine until the movement started. We were having a poster walk on Clinton Street, and I was carrying the poster that said, "Khrushchev Can Eat Here, But I Can't." I looked up and saw this surgeon coming out of Universal Photo, and as I got ready to say hello, his eyes traveled down to my placard, and he never said a word, just walked on, and never accepted any referrals from me again.

Oh, there were some who would meet me in the hospital hallways and privately congratulate me on what I was doing, even urge me to go on, but they were always looking over their shoulders, making sure nobody heard them.

Other doctors were openly hostile. They wouldn't get on the elevator if I were on the elevator. If they started to get on and saw me already there, they wouldn't get in. Some would not sit at the same table with me in the cafeteria.

If I came up, and two of my friends were sitting there—and I say friends, but it was mainly just the guys I had referred patients to, particularly the surgeons—and I sat down where they were, not realizing that some of the guys who were sitting with them did not necessarily want to sit with me, some of the doctors would just get up and leave.

This hostility extended to a few members of the hospital staff as well, like the head nurse down in the emergency room. I was working with a patient one day, and she passed by, and she said, "Dr. Hereford, I heard you've been downtown there picketing." I said, yes. She said, "That is really ridiculous for all you colored people to act like you're acting. And you have two colleges, and we white people don't even have a college." I made no answer, but I thought what *she* said was ridiculous. Besides, Oakwood College had nothing in the world to do with the state. It was a private Adventist school. But in her mind, just the existence of Oakwood and Alabama A&M should have been enough to keep us from protesting against anything.

Once we got the lunch counters open and Huntsville Hospital integrated, we turned our attention to the schools. During his visit, Dr. King had urged us to get some students and try to enroll them. Mr. Blackwell had told us later, "Yes, we're gonna do just that, but with our small force, we have to do one or two things at a time." He said, "The integration of the lunch counters might take a hell of a long time. But [on] the school situation, the Supreme Court has already outlawed segregation. All you have to do is get the kids and take 'em to the school. You might have to file suit, but you're not gonna have to get out here in the streets and march and be arrested."

So we began looking hard at the school situation. Now, the *Brown v. Board of Education* suit had been settled back in 1954, but Huntsville had made no strides whatsoever in school desegregation. There were now actually three black schools in town: Councill, which still taught grades one through twelve; Cavalry Hill, which taught one through nine; and West End, which was one through six. Those were the sole choices for black children.[1]

When the CSC had been formed and I'd been made chairman of its subcommittee on education, Mr. Blackwell helped me write out our goals, the main one being complete integration of the city's school system.[2] During the fall of 1962, we began conducting meetings with parents of black families all over the city, wanting to know who would be interested in signing a petition to carry to the school board to ask them to integrate the schools.

We had expressions of support from many, but as the petition began circulating all over the city, some parents hesitated to sign because they were afraid they would lose their jobs. We finally got thirty-five parents to sign, which we thought was really an accomplishment because a lot of people didn't want their name to go on a petition that was going to be made public. The local newspaper was finally starting to print things about what we were doing, and many of the parents were thinking, well, gee whiz, if they print my name in there, Mr. Charlie's gonna know it, and he's gonna retaliate.

So we got thirty-some-odd parents to sign that petition, and we carried it to the school board and told them that the parents wanted the schools integrated, that the Supreme Court had already outlawed segregation, and that it had been almost ten years. The first time we met with the Huntsville Board of Education, they had about six items on the agenda, and they made ours the last. They covered everything on there—who's gonna pay for the football uniforms, who's gonna fix the leak over on that school, what the budget's gonna be, and so on— and after we went through all that, they asked us to speak.

Our spokesman, Reverend Bell, got up—we had about ten members from our committee [the CSC] at the meeting—and he asked the board if it would integrate the schools, and after he got through speaking, they made several statements. I don't remember what they said, except I know they didn't say they were gonna integrate the schools. So Reverend Bell spoke another ten or fifteen minutes, and the response from the board was about five minutes, and then one member of the board moved for adjournment. It was seconded and passed unanimously. And they walked out of the building and just left us sitting there.

So we decided to file a suit. We contacted the NAACP Legal Defense Fund in New York, and the NAACP sent down its lawyer to meet with us and help us prepare to file a suit, and by the time the lawyer came, only five families were left to actually file the suit, and then one of those dropped out.[3]

That left four families to file the suit. Of those who dropped out, I know in several instances their employers pressured them to drop out. Others came and asked that their names be taken off the suit but gave no reasons. Some just stopped coming to the meetings.

On March 11, 1963, we filed a class-action suit against the Huntsville Board of Education in federal court to desegregate schools in the city. The final four people named in the suit were me, on behalf of Sonnie IV; Mrs. Sidney Ann Brewton, on behalf of her son John; a beautician named Mrs. Odell Pearson, on behalf of her daughter Veronica; and Rev. C. Alexander Piggee, on behalf of his son David. The suit was scheduled to be heard in federal court in Birmingham in August.

That June, while waiting to go to court, Martha and I took another trip organized by Dr. Phil Manning of the University of Southern California. This one was a three-week tour of medical centers in London, Paris, Copenhagen, and Stockholm. We visited the Royal Free Hospital in London, the American Hospital in Paris, and the Karolinska Institute in Stockholm, but worry over what might happen in August with our lawsuit, and what might happen should we win the suit and then try to register our son, was never far from our thoughts.

We got back to Alabama in July, and it was getting time for school to start. In court, the school board had made several motions, and I think one of those they filed against me was that they shouldn't have to admit my son because he wasn't old enough. He was five, but his birthday was August 30. Then they said they didn't even have any record of his birth in Montgomery. And they didn't, because he was born in Indiana. They were just doing anything they could to delay having any black children come into their schools, you see.

We went to Birmingham to plead our case before a federal judge named H. H. Grooms. Our lawyer was a woman named Constance Baker Motley, who took Thurgood Marshall's place on the NAACP Legal Defense Fund.[4] She worked with our lawyers in Birmingham who had pleaded the cases for the Huntsville sit-iners. They also had other cases in Birmingham, Tuskegee, and Mobile, and Judge Grooms decided to hear all of them at once.

I testified for the Huntsville group. They tried to get me to say that it was dangerous for my son to cross that street to go to the Fifth Avenue Elementary School. It was real funny, the stuff they tried to say. I even had to tell them how many feet it was across the street. And they wanted to compare it to how many feet it was if he went across the street to a black school, you know.

Constance Baker Motley was really something. In her mannerisms she reminded me a little of Dorothy Brown, the surgeon at Meharry. Motley was tall and had a commanding voice, and she always seemed to know what she was doing. In court, the fact that she was a woman, and a black woman, seemed to work in her favor, because all the lawyers for the Huntsville School Board were white men, and somehow or another they underestimated her ability, and the first thing they knew, she'd have them on the ground, and she'd be on top of them. I suspect that if Thurgood [Marshall] had come, they would have approached the case differently. But they dropped their guard, and by then, it was too late.

When Judge Grooms made his ruling, he gave it right there from the bench, immediately after the case was heard. He asked the Huntsville lawyers, "And you're telling me that you're gonna have the whole school system disrupted?"

They said, "Oh, yes, yes, Judge, it's gonna be torn *all* to pieces."

He said, "These four little Negro children? You mean to tell me, you're an administrator of the school, and you're gonna let four Negro children disrupt your whole system?"

And that embarrassed them. And Orzell Billingsley, our lawyer from the sit-ins, was there with Constance Motley, and, referring to a couple of the attorneys for the school board in Huntsville, he says, "I see Mr. Joe Payne got attorney Barnes to help him. Attorney Barnes has been pleading these cases all over the state. He pleaded down in Tuskegee. He pleaded in Birmingham. He pleaded in Mobile. And do you know what? He's consistent. He's lost every one of them."

We felt like in the end, it would be ruled in our favor. And that's what happened. Judge Grooms ruled from the bench. He told the school board, "You go back to Huntsville, admit these four students to the four schools that are involved, and by January 2, supply me with a plan for *total* desegregation of all the schools in Huntsville and Madison County."

This was the middle of August, and it was getting time for the schools to open, which was scheduled for the Tuesday after Labor Day. That's when the four parents named in the suit would bring their kids to school. The four target schools were Fifth Avenue Elementary School, on Governors Drive; Rison Elementary, on Oakwood Avenue, which Veronica Pearson would be entering; Terry Heights Elementary, on Barbara Drive, which David Piggee would be entering; and East Clinton Elementary School, on Clinton Avenue, which John Anthony Brewton would be entering. I would be enrolling Sonnie IV at the Fifth Avenue school.

Now, you have to remember, this had been a year of violence in Alabama. It had started with Wallace's segregation now and forever speech on the capitol steps in January. In April and May came the dogs and fire hoses in Birmingham and then the governor's stand in the schoolhouse door [at The University of Alabama].

We'd had only small, isolated incidents so far in Huntsville, but with the continuing troubles throughout the state, anything could happen. With all the publicity about school integration, I was starting to get more threatening phone calls than usual—the KKK calling my office, calling my house.

You know, when you're practicing medicine, and especially when you're delivering babies, you have to answer that phone. And when you pick up your phone, you don't know if someone's calling you to say Mrs. Susie Brown's in labor, or somebody's calling you a low-down, dirty son of a bitch, telling you where they were gonna plant a bomb, or that there's a rifle pointed at your head.

The phone would ring all times of the night. A fellow woke me up one time at three o'clock in the morning. A voice said, "Dr. Hereford, you're dead. And your son's dead, too."

Another time, someone called and said, "We're gonna put a bomb in your car. We're gonna blow up your office."

It got so bad I took to answering the phone and pretending I was a policeman. The phone would ring, and I'd answer and say, "Dr. Hereford's residence. Officer Parker speaking." Sometimes I said, "Officer O'Reilly," but it was usually "Officer Parker." And if it was a threatening call, you'd hear a click. But a legitimate call could still get through, and so I was able to keep doing my job as a doctor. I tried not to let anything affect my practice in terms of my ability to continue treating my patients.

I do remember that there were many people who said I shouldn't have gotten into it in the first place, that nothing was ever gonna come of it. One of the white farmers who lived near my mother kept telling her to tell me, for God's sake, get out of it, distance myself from those communists, you know, I was just going to ruin my reputation and my medical career.

It was the Tuesday after Labor Day, September 3, 1963, that Sonnie and I went down the first time to the Fifth Avenue school. We got up and got dressed and walked on down. He'd just turned six, and he was anxious to go, and I can remember how happy he'd been when we came home from Birmingham that day and told him we'd won the case. He was thrilled, though, of course, he didn't understand any of it; he just wanted to go to school.

We walked from my house, which was directly in front of the Huntsville Hospital, to the Fifth Avenue school, and when we got there, the school was closed. There were a lot of other parents there, and they were upset that the school was closed. What none of us knew was that the previous day, the school board had decided to delay opening of the local schools until Friday in response to a request from Governor Wallace. So we couldn't get in that day. We promptly informed our attorney, Constance Motley, and she said, try again tomorrow because if they turn you around, we'll have a case.

So the next day we returned, and the school was still closed. The same thing was happening in Birmingham, Mobile, and Tuskegee, where Wallace had ordered in the state troopers. Everything was getting a little confusing by now, because the school board was telling everyone they're gonna open the schools on Friday, but the paper was saying that Wallace was planning to send in state troopers to keep them closed. But we decided to try again on Friday anyway.

Thursday night, as we got ready, I had no idea what might happen, and as you can imagine, my wife and I were concerned about our son, though we couldn't imagine anyone trying to do him any harm, and we'd been assured by Mr. Macon Weaver, who was the U.S. attorney for northern Alabama, that there'd be FBI agents to accompany us. But we believed what we were doing was something that had to be done, something important for all black children in the city. And then, I was one of the leaders of our movement. Why should I ask somebody else to send their son, when I had a son?

My brother, Tom, had come down with some of his friends, and they spent Thursday night with us in the house. We'd gotten all kinds of threats, and we were a little worried about what might happen. Tom had brought his shotgun, and we teased him about it a little because he forgot and left it out in the trunk of his car.

The next morning, after Tom left for his teaching job in Decatur, Sonnie and I again headed off to the Fifth Avenue school. It seemed like the longest walk of my life, because despite having the FBI agents around, I got to thinking about all the things I'd heard about sharpshooters and snipers and people running up on the sidewalks with Jeeps, running people down.

As we approached the school, I could see a crowd of 150, maybe 200 people, and the state troopers already there—ten or twelve state trooper cars, and each one with at least two officers standing beside it—and they kept us from going in. As he had promised to do, Governor Wallace had sent in the state troopers and closed all four of the schools, and they were not letting anybody in, black or white. And some of the Caucasian people were shouting obscenities at us, and some of them were mad because we wanted to get into the school, and others were mad because their own kids couldn't get in the school.

So no one was permitted to enter. Governor Wallace had simply closed Fifth Avenue, Rison, Terry Heights, and East Clinton. He closed all four of them. He would not allow the black students to go in, but then the white students couldn't go in either.

And, as I say, they were mad at me because I wanted to go in the school and take my child, and they were also mad because they couldn't get their own children in the school. They yelled at us, and at the other schools they yelled at the other black kids and their parents, and I know that at the other three schools, a few of the whites said things like nigger, we don't want you here, and things like that. I don't remember what all they said to us, but my wife and I had tried to prepare Sonnie the night before to deal with it, how to let the words just roll right off his back.

So we came back home, and I let Constance know what had happened. At first, she told me not to go back, but later she called and said, "Go back over there on Monday." She said, "Go to the Western Union, and send a telegram to Judge Grooms, and tell him exactly what happened, that they refused to let you in." By Saturday, she was in federal court trying to get a restraining order against Wallace, and Judge Grooms had set a hearing for Monday.

Monday morning, Sonnie and I went back to the school. This time, there were only a few people around, mostly the police chief and a few plainclothesmen and news photographers. Not a trooper in sight. So the school officials enrolled my son at around 8:30 A.M., and they enrolled the other three kids in stages throughout the morning—Veronica Pearson at Rison, John Brewton at East Clinton, and David Piggee at Terry Heights.

One hundred years of desegregation hopes were fulfilled that day. And there was this guy from ABC News who came and interviewed my son, there in my backyard, sitting on a swing. And Mike Wallace's team interviewed us, and he showed the interview on CBS. But what I liked best was the way *News-week* described the scene: "A wide-eyed first grader, Sonnie Hereford IV, his hand clasped in that of his father, Dr. S. W. Hereford III, had walked unhindered into a Huntsville elementary school to become the first Negro to break the grade-school color barrier in Alabama."[5]

Things were different in Birmingham. They were different in Tuskegee, in Mobile, too. There, the troopers continued to bar black kids from entering the schools. Huntsville had escaped the worst of it.[6] Later, I heard stories about how a deal had been made between the city and the governor to get the state troopers out of Huntsville after that one-day show of defiance on Friday. I would say if any deals were made, it was because we'd kept up the pressure—you might lose Redstone, you might lose Redstone. They didn't want to lose Redstone Arsenal. They didn't want to lose those federal contracts at Marshall. They didn't want to cut off all the money flowing in to support the space program. This was leverage for us, because they wanted to keep their federal contracts, and we'd made it clear they couldn't do it if they continued to deny us our freedom.

All of us understood that there were dangers because we knew that even the federal presence here was not enough to prevent violence against black people. You need to recall those days, all the bombings in Birmingham, and my wife thinking they might attack us in our own house, too. Two days before I tried to enroll Sonnie, the Klan dynamited the home of a black attorney in Birmingham named Arthur Shores, and just six days after I got Sonnie registered they killed the four little girls in church in Birmingham [the bombing of the 16th Street Baptist Church on September 15]. We got the four kids in Huntsville enrolled on a Monday, and the four little girls in Birmingham were killed, I think, the following Sunday. And I've often wondered if that might have prompted the bomber to plant his bomb at that time because you had integration in Huntsville, Mobile, Tuskegee, and Birmingham. Those were the four cities, you know.

Then in November came the news of President Kennedy's assassination. That really hit me hard. I'm glad we had all the Kennedys back then, John and Robert, and then Lyndon Johnson. They at least created the climate for us, sort of encouraged us to continue what we were doing, made us want to do what we were doing. And I suspect that if some of the other presidents had been in office then, we probably wouldn't have had the enthusiasm and the energy to do what we did.

So the Kennedy assassination, that really hurt me. I was making a house call in Northwood, and I had my radio on, and when I got word, it was about 1:15, something like that, and the guy said it. I had to stop my car. I couldn't go to that patient's house right then. I sat in that car about fifteen or twenty minutes before I could go on.

As for George Wallace, I remember how Constance Motley told me just after we got Sonnie enrolled, she says, when you get in there, don't say anything negative to reporters about Wallace. You can say anything positive you want to but nothing negative. And I didn't say anything negative, though it was tempting because here I was, trying to get my kid in school, and I thought he was the low-downest, orneriest son of a bitch that ever lived to send the state troopers here to keep us out of the school, and all he had to do was just give the word, and we would have been in the schools. It was just causing us so much agony and money and time.

I could have been taking care of sick people rather than spending all this time going back and forth to the school, carrying the boy and trying to get him registered, all that tension. And the KKK—them calling my office, calling my house. I do believe that Wallace later regretted what he did. I do. But I suspect if he hadn't been shot, he wouldn't have been asking for forgiveness.

At the Fifth Avenue Elementary School, Sonnie did very well, despite an occasional problem here and there. One day, he came home from school and said, "Daddy, you know they have Cub Scouts over there. Could I join?" I said, "Yeah, if you want to."

So the next day, I was in my office, and I got a phone call, and this guy says, "Dr. Hereford, I'm so-and-so." Says, "I'm a real estate man here in town. I heard that your son wanted to join the Cub Scouts."

I said, "Yes, he told me that last night."

He said, "Well, Doctor, you know that he can't join the Cub Scouts. Why don't you sit him down and explain that to him?"

I said, "Sir, I'll tell you what I'll do. I'll put him in the car and bring him up there to your office and let you explain it to him."

He said, "No, no, no, I don't want to explain it to him." And what they finally did was dissolve the Cub Scouts in that school.

After two years, we decided to transfer Sonnie to St. Joseph's Catholic School, but it was not out of disappointment with his teachers or his treatment. It was a personal decision, based on the fact that our children were being reared in the faith of their mother. From an early age, Sonnie's dream was to go to Notre Dame, and it was one he eventually saw come true. Many years later, they even put him on the board of trustees.

Despite everything that our movement had accomplished, there was still a lot of work to be done, starting with the removal of all the old segregationist signs that were still up all over the city. We also asked the city to hire black policemen and firemen, and we wanted to get into the theaters and hotels like the Russel Erskine.[7]

We'd tell the merchants, you need to hire some blacks to be clerks and cashiers, and they'd say, you don't have anyone qualified to do these jobs—they don't know how to greet the customers and how to dress, and they can't run the cash register. So we set up a place where we trained young women to work the cash registers. Then we'd say, okay, here's this person, she's been in training for four months. Can you hire her now? We were able to get a lot of people hired in positions like that.[8]

We also kept asking that more blacks be hired in the high-tech jobs out at Redstone and Marshall. The director of NASA came to town one day and talked to some of the big contractors out there, because all these big companies like Chrysler and Boeing had government contracts or were associated with the space program. We'd gone to them, talked to them, and said, why don't you hire some blacks? They'd say, well, we don't have any qualified here. So the director of NASA came from Washington and said, "Find some." And they sent to Seattle. And they sent to Houston. And they sent to New Jersey. And the next thing you knew, we had some black engineers.

For me, another good sign came in the spring of 1964 when Dr. Drake, Dr. Belle, and I were finally admitted into the Madison County Medical Society. I think the members realized we could no longer be denied, and some of the old gang that had resisted so long had finally retired or died. So we were admitted, and later that same year I attended my first meeting of MASA [the Medical Association of the State of Alabama] down in Mobile. There were ten or fifteen other black physicians in attendance, and what was remarkable was how few problems we had. We were able to stay in the convention hotel, since the meeting occurred after President Johnson had signed the bill outlawing segregation in public facilities.

I don't recall having any problems in the Madison County Medical Society after that, if you exclude its Medical Auxiliary, which was an organization for the doctors' wives. It seems as though they shut it down when we got in. Then, after some time had passed, they started meeting again. My wife joined, though, of course, she was never asked to attend any of their tea or bridge parties.

This didn't bother either of us. After all those years of being shut out, I considered our admission a victory, and I remember making the announcement about it when I went to the Southern Christian Leadership Conference's meeting in Savannah in October 1964. I was there to participate in a panel discussion on poverty and its effects on health, which I'd been asked to do by Dr. King through Mr. Blackwell, and when I made the announcement about us getting into the county medical society, everyone stood up and applauded.

For the integration of public facilities in Huntsville, it took about twelve months, that's all, until almost everybody was complying. And many of the business establishments, on the very day President Johnson signed the Civil Rights Act of 1964, were ready to serve people. You had a lot of white people who had wanted to do the right thing all along but were afraid they'd be boycotted by the other side.

The one big exception was the pharmacies, mainly the ones with lunch counters. Several had refused to go along with the mayor's request in July 1962 to desegregate, and even after President Johnson had signed the 1964 law, they still wouldn't serve black people.

I used to post a sign in my waiting room that said, "Some pharmacists in town still discriminate against Negroes." I didn't say which ones, because I didn't want to be charged with violating the anti-boycott law. But once I got the patient inside the examination room, and if he asked me, I would tell him the names, and many would go elsewhere to have their prescriptions filled.

There was one pharmacist who was more outspoken than anyone else, a man very highly regarded by the other pharmacists in town. Since opening my practice, I'd had good relations with him, and he'd always treated black people fairly. Then the sit-ins started.

Well, I called him one day—my uncle had been sitting-in there, and this pharmacist had been very mean to him—and I spoke to him about it, and I said, I had thought you would be more cooperative than that, especially with all the prescriptions I've sent you.

He said, "Well, I'll tell you. He came in here talking about this was Custer's Last Stand and all that, and I said, hell, I don't see no goddamned Indians. And I told him, I said I wasn't gonna serve him, would never serve him, and I'm telling you the same thing. If you ever come in here and try to get served, just will your soul to God and will your ass to me."

Well, I never had the desire to go over there and confront him, but eventually he had to come 'round, just like everybody else. I did pay a visit to his partner's establishment—remember, this is *after* President Johnson had signed the deal [the Civil Rights Act] in 1964—and this particular drugstore was also one of those places that had refused to go along with the mayor's request to desegregate two years earlier. I'd earlier called him and politely asked him to desegregate—said, I've sent you all these prescriptions, and you've got a lot of black customers.

He says, "Well, I'm not gonna open my counter. And the reason why I don't want to do it—well, your folks are just so nasty. They're just so nasty and dirty when they come in and sit at my counter. And I'm not gonna open my place of business to them."

I said, "Some of them are clean, aren't they? Aren't some white people dirty?"

He said, "Yeah, but it's more dirty blacks than it is white."

Now, Reverend Bell had warned me never to go anywhere by myself to try to get somebody to serve me, but one day, I went over to this man's place, and I sat down at the counter. I waited about twenty minutes, and the waitress never did come up to me to serve me. So I got up and walked over toward the rack where they had some cosmetics or something and just started looking at them.

And the next thing I knew, a guy came up to me and hit me just like an offensive tackle from the Green Bay Packers and almost knocked me down. He said, "'Scuse me." Then, before I could recover, he came back the other way and hit me again with his shoulder, just as hard as he could, and he said, "'Scuse me."

See, I think he wanted to be sure that he said "Excuse me." I think he was covering himself. In other words, if I bump into this guy, regardless of how hard I bump him, as long as I say "Excuse me," it means that it was an accident. I just stayed right there and stood my ground and never raised a hand to him. I have no idea who he was, and I doubt if I'd know his face if I ever saw it, and I'm almost sure that nobody in that drugstore would have told who it was because, like I say, I suspect he was the designated hitter against agitators. The manager had probably told him that if any black person comes in here and tries to sit at my counter, I want you to go over there and knock him down.

I remember one weekday night in March of '65—this was when the struggle for voter registration was going on in Selma and state troopers had attacked the marchers on the Pettus Bridge—we got word that the White Citizens' Council was having a meeting at Big Spring [Park]. It was a public meeting, so several of us decided we'd go. I don't think we would have dared go down there if it had been five years earlier, even two years earlier. But we went down and listened to what they had to say at the Big Spring Park.

They said a lot of bad things about us, especially a prominent lawyer in town whose name and face I knew well. I don't know if he was the leader or just one of the speakers, but he's the only one I knew because some of my patients had hired him on injury cases. And this lawyer says, "I see some black people scattered out here. I know they're bastards because most of the black people don't know who their daddies are anyway." He got a big hand for that one.

I remember how that same speaker said that the reason Jimmie Lee Jackson had died—this was the young man who'd been shot by state troopers during a march in Marion, Alabama, in February and had later died at the black hospital in Selma—was because of the incompetent care he'd gotten from black doctors in a black hospital. Nothing about him dying from gunshot wounds at the hands of a state trooper.

After Dr. King had won approval from the federal courts to have the Selma to Montgomery march, I just couldn't stay in my office. I didn't participate in the whole march, just toward the end as the marchers were coming into the outskirts of Montgomery. About twelve or fifteen of us left Huntsville at three o'clock in the morning.

When we arrived, we found the people camped out on the outskirts of Montgomery, and about nine or nine-thirty they had some speeches. Mrs. Viola Liuzzo, the white volunteer from Michigan, had just been killed by the Klan in Lowndes County, and I had two cameras and was taking pictures of the speakers, and I got up on a roof so I'd make sure I could get Dr. King and his group as they passed by.

We started marching, and we slowly made our way from the outskirts of Montgomery on to the capitol, and some of us doctors had on our white pith helmets. I put a red cross on mine because I had told Dr. Abernathy that I would do whatever I could if anybody needed my assistance. We marched all the way to the capitol, and we expected Wallace to come out, but he would not come out and say anything to us. So several of the march leaders made speeches on the capitol steps. We got there around noon, and we stayed until two or two-thirty and left.[9]

I continued to follow Dr. King's career and was aware of his visit to Memphis in support of the sanitation workers' strike. Then one day in early April 1968, I was driving down Whitesburg heading out to Farley on a house call when the word of his assassination came over the radio. It was a repeat of the Kennedy assassination, and I had to pull off the road again. I wanted to go to the funeral in Atlanta, but there was no way I could get away, though Tom was able to go.

After that I tried to stay active in civil rights as best I could, but with only three black doctors in town, my practice had grown so large that it left me little time, plus all my volunteer duties for programs like Head Start and Upward Bound.[10] I finally got to where I almost had to stop taking new patients, but I found it hard to say no and rarely turned down anyone. In 1968, I did ask to be relieved of my teaching duties at Alabama A&M. I continued there as the clinic physician until 1973, at which time I asked to be relieved of that, too, as well as my duties at Oakwood. I did stay on as A&M's team doctor, which is something I greatly enjoyed.

Having Dr. Sonny Belle in town helped a lot, and for a time, he, Dr. Drake, and I worked together, covering for each other, until Dr. Belle passed from lung cancer and leukemia in 1970. He was shaving one day and cut himself and wouldn't stop bleeding because he didn't have adequate platelets and his white cells were developing too fast, bringing on anemia. At that time, some of Dr. Belle's patients came into my practice.

Then Dr. Drake had a heart attack, and he was supposed to cut back, but he didn't really cut back. He took his medications and exercised, and that was the thing that led to his demise because he was out exercising early one morning on his bicycle when he was struck by a car. He died in November 1979. At that time, many of Drake's patients also came into my practice.

By the early 1970s, my load was around forty-five patients a day. I would see twenty or twenty-five before lunch, then probably about that same number in the afternoon. My hospital practice was heavy, too. They used to print cards for us indicating the number of patients we had and their location and how many days they had been in already. We would come in the entrance to the hospital and reach up to our cubbyhole to get our cards. My card sometimes would have ten or twelve, maybe fourteen or fifteen patients listed, and if I made rounds for myself, and sometimes for Dr. Drake, I might see thirty in one day just on the hospital rounds.

Later on, just out of curiosity, I counted up my charts at the office, and there were 11,000 charts. Of course, some of those patients had moved out of town, some had become inactive, and some of them had expired. Still, I think my active load of patients was somewhere in the neighborhood of 6,000. Most of the family practitioners I knew had 2,000 or 3,000 patients.

As I look back now, and as I try to understand what has happened to me since, I've come to the conclusion that of all the things I did in civil rights, nothing stirred up more anger toward me, more personal resentment, than the part I played in school desegregation.

A year after we'd won our case, under pressure from Judge Grooms, the school board finally came up with a plan to integrate classes. But objections over transfers and teacher assignments kept desegregation to a minimum. It went on like this for years. By then, I knew few details of the suit, only that it still had my name on it. And every time it came out in the paper, where it mentioned *Sonnie Hereford III et al. v. Huntsville Board of Education,* that kept my name in the limelight.[11]

Some of the staff doctors at the hospital never spoke to me after 1963. All of a sudden, my work at the hospital was more closely scrutinized, and I was called on the carpet whenever I failed to dot an "i" or cross a "t."

Then, my malpractice insurance was canceled by a local company, though I'd always paid my premiums on time and had never had a malpractice suit filed against me. I just got a letter one day telling me that they were canceling. I called them up and spoke to one of the people at the company, and he told me that he would not give me a reason. When I pressed him, he said, "We don't have to give you a reason." As a result, I had to seek malpractice insurance from Lloyd's of London at a cost of three times what the local doctors were paying.

There were other troubling incidents, which, to this day, I remain convinced were petty acts of retaliation against me and my family, in this case from the police. Approximately two years after cancellation of my malpractice insurance, someone broke into a Coke machine near my home and damaged the machine in such a fashion that you could receive both a Coke and your dime back. The person who did it was arrested and was in custody of the police.

Well, my son went to the Coke machine, put in a dime, got out a Coke and his dime back, put in the dime again, another Coke and another dime back, and he did this a third time. A policeman came up, saw him putting the dime in, getting the Cokes out for the same dime, and arrested him for petty larceny. We had to go to court, pay a lawyer, and my ten-year-old son now had a record of petty larceny.

Despite all this, my participation in the civil rights movement was one of the proudest moments of my life. If I had it to do again, I would do it again and in the same fashion as before, except with more experience and more determination.

6
Troubles and Trials

It was about 1970 when Medicaid came to Alabama, and when you think about it, it should have been a good thing for me because Medicaid was supposed to help poor people pay for medical care. That should have helped my situation, but that's not the way it turned out. It was the start of a lot of trouble for me.

For one thing, it was hard to keep up with the paperwork. We had some patients with no insurance whatsoever; we had some with Medicaid only and some with Medicare only; and we had others with a combination. We had those four categories, and we had to try to remember that when we filled out the claims. That extra paperwork affected how you dealt with the patient. If you spent ten minutes with the patient's examination, then you'd have to spend at least five or ten minutes filling out the forms, especially those of us who didn't have the new technologies in our office.

In retrospect, my informal way of doing things wasn't the best way to go about it, and certainly some of my record keeping was not up to par because I did not keep the records in every single instance, 100 percent, like they should have been.

By the mid-1970s, I think about 75 percent of my patients were on Medicaid, and I believe I was the only doctor in town that had that figure. Others didn't even approach it. In fact, some of the physicians had said initially that they were not going to accept Medicare and Medicaid patients. Dr. Drake had expressed that thought. He finally did, but neither he nor Dr. Belle ever had the volume of Medicaid patients I had. And many of the Caucasian physicians never did accept Medicaid patients.

There were about four of us in the whole state that were the top providers of Medicaid. Because of that, we made more Medicaid income than the other doctors. I was probably number three or number four. But when you scrutinize it, you'll see that Medicaid was about four-fifths of my total income, whereas, with some of the other doctors, it may have been 10 percent of their total income. My patients were poor, and they're the ones who had Medicaid.

One morning, I got up and went out on the driveway to pick up the newspaper, and there on the front page it said that there were doctors who were making a fortune off Medicaid and that the previous year I had made $85,000. And they were right, because that was the bulk of my practice. I collected $85,000 from them, and my overhead was probably $60,000. So my net was about $25,000, and when you take income tax from that, I really wasn't making much money. Some people would meet me on the street and say, Dr. Hereford, I didn't know you were making that kind of money.

The fact that I seemed to be making money off a program meant to help poor people—that's probably what got me singled out when the time came to cut costs. I've thought about all this a lot since I lost my license, and I think that was one of the reasons.

It probably didn't help matters that I enjoyed gambling occasionally. My wife and I used to go to Las Vegas pretty regularly, and then we'd go down to the Bahamas because we loved to play Black Jack, you know. At first, we just liked to play slot machines. We would sometimes go to Las Vegas, and we used to go down to Puerto Rico.

Some people actually saw me in the gambling places. They were there gambling themselves. And some other people had heard that someone had seen me there. And then, maybe they had called for an appointment and the answering service referred them to my alternate doctor who was covering for me, and they may have become disgruntled on that point—well, you know, he's not here, and in my opinion, he ought to be here. But I was only away on my off days. Not every single off day. It was once or twice a year. And then finally, there was one point where I would go once or twice a month.

When my Medicaid problems started, that [the gambling] was something that scared my lawyer. He thought being in Montgomery, even if you had a jury trial, coming from the Bible Belt, that these people were going to say, okay, this guy is charging us our tax money, and he's in Las Vegas gambling. Plus the fact that this would give you a great incentive to steal in the first place. The investigators and attorneys never said I was using Medicaid money for gambling in plain language, but they did in innuendos.

I also suspect that I may have had some disgruntled patients, some individuals in the black community who had some sort of grudge against me simply because you can't practice medicine for as long as I did with as many patients as I had without making a few enemies, especially when they find out how much money you're making.

There were many ways a doctor could make enemies. You take what happens when families get together and the kids start fooling around out of curiosity about sex, and one or the other ends up in the ER and the doctor has to come in and make a determination as to what happened and then write a report. That is what you call today a no-win situation, because whatever you write, you're going to lose some friends. Rape cases, or alleged rape cases, now those are the worst, and I had to testify in court at least a half-dozen times.

There was one case—and I just refused to get involved in this one because by then I was starting to have my own problems with Medicaid—of a robbery at one of the local motels, where the desk clerk had been raped. She told police that the rapist had a very large sex organ, and somehow or another, the police found the man they thought did it and put him in jail, and his relatives called wanting me to go down to the jail and actually to measure his penis, just to show he was average size. Can you imagine getting involved in something like that? I know I made some enemies when I told them, no, I won't do that.

My first indication that I was about to have some problems was when I got a letter from Texaco. I had several credit cards from them, and I got a letter from them saying they received a subpoena from the Medicaid Fraud Division of Alabama asking them to turn in all of the records of my gas expenses. I wondered, what in the world does that have to do with Medicaid? So it seems like what they did was go behind my back [to review] all the expenses that I had listed for house calls, as I had included those in my claims.

The next indication I got was when I received a letter from my travel agency. The Medicaid people had gone to the agency and found out every single time I had traveled. And then, say, if I had traveled on February 19, and they had a claim for February 19—well, they had me dead to rights, a claim for somebody being in the hospital, not for an office visit. There's no way in the world I would have sent in [a claim] for an office visit. But I would send in for the hospital [visit] for somebody from the twelfth through the twentieth, and that included the nineteenth. And they said, how in the world could you be taking care of this patient while you're in Las Vegas?

The truth was that someone was covering for me when I was out of town, just as I covered for them when they were out of town, so that whatever amount I collected when he visited my patient I returned by visiting his. Doctors covered for each other all the time or you would never get a break. We didn't exactly have a group practice, but we covered for each other, the doctors, you know. Dr. Belle had passed, and another black doctor had come to town, an Oakwood graduate, and he was in our group. So we started covering for each other. And then, sometimes I would go out of town.

And just say, for instance, that I put a patient in the hospital on the tenth of the month, and then maybe Saturday, the thirteenth, and Sunday, the fourteenth, I was out of town, and then I came back that Monday. In the meantime, one of the black doctors would make rounds through the weekend for all of us. And then, say, the patient went home on the twentieth. Now, when I would send in a claim, I would say: "Mrs. Mary Brown, admitted on the tenth and discharged on the twentieth, and if you're going to pay me five dollars a day, then you owe me fifty dollars." And then they would give me a percentage of the fifty dollars.

But then later they said if I didn't actually *see* Mrs. Brown that Saturday and Sunday I couldn't charge, and my colleague, the other black doctor, couldn't charge either. And [they said] I had no business charging, since I didn't actually see the patient.

One day—this was after my legal troubles had started—we were having a hearing before an administrative law judge in Montgomery about all these things, and I was talking about how unfair I thought all this was. The attorney who was prosecuting the case says, "Your Honor, this man has sent these claims in, and he didn't actually see the patient, although he says his partner saw him in his stead."

And the attorney talked about how terrible this was and how that was actually fraud. And now, it's approaching the end of the afternoon session. He says, "Your Honor, this case is to be continued until tomorrow, but I won't be here tomorrow. I have to go to Rhode Island and take a deposition. But my partner will be here to prosecute this case tomorrow." Now, me being a doctor, my partner can't work in my place, and at the same time, he's telling the judge that his partner's coming to work in his place.

Eventually, they started asking me for invoices to prove that I had purchased such-and-such medications because they were saying that if I was claiming I gave thirty-five of these injections to these patients, then I certainly had to have purchased these medications, somewhere, sometime. There was a drug salesman, a detail man from Gadsden, who actually was a co-partner of a drug company, and he got out in the field and peddled his own medications. He covered Huntsville, and as a goodwill gesture, he wanted to do something for the black community. So whenever he had any medications that were slow moving, he would give them to me. And though some of them might have been approaching the expiration date, they may still have had fourteen or fifteen months, and rather than trying to sell them at the regular price, he'd just bring them by my office.

And then, sometimes people would bring medications that they would have reactions from, and they'd just bring them down and say, "Doctor, these medications are giving me a rash, or giving me the headache, or something, and I don't think I ought to take them." Well, okay, Mr. Jones, let me give you a sample here, and you leave that bottle with me. And then I would use it for some other patient who couldn't buy any medicines at all.

Or maybe somebody needed prescription X, and maybe there are twelve pills left in this bottle and eighteen pills left in another bottle. Well, when you combined those, this indigent patient has enough for his whole regimen.

I thought I was doing a service. But the Medicaid people had the impression that, number one, I was selling these medications and, number two, that I was furnishing them to patients for the relief of pain or insomnia and claiming I had given them injections for the pain when they in fact did not get an injection. But that would have been difficult to do because they had standard fees for procedures—so much for a urinalysis, so much for an injection—and they could come into your office and check the charts to find out if you had actually documented everything you said you did on the claim.

They had what is called the Medicaid Fraud Division, and, you know, it's a funny thing, too, whenever they communicated with you, they wrote you a letter. Your name and address would be in fine print. But their name would be in boldface. In other words, if anybody had happened to see your mail, there was no way that they could miss, at the top of that envelope, top left, "Medicaid Fraud Division." And I thought that was a bad thing for them to do. Why do they want to make that name three times or four times as large as the addresses on the envelope?

Once, when I went to their office in Montgomery to talk to them about a situation, I sat and talked with an investigator face to face. But all of the other investigators in the office stood in such a way that they could view me, but I couldn't view them. They were peeping around corners and standing— somehow or another, I don't know exactly how they did it—they had plywood or something like that so that it would obscure you from seeing their faces, and I think some of them had one-way mirrors and that sort of thing, you know, because I think they wanted to go into the communities, and sometimes they did not necessarily want the doctors or their staffs to recognize them.

And then they would come into your community—say, for instance, they suspected some physician of doing something wrong—they would come into the projects, and they'd flash a badge. Well, here's a big, tall white man flashing a badge in a black person's home, at the door or sitting on a couch, flashing this big badge and saying, I'm from the Medicaid Fraud Division, and I want to talk to you about Dr. Hereford, or Dr. Jones, or whomever. We suspect him of fraud, and we think you may be involved. Can you tell me such-and-such a thing?

Do you think they're going to get answers from that person? They'll get that person to say almost anything. Although they said, "We think you may be involved," what they actually may have been meaning is, "We think the case may have been your case." But the person gets the impression he's saying, maybe I'm in cahoots with the doctor.

And if they thought they had probable cause, they could come to the Madison County courthouse and set up an office and subpoena certain patients to come and talk to them. Now, those patients are scared to death. You're living in a housing project. You're already afraid of the power structure. Then you get a subpoena that says you have to come to the Madison County courthouse at such-and-such an hour on such-and-such a day. Now you've got to miss your job and go up there, and you don't know what you're going up there for. And then they get you in the room and start grilling you about what did the doctor do and what did the doctor say and all that, what sort of treatment did he give you and on what date.

The Medicaid people had a whole staff, just like the FBI. As a matter of fact, they hired people who had been detectives in other agencies. One of the investigators told me one time, "We'll be back, but we can't come Wednesday, we got to go to Cullman and bust a nursing home." Those are the words he used. He's got to go and *bust* a nursing home. At the time, Graddick was attorney general,[1] and he was pushing Medicaid fraud prosecutions because he wanted to be governor. If he could nail this guy up here in Huntsville for Medicaid fraud and then get several nursing homes, well, you see how this would boost his popularity, and people would think, well, my God, he's really looking out for us taxpayers, you know.

They [Medicaid officials] came to my office one time and asked me to produce my sign-in sheets. Well, I didn't keep sign-in sheets. I mean, maybe I should have, but people would come, and I had sheets out there, and the people would sign in—that they arrived at such-and-such a time, so that the nurse could keep the order and pull the charts and so forth—and then I would go ahead and see the patients, and as near as possible, I tried to keep accurate records *on the chart*.

But I never kept a "sign-in sheet." They kept asking me for my sign-in sheets, but I didn't maintain any because I didn't think it was necessary at that time. I didn't even make any attempt to keep any. After the patients had registered, and we had seen them, we just put the sheets in the trash.

I didn't have any appointment sheets either because we did not take appointments. People came to the office when they could get off their job, late at night, on weekends, whenever they were able to come to the office. If I had known then what I know now, I would have kept the sign-in sheets because they were going to use the absence of sign-in sheets to say that I didn't actually see the patients listed on some of the claims I had sent in.

In the summer of 1979 I was to go and have a meeting with the Medicaid people because they had alleged that I had gotten some funds that I was not due. This was before I had a lawyer, and they had written a letter to me that said something like, "We have these allegations against you. Would you like to come down and discuss these with us?" So I thought I would go down and discuss it with them. I got my files, put some records together concerning certain patients and how little I had been charging before the Medicaid.

And so I'm going down there to talk with them, and the meeting was scheduled for about ten o'clock, say, on a Thursday morning. Well, Wednesday, around sundown, I drove down to Montgomery, and when I got there, I dialed my wife, and she said, "Do you know what happened after you left?"

She said, "Well, the sheriff came with a warrant for your arrest—said you'd been stealing from Medicaid—and I told him you were in Montgomery to talk to the Medicaid people. And so he wanted to come and search the house because he thought you were hiding in the house. And I was embarrassed because the relatives were here, my mother's folks from Kentucky."

And I thought to myself, I don't know a lot of law, but this is stupid, for me to meet with them tomorrow morning, and then, when I drive back home, I'm gonna go to jail. So I called them the next morning and said I was not coming to the meeting, and they said, "How come?" And I said, "Because you already got a warrant for my arrest. You want me to come down for a discussion, and then, when I drive back home, I'm gonna have to go to jail."

After I hung up, I drove back to Huntsville and went to the courthouse and turned myself in. I didn't want them to come to my house again. There was a reporter who took pictures for the newspaper, and he had access to the jail, and whenever they were going to arrest a well-known person, he'd come and take their picture. And he took my picture, and they also had it on television, that I had been arrested for Medicaid fraud.

I was in jail for only about thirty minutes, and they let me sign myself out on my own recognizance. I was booked on Medicaid fraud, one count for each patient they claimed I had charged for and not treated or where I allegedly hadn't done the lab test or had injected patients with Demerol, when their condition in the opinion of investigators did not warrant so strong a narcotic.[2]

The trial date was set, and now I did get a lawyer. The first one I called was the guy who had been the family lawyer for years. Of course, he was white because, as I recall, there were no black attorneys in town. This lawyer sent the junior partner down to my office—the investigators were in my office with a search warrant and going through all my files, and I had called him. Can you imagine that? You've got a waiting room full of patients and they're in there reading you your Miranda rights and the patients are looking up and seeing all these detectives.

So he sent the junior partner down there, and he looked at me and saw these people, and we went into my private office, and you know what he asked me? He said, "What must I do?" This is my attorney, asking me what to do. And I was thinking, if he had appendicitis, I wouldn't be asking him, "What must I do?"

Later, someone recommended another lawyer, and I went to talk with him, and he accepted my retainer and got all of my confidential information. Then, in about three weeks, he called and wanted to know if I could come by and talk with him.

When I went up to his office, he tells me that Graddick, the attorney general, had asked if he would represent him in a lawsuit being brought against his office after he had ordered a break-in at a bootlegger's house, and the lady there had taken him to court, saying this was her residence. My lawyer says, "I want to advance my political career, and so I accepted the case, and I can no longer represent you because it would be a conflict of interest."

And he still had my retainer. So now I have no attorney and no money. Not only did he not handle my case, but he also had all my private files, and even if he had given me back my private files, now he's in cahoots with Graddick. He could have copied everything before he handed them back, plus he's told me that he has political aspirations.

So I decided to just go bare, no attorney at all. Dr. John Cashin called me and said there was a young black attorney who had just come to town, and he'd done some work for him. John said, "I'd be afraid if I were you not to have any legal representation." I told him, okay, and the black lawyer came to my office, and I allowed him to take the case. What I didn't know was that he was going to be submissive and timid, wanting to plea bargain everything in a way so as to give the other side all the advantages.

After the Medicaid people claimed that there were patients that I had billed for that I didn't see, they had turned that information over to Medicare, and Medicare began its own investigation. And the Medicare people said basically the same thing—if you weren't here, say, on March 15 to see Medicaid patients, then as far as we're concerned, you didn't see the Medicare patients either.

Then Medicare turned their files over to Blue Cross, and Blue Cross made the same accusations. So I took it upon myself to research every single case that the Blue Cross people had said I had sent in fraudulent claims for. Initially they said I'd stolen $8,000 from them. And then, as I began to disprove these claims, I got another letter that said, well, you owe us $250, or something like that.

Finally, I got the man who was second in command down in the Birmingham Blue Cross office to come to my office, and I showed him documentation I'd gotten from Huntsville Hospital, which had taken me hours and hours going through all the microfiche. We went over all these sheets, and he took copies back to his office. Then in a week or so, I received a letter of exoneration from him stating that I didn't owe Blue Cross anything.[3]

In the meantime, Medicaid had cut off my payments, and the investigators had gotten a grand jury to go ahead and indict me. My attorney advised me to plea bargain—in other words, to plead guilty and pay back double the amount of the claims I had submitted. Medicaid and Medicare were federal programs, he said, and unlike Blue Cross, they could put me in jail. He was reluctant to challenge them, and he let them bully him into persuading me to agree to pay back a certain amount, which they would accept only if it were two times what I had allegedly stolen.

And, as I said, the thing that really seemed to bother him was whenever the Medicaid investigators mentioned the gambling, or whenever discussions came up about injections of Demerol, which I had given patients who were in severe pain. He was afraid of the narcotics aspect—afraid to death of that. So when he went for discovery, they showed him some things that they allegedly had, and it seemed like whatever they said they had, he took it at face value.

By now, people in the black community in town were starting to come to my defense. They had been used to being discriminated against for so long until it seemed like most of them assumed that this was discrimination because they knew about all my civil rights work. I believe many of them were thinking—this is their way of getting even.

By the fall of 1979, people in the black community had started circulating a petition on my behalf, which even some of the white doctors signed.[4] That didn't surprise me, because I'd been referring patients to a number of them, and besides, they all knew that I was doing an overload of charity work and that if I weren't doing it, someone else would have to do it. And there were letters on my behalf from people like Dr. Morrison, president of Alabama A&M, and Dr. Mary Chambers, who had taught me biology, plus several black businessmen and Boy Scout leaders.[5]

Meanwhile, my attorney was starting to plea bargain the whole thing, and we ended up giving away the house and lot. I was to pay the Medicare people double what they alleged, and for Medicaid the total I owed amounted to around $80,000, plus some fines and sanctions. So the whole thing, I think, was way over $150,000, and for a person who's seeing patients for five or six dollars a visit, it takes you a long time to make that much money. My lawyer told me later, "After all, you're back in practice. I didn't let 'em take you out." Those were his exact words.

The alternative would have been to take my chances in court, and that could have turned out much worse. So I decided to plead guilty to some of the charges and accept whatever fine and penalty the judge imposed. I did so because I was concerned about my family, my patients, and my own well-being. Also, if I did go to court, and if I weren't able to disprove what they were saying, then I might have to go to prison. And I'm thinking, well, by making this plea, it's going to cost me an enormous amount of money and embarrassment, but I will still be in practice, and I can continue to support my family. I thought I had no choice but to follow my lawyer's advice and plead guilty to two counts of Medicaid fraud, though I never did anything intended to defraud the program.[6]

The plea bargain was three years' probation and report to the probation officer every month about how many Medicaid patients I was seeing. Stay out of bad crowds. Don't cross the border. Don't cross the state line. We had a twenty-five-year class reunion at Meharry, and I had to get special permission to go to Nashville. When the Alabama A&M soccer team played in the national tournament at Stanford University, I had to get permission to go as team doctor.

Then the thing I had feared most—that the Alabama Board of Medical Examiners would get wind of what had happened—came true, even though my attorney had said that when he told the Medicaid people that he wanted to plea bargain, they had assured him that they didn't intend to send any information to the board. That was in February 1980, and about a month later, he got word that they had done so.[7]

That same afternoon, I felt so bad I decided to go see a psychiatrist because I thought the thing had been resolved, or 90 percent resolved, and now, all of a sudden, I still have to do all the terms of the probation and face the board of examiners. That was the only time in my life I ever had to go to a psychiatrist, and it was just that one time, and my attorney was about to go to pieces as well because we had thought we had the whole thing resolved, and then we find out it's worse than it was before. We had given away the house and the lot, and the man says, well, I want your stove and your refrigerator, too.

The Alabama State Board of Medical Examiners said I could appear before a panel of medical doctors with an administrative law judge in charge to show cause why my license shouldn't be revoked. Or I could go before a three-man panel from the government side—the [Alabama] secretary of state, the attorney general, and I believe the lieutenant governor. Now, here's the man [the attorney general] who brought the charges against me, and he's going to sit in judgment? We thought we would have a better chance with medical doctors.

So we went down to Montgomery, and we brought along the petition and some of the medical charts showing my fee charges, plus a few witnesses to testify about my work in the community. We finished about two o'clock, and my attorney knew somebody in Montgomery who would have the word. About sundown, this person let him know that the board had decided to revoke my license for three years but to stay the revocation and make it for thirty days. I was to meet with the board every quarter for the three years of my probation, and I was to bring my probation officer's report to each meeting and an accounting of all the patients I'd seen, including Medicaid patients.

So I went and reported in Montgomery every quarter. I was still able to work with patients, and I could now turn in claims to Medicaid again, but they applied these against what I owed. So $40,000 up front, and then give them money as I accumulated it. I got part of what I owed paid off in the first few months, but I was still short by about $25,000. I borrowed all over town, and people from the black community created a committee to help with the legal expenses.[8]

That summer—this was in 1980—the committee gave me a testimonial banquet, and Dr. Joseph Lowery, a native of Huntsville and now president of the Southern Christian Leadership Conference in Atlanta, came and spoke. They were able to raise about $4,500, which helped, but I still didn't have as much as I needed.

In the fall, the board called a hearing for revocation of my probation because I had been able to pay only half what I owed by the deadline in August, and I had to promise to pay $2,500 a month until the balance was paid. I got behind on that, too, even though I was seeing as many patients as possible.[9] Only with the help of a physician here in town, a man originally from India to whom I had referred patients, was I able to make the last payment.

As far as my hospital activities and pharmacy prescriptions were concerned, by now I was operating under a microscope. Some hospital officials, the chief of staff and his people, were scrutinizing me. One time they called me on the carpet after the Medicaid situation, and they were saying some of my charts were sketchy and didn't give enough information on what was happening to the patient, that the write-ups should be a little more thorough. And they had a charts committee to oversee this, and one of the members was an internist. So I went back and looked at some of his write-ups when I had referred patients to him—-some relatives or patients who had been friends of mine—-and his were much more sketchy than mine. If fact, there were some records he dictated where the person taking the dictation could not understand what he was saying and just left blanks, and later the sheets got signed with the blanks left in. To me, that seemed very haphazard and slipshod—not even looking to see what the person had typed. Or perhaps he had forgotten what should have gone in the blank. I started to confront the charts committee with that, but I didn't. There are a number of things I look back and think I should have done.

Sometime in the mid-1980s I realized that I might be in trouble again when one of the people from the Alabama Board of Medical Examiners, a member of its Medical Licensure Commission, came by my office and said he was concerned that there were some persons who were getting certain medications, and he wondered if their conditions warranted them having those medications. And I was suspicious that some of the pharmacists may have said that to him. The way it worked was that the drug inspectors would go around the state from city to city, and they'd usually go to the pharmacists first and find out who had been prescribing such-and-such a medicine and especially inquire about somebody who'd had some problems before. In other words, a red flag goes up—you know, we're going to scrutinize this person.

So this guy comes by, and he had some names with him and the pharmacies where the patients had filled the prescriptions. He didn't ask to see any files, I guess because he knew they were going to subpoena them. Sure enough, a few days later the Medical Licensure Commission asked me to send them copies, and they got independent doctors to look over these and say whether they thought these patients should have gotten the particular medicines I prescribed.

At that point, I just told them I would voluntarily restrict my prescriptions. Anything in Schedule I, II, or III, for example, anything with Demerol, morphine, and so forth, I just would not prescribe at all. I agreed just to prescribe from Schedule IV and V drugs. Schedule V is like taking half an aspirin, almost nothing. Schedule IV would be something like a Darvon, very, very mild. Once again, this was a sort of plea bargain on my part. I didn't want to fight it anymore, didn't want to be bothered with going back to Montgomery.

So the Medical Licensure Commission went along with this and said I was to prescribe only from Schedule IV and V drugs. And I had to give them monthly reports of every single person who received prescription drugs, anything that was in any schedule. But not long after this, they got me for prescribing Lortab, which is hydrocodone, similar to codeine. They had a drug task force in town from Montgomery whose job was to arrest all the pushers and peddlers, and I guess they saw it in the drugstore that I had prescribed Lortab, and they knew that to be a very strong one, though I was able to show them from their own manual that this was in the schedule of drugs that I was allowed to prescribe.

The Lortab prescription really hurt me. They came to my office, and they put me in jail. And when they were getting ready to put me in the police car—they didn't put handcuffs on me, but they wouldn't let me drive my own car—I tried to show the arresting officer the manual, but he didn't want to see it. They took me into a holding area, and my brother came and bailed me out. He bails out people almost every day, and so he came and bailed me out.

I got another lawyer to represent me, and I showed him the manual, and I said, "Here it is in their own manual, it says it's okay."[10] My attorney and I met in court twice for preliminary hearings. I wanted to plead the case on the basis that I followed their guideline, but he said to plead the case on an error they made in charging me. They didn't say I prescribed but that I dispensed. Well, there was no dispensing. So the case never came up.

The final blow came when the Board of Medical Examiners charged me with practicing medicine in such a way as to endanger the health of my patients. They cited specific cases since 1985 for which they said I had prescribed controlled substances for no legitimate medical purpose. But the things I was pre-scribing were mild to moderate pain relievers, not anything that's real strong. You're not talking about morphine or heroin or anything like that. I'd say, on a scale of one to ten, the ones I prescribed for patients suffering from injuries of some sort were maybe three or four.

The board also said that some of the patients were getting the pain relievers too frequently. But there was no time when they could say they [the patients] got too many at one time, because Dr. Donalson and I had spoken about that way back in the 1950s, that we would never give a person more than either two dozen or two-and-a-half dozen. Thirty was usually the limit. I don't believe I've ever written a prescription in my life where I would give sixty, unless it's something like blood pressure medicine that had to be taken twice a day. But no kind of sleeping medicine, or pain medicine, or weight-reducing medicine--not even once did I prescribe more than thirty, and frequently it was less.

Do I believe I sometimes made mistakes in prescribing medicines for pa-tients that they probably should not have gotten? I suppose it's possible. And I imagine all doctors do. For instance, if a person comes to you and is having pain in a certain area, from an automobile accident or a farm accident or an athletic injury, maybe cancer, you try to diagnose what's happening. And if you can't do it, then you refer him to a specialist, and the specialist recommends a cer-tain treatment, but then the patient comes back to you, and he's having the same type of trouble.

So you say, maybe I'll give him something to ease him while we can have further study on this. Maybe we can do some more lab tests or some more X-rays or something. But let's do something to ease his pain. Don't let him lie awake all night hurting.

The Board of Medical Examiners also accused me of not doing adequate follow-up on some of my patients—labs and physicals and so forth. In fact, a lot of those patients were referred to specialists, who did the follow-up. I sent so many patients to so many specialists, I almost got embarrassed about asking them to go because I thought they might think I feel I'm incompetent to diag-nose their case.

I tried to explain all this to the board. I had the hearing down in Mont-gomery, and though I had an attorney to assist me this time, I appeared before the board on my own behalf. There were doctors who came and testified about the cases on which I was charged. They testified, and I testified, and the board members seemed to believe me while I was talking.

But a few days later, the registered letter comes telling me that I could no longer practice medicine.[11] The mailman comes to my office about 11:30, and then about 12:15, the man is there to pick up the license. This was the same man from the board's licensure commission who earlier had come by for a friendly visit. I wasn't tempted to fight it. You just get sort of worn down, and it's embarrassing with your family and your friends to have to keep running down to Montgomery, and I was just sort of worn out with the whole thing.

It seemed like the roof just caved in on me. And my wife was out of town—her mother was ill, and she was in Kentucky—and it was just terrible. My wife had been sort of conditioned to something every three or four years, like that first time, with my son's arrest over the Coke machine situation, and then their refusal to give me my malpractice insurance, and the Medicaid-Medicare thing.

The only hope I had left was that the Medical Licensure Commission had said that I could get my license back if I did extensive remedial training.[12] That meant five hundred hours in family practice or primary care. That's the figure that had been thrown around at the meeting in Montgomery.

Now, how they arrived at five hundred hours—I may have had something to do with that myself. In my summation, I had said that I didn't think that the evidence presented was enough to revoke my license, but that if the commission did feel it was enough and wanted me to have additional training, I didn't mind even taking a residency. I would have been willing to take a residency if they had allowed me to keep my license so that I could still support my family.

But they decided, no, we're going to ask him to do [the equivalent of] a residency and lose his license at the same time. But five hundred hours, these are real clock hours—seminars, workshops, conferences, and rounds. I would have had a problem finding five hundred hours, then a problem of my own stamina, then a problem of the well-being of my family. I had three girls in college and a mortgage I was behind on.

I had a second meeting with the commission about a year and a half later. I had done a number of seminars and workshops and grand rounds at the School of Primary Medical Care of The University of Alabama in Huntsville, and I had a letter from Dr. James Chandler, the chief of medicine there, on my behalf.[13] I asked the commission to reconsider the five hundred hours. I told them that Dr. Chandler also believed this was excessive and would take me at least ten to twelve months. I even offered to prescribe medicines only from Schedule V.

At some point, one of the doctors asked me if I would be willing to take the medical boards again, just as if I were fresh out of medical school. And I said, yes, I'll take the boards any day you want me to take them. But nobody ever mentioned it again. About a week later, the answer came. The commission told me that there wasn't enough effort [on my part] toward getting the recommended number of seminars and workshops. I still had to take five hundred hours.

I made one last effort with the commission. I had spoken with a doctor who had a nursing home in Cullman and who was interested in my coming to work under his supervision. So the commission said I could come down and talk to them about it. Tom went with me, as well as my daughter Martha. So we're sitting out in the hall waiting, and when we went in, we found it was their last meeting before Christmas and that they had planned a party in another building. They met with us a little while, and then they hinted that they wanted to close the meeting and go to the party.

We talked awhile, and I was getting more and more disgusted because they wanted to end the meeting and were perturbed with me for not approaching that five hundred hours. So I began to gather up my papers, and Tom reminded me that Kita [Martha's nickname] had a presentation she wanted to make. So they allowed her to make her presentation, and it was a beautiful statement that she had written in the car on the way down.[14] Still, my appeal was denied.

By now, I had been out of practice for four years. When I closed my practice, the landlord had wanted my space for another doctor, and he agreed to let me store my stuff in a smaller suite while I made arrangements to sell as much as I could. A great portion of it we brought and put in the garage here, like the waiting room furniture. The medical equipment, the examining tables, we took some of it out in the country to my mother's farm. We stored them in one of the rooms, but then my brother rented out the rooms, and we moved the equipment outside and it just sat out there and rusted.

One of my hardest memories is the day Tom and I went and burned all my patient files, all the way back to 1956. I had to decide what to do with them. You can't just throw away somebody's medical files. So we called the Brown's Ferry people, the people who pick up and destroy trash, and they were going to charge us for destroying them. And then, Tom and I went to the hospital to get lunch, and I thought about the incinerator that they have at the hospital. And I asked a black man who was in charge of the incinerator if he'd let us bring those files up there and put them in that incinerator, and he said yes.

Tom's son had a large pickup truck, and we brought a load of files to the hospital and threw them all in the incinerator. This was about six or seven years after the office had closed; it was my understanding that you're supposed to keep the records for at least five years. We just threw them in. I didn't feel like looking at any of them. It was gut-wrenching to do it. I guess I just can't put it into words.

It was like a part of my body was being cut out. And knowing that I probably would never get back in practice again, and thinking that even if I had the opportunity to practice again, how old would I be, and where would my patients be? I had been practicing a long time because I went to college for two years and then into medical school, and I had always felt that I was really blessed to get started in my practice that early.

And somehow or another, deep down, I thought something was going to happen to give me a setback toward the end of my career. I don't know why, but I felt maybe a sense of guilt, like I had cheated the system by being able to go in so fast, to finish up at Alabama A&M in two years and then go right to Meharry and finish near the top of my class, and I didn't know anybody else who was able to do it like I did. I felt like something would probably happen, something I can't explain. I was the first physician in our family, and maybe I was thinking it was just too good to be true.

In the meantime, my wife and I got by as best we could. And then, Dr. Waymon Burke at Calhoun Community College, who had helped me produce my film, *A Civil Rights Journey,* based on the footage I took during the 1960s, learned that I wasn't working, and my daughter asked him if her father could get some part-time teaching, and in the fall of 1996 I was hired part-time at Calhoun to teach anatomy and physiology.

But there were financial problems, and the mortgage was so far behind that when I finally got caught up, I had to pay several thousand dollars at one time. And to do that, I had to sell off part of the land that my father and great-grandfather had purchased back in the 1920s.

The teaching has helped me in many ways, not just financially but also in helping me to feel like I have a purpose in life. In a way, what I've done in educating young people and premed students and teaching young people about the civil rights movement could be more beneficial than if I had been working in the office, because every semester I have one or two premed students and around thirty nursing students. And my evaluations have been very favorable.

And every year, I go around showing my film and telling young people about the old days, the time of segregation and what my generation went through and the battles we fought. I talk to churches and schools and libraries. I tell people we weren't trying to get into their country clubs. We wanted to get into Shoney's and to get into their libraries and their universities.

Still, these events cost me a lot of heartache, a lot of money, and a lot of bad publicity. Everything bad that has ever happened to me has been in the paper. Just to give you an example: one of the local TV channels not too long ago asked me to come down at six in the morning to talk about the 1960s and the local civil rights movement, and I went down there, and we talked about civil rights.

Then, about four or five days later, they presented a program about doctors who had lost their licenses, and they used the picture that they took when I went to do them a favor in talking about civil rights—they used that to degrade me. So I felt like asking the people there, why is it that every six to twelve months they want to mention the fact that I lost my license? I've lost it, and I can't practice anymore. Why keep drumming it up every five or six months?

And whatever my life has been about, in everything I've done, I think that my civil rights work has to be factored in.

Right now, I'm just trying to push all this out of my mind because a lot of people have a misconception of what happened to me. A lot of them have formed their own opinion, and it's a bad opinion. But I made up my mind to tell this story, to go ahead and do it.

Afterword

Unable to earn a living through the practice of medicine, Hereford faced extraordinary hardships in the years after 1993. Adding to his financial woes was the painful loss of his place in the black community and the special status that physicians had traditionally enjoyed. As his former patients drifted off to other doctors, he struggled with how to reaffirm his own sense of worth.

Over time, Hereford began trying to define a new role for himself, much of it focused on his earlier civil rights activities. During the 1990s, as Huntsville began pondering the meaning of the civil rights movement to its own history, he became a frequent guest on local radio and television shows, explaining what life had once been like in the city that now prided itself on its progressive spirit. Every January and February, as part of events celebrating Martin Luther King Jr.'s life and Black History month, his calendar began filling up with appearances at local schools, libraries, and churches. The young Councill student of the 1940s whose stuttering had been so bad that he could not give the valedictory address proved to be a formidable speaker.

Providing powerful visual confirmation of Hereford's testimony were his homemade films, which until now had sat largely undisturbed in boxes, fifty spools of unedited footage documenting the lunch-counter sit-ins of 1962, the marches on the square, the mass meetings at the black churches, Martin Luther King Jr.'s visit in March, the integration of Big Spring Park on Mother's Day, and the counterdemonstrations during George Wallace's speech on the courthouse steps during Armed Forces Day. Using inexpensive videocassette recording machines, Hereford copied portions of the footage to VCR format, from which he produced a film that ran eighty minutes.

Hereford received much-needed help from a historian at the Huntsville branch of Calhoun Community College named Waymon E. Burke, who had earlier taught Hereford's children at Butler High School. As a native of Huntsville, Dr. Burke had been moved by the civil rights story told in Hereford's homemade film and had used it as a primary document in his Advanced Placement history classes. Now, as division chair at Calhoun's Huntsville campus, he hired Hereford as an adjunct instructor of biology, physiology, and anatomy. The teaching brought in only a modest income, but it helped Hereford survive, and he took pride in the positive evaluations he received and in the opportunity to make his medical knowledge useful to others.

Burke also conceived a plan to produce a more polished, classroom length version of Hereford's eighty-minute film, this one supplemented by interviews of Hereford and other local civil rights leaders. In his role as director of Calhoun's Center for the Study of Southern Political Culture, Burke secured funding for the project, including a grant from the Alabama Humanities Foundation. In February 1999, the forty-six minute documentary, *A Civil Rights Journey*, had its premiere on the Calhoun campus and was soon part of the holdings of many local schools and libraries. Several years later, producers of a documentary on the civil rights movement in Birmingham used assorted scenes from Hereford's footage on Huntsville as historical background. The film was called *Mighty Times: The Children's March* and went on to win an Oscar for Best Documentary Short Subject in 2005.

Slowly, the city began to accord belated recognition to the black activists who had provided a model for peaceful change during the 1960s and had thus helped Huntsville avoid the images of violence and bloodshed still associated with cities like Birmingham. On August 28, 1995, in recognition of the thirtieth anniversary of the Voting Rights Act of 1965, an honorary resolution, signed by the mayor and members of the City Council, paid tribute to Sonnie and Martha Hereford and to their son, Sonnie Hereford IV, along with Dr. John Cashin, his late wife, Joan, and fifty-one others who had been involved in securing voting rights "for citizens in the Huntsville community and the world." Nine years later, a marker was dedicated at the site of the now demolished Fifth Avenue Elementary School, where, on September 9, 1963, as duly noted in the inscription, "Sonnie Hereford IV became the first African-American student to integrate public schools in Alabama."[1]

For Hereford, the role that he played in the civil rights movement represented the crowning achievement of his life. Clearly, his efforts were important to the struggle in Huntsville, and the documentation that he has left behind through his films and his oral accounts confirms a fundamental truth about the movement as a whole—namely, that the victory in destroying the legal discrimination still in existence a century after the close of the Civil War came not just through the intervention of a few heroes like Martin Luther King Jr. but through the work of local people who had been preparing the ground for many years.

That the presence of Marshall Space Flight Center, Redstone Arsenal, and other federal investments in the city provided leverage for the victory of civil rights demonstrators is indisputable. To their credit, local white leaders used their influence on behalf of nonviolent change, though they did so only after prolonged resistance and only because Huntsville's black community left them with little choice. Early in the sit-in campaign, local black leaders had recognized the vulnerability of a city that owed its growth to the federal presence and had adapted their tactics accordingly—in their placards, their boycotts, and their picketing outside the Midwest and New York stock exchanges. Black ministers, professionals, students, businessmen, and workers forged a powerful sense of unity, and despite the repeated harassment and arrests of protestors, their efforts had broken the back of segregation in Huntsville two years before the Civil Rights Act of 1964.

The city's subsequent reputation for racial tolerance and political moderation, both essential in its quest to become one of the state's leading economic centers, owes much to people like Hereford. As a member of the Community Services Committee and as chairman of its subcommittee on education, he helped formulate strategies for the peaceful integration of the city's restaurants and schools. In addition, he played a key role in breaking down racial barriers at Huntsville Hospital. Its relatively trouble-free integration stands in marked contrast to what happened in other hospitals throughout the South, even for those whose federal funding for Medicare and Medicaid and for hospital construction under the Hill-Burton Act was conditional on ending discrimination in the wards. According to John Dittmer, in 1966 nearly two thousand southern hospitals and clinics were still not in compliance with federal requirements.[2]

Despite these achievements, it is not possible to assess Hereford's career in isolation from his Medicaid troubles of the early 1980s and the later charges he faced regarding his prescribing practices. Regulation of the profession and the power to revoke a practitioner's license for serious misconduct are essential to protecting the people's health. On the other hand, citizens have a right to expect that such powers are applied equally, without regard to race. To believe that this was always the case during the era when Hereford practiced is to ignore longstanding patterns of racism on the part of Alabama's medical corps.

While the modern perception of the doctor is that of healer and counselor, one who sees suffering on a daily basis and whose scientific training has raised him above the prejudices of his time, history offers a less flattering portrait. In Alabama, blacks who tried to gain access to the professional privileges enjoyed by white colleagues often encountered a wall of rejection built on deep-rooted racial prejudices. Here, medical objectivity masked an intensely conservative social and political ideology.

In such an atmosphere, it is easy to understand why black doctors believed that their performance was scrutinized in ways that did not apply to white doctors and that professional misconduct was punished with greater severity among blacks than among whites. In Huntsville, stories circulated within the medical

community of white colleagues whose negligence or outright fraud went un-
reported and unpunished—of the doctor who refused to keep patient records
at the hospital; of another who removed gallstones without justification; of another who performed unnecessary appendectomies.[3]

Hereford's recollections of how the monitoring of his activities at Huntsville Hospital seemed to intensify after the 1960s instead of being diminished
by new civil rights laws reflected a broader pattern that stemmed ironically
from the very movement in which he had played a part. In their study of race
and health care in America, W. Michael Byrd and Linda A. Clayton note that
new and more intense levels of scrutiny often awaited black doctors after the racial barriers came down. Far from achieving equality, many now found themselves vulnerable to new forms of professional and legal sanctions from white
practitioners who had once tolerated their presence in the black wards or who
had been content to refer their poorest patients to them. In cities like Detroit,
Chicago, Houston, and Fort Worth, veritable "purges" of black physicians from
hospital staffs occurred under the guise of peer-reviewed quality controls.[4]

In Alabama, oral histories of black doctors echo Hereford's account of his
hospital experiences, as they do his prolonged frustration in gaining admission
to the county medical society and his ensuing problems in being able to keep
up with developments in medicine.[5] They confirm other parts of his testimony
as well, such as the ways in which, as a matter of necessity, a black doctor's office functioned, from its irregular hours to the absence of appointments, which
often stood in contrast to the more predictable routines seen in the offices of
white colleagues.[6]

So informal a style made Hereford ill prepared to meet the record-keeping
demands of one of the state's largest Medicaid practices, though his willing-
ness to treat such patients set him apart from many of the town's white doctors. That fact was stressed by a local white surgeon named Clement P. Cotter, who, writing in October 1979 in support of Hereford's reapplication to
the hospital staff, stressed that his "medical knowledge and clinical experience
are vast and as good as any other physician of his type in the community" and
that he "has a tremendous practice and little, if any, help." Cotter added that
since Dr. Belle's death and Dr. Drake's partial retirement, Hereford had become "the prime source of care for the vast majority of the black population of
our community. . . . [He is] literally swamped since it is difficult to get any other
physician to accept these patients from the lower rung of the socio-economic
strata. I feel that this is a direct contributing cause of some of Dr. Hereford['s]
present problems."[7]

That law enforcement officials may have regarded large Medicaid providers like Hereford with suspicion is not surprising in light of periodic attacks
on the quality of training received by Meharry and Howard graduates, despite

their successful record on state and national licensure board examinations.[8] Especially damaging were studies in the medical press that appeared to magnify their place among those accused of wrongdoing.

A 1985 demographic analysis of physicians sanctioned for Medicaid fraud, for example, found an "overrepresentation" of black and foreign-trained physicians and psychiatrists among 147 cases occurring between 1977 and 1982. According to the authors, of the eighty-eight who had trained in the United States, a total of six were Meharry graduates, though blacks made up just 2.8 percent of all doctors.[9]

A follow-up article published six years later in the *Journal of the American Medical Association* repeated these claims, which drew a pointed response from Chicago internist Matilde Rios, who had trained in Uruguay and the United States. Rios pointed out that the term "overrepresentation" could be defined only with regard to a particular population, which in this case should be Medicaid providers, where minorities abounded. Because the authors had failed to provide comparative data on minority percentages among these providers, their findings were meaningless. Worst of all, they perpetuated the myth that minorities cheated more than their mainstream counterparts at a time when they were providing the bulk of care for the nation's poorest patients.[10]

In subsequent years, such distorted portrayals of minority culpability in fraud cases also appeared in the popular press, such as a two-part series published by the *Hartford Courant* in 2003.[11] In response, black professional groups like the Association of Black Cardiologists pointed out that Meharry and Howard graduates often served poor areas and thus had large Medicare and Medicaid clienteles, that these patients suffered from high rates of chronic diseases, and that the legal system tended to target such practices because of the large numbers of claims submitted.[12]

As to how typical Hereford's drug-prescribing problems with state medical authorities may have been, existing information does not provide a clear answer, though some oral histories share Hereford's suspicion that drug enforcement agents regarded black physicians as potential sources for illegal drugs and were not above trying to entrap them.[13]

Incomplete figures provided by the Alabama Board of Medical Examiners through its automated database indicate that black physicians accounted for a little over 11 percent of the total number of doctors disciplined between 1960 and 2007.[14] At any given period, that figure is significantly higher than the proportion of black doctors relative to all doctors in the state. Other information available in the board's quarterly newsletters that contain actual names of doctors facing sanctions provides more precise numbers. During the years 1995 to 2001, for example, the newsletters reveal a total of fifty-eight doctors whose licenses were revoked or surrendered voluntarily. Of these, seven can be identified as African Americans—four in Birmingham, two in Mobile, and one in Tuskegee.[15]

Finally, the state-by-state findings in a report by the Public Citizen Health Research Group reveal that between 1991 and 2000 Alabama medical authorities took a total of 366 disciplinary actions against physicians (this figure often included multiple actions against a single doctor). In 41 of these, or just over 11 percent, the practitioner involved can be identified as African American. Of the 84 individuals who actually surrendered their licenses or had them revoked, a total of 9 can be identified as African American.[16]

This data suggest that the percentage of black doctors who experienced disciplinary actions by the state was indeed higher than that of white doctors relative to their overall numbers. Whether there existed parity in sanctions—whether white practitioners guilty of the same infractions escaped with milder forms of punishment such as probation, restrictions, fines, or reprimands—is far more difficult to determine. In punishments accorded for blatantly inappropriate or illegal activities, there do not appear to have been any visible patterns of discrimination in that both blacks and whites suffered similar penalties.[17] What is less certain are allegations in which black doctors were charged with wrongfully prescribing controlled substances. In six of the known cases in which black doctors lost their licenses between 1995 and 2000, this constituted the main allegation. It was the same accusation that had cost Hereford his license and that he insists was unjustified.

While the loss of his license spelled the end of Hereford's medical career, the event should not eclipse the many years that he had spent in service to others, mainly poor people. That fact is borne out in his own private papers and in numerous awards and citations lauding his work on behalf of one group after another. None of this included the many nonpaying patients who thronged his waiting room every day. On balance, his efforts helped improve the lives of thousands of ordinary people and were undertaken in the face of formidable racial barriers.

In this regard, Hereford's career typifies what black doctors, dentists, pharmacists, and other health care professionals faced in the South. The details of his experiences—growing up the great-grandson of slaves, sharecropping as a child during the Depression years, surviving the rigors of Meharry, struggling to gain hospital privileges, and, most of all, overcoming the racism of the state's white medical corps—tell us a great deal about the history of Alabama, the history of African American health care, and the history of medicine in general. They serve as just one small example of an historical inequality of access to health that continues to the present in America and throughout much of the world.

Notes

INTRODUCTION

1. Hereford's discharge shows that he was inducted at Huntsville on 17 July 1918 and served with the American Expeditionary Army between September 1918 and September 1919. For information on African Americans during the war, see Arthur E. Barbeau and Florette Henri, *The Unknown Soldiers: Black American Troops in World War I* (Philadelphia: Temple University Press, 1974).

2. John Lewis with Michael D'Orso, *Walking with the Wind: A Memoir of the Movement* (New York: Harcourt Brace and Company, 1998), 13.

3. Theodore Rosengarten, *All God's Dangers: The Life of Nate Shaw* (New York: Vintage Books, 1974).

4. Probate records show numerous purchases of land: two acres for $20 by Bettie Hereford in March 1916; five acres for $700 by Sonnie Hereford Sr. in May 1919; one acre for $300 by Sonnie Hereford Jr. in October 1919 (shortly after his discharge from the army); and around ten acres for $3,000 by Sonnie Sr., Bettie, Sonnie Jr., and Jannie in December 1924. See *Deed Record: Madison County,* vol. 121, pp. 122, 655; vol. 123, pp. 587–88; vol. 131, p. 114.

5. Thomas Edward Hereford, interview by Jack D. Ellis, Huntsville, Alabama, 27 February 2000.

6. See probate documents in *Mortgage Record: Madison County Alabama,* vol. 242, pp. 205–06 (1931), and vol. 255, p. 117 (1934).

7. C. Erick Lincoln and Lawrence H. Mamiya note that white churches had nothing comparable to this office, which was "derived from the kinship network found within black churches and black communities." See *The Black Church in the African American Experience* (Durham: Duke University Press, 1990), 275.

8. In 1940, public spending per black pupil in Alabama was only a third of what it was for whites. See James T. Patterson, *Brown v. Board of Education: A Civil Rights Milestone and Its Troubled Legacy* (Oxford: Oxford University Press, 2001), xvii, 9, and James D. Anderson, *The Education of Blacks in the South* (Chapel Hill: University of North Carolina Press, 1988), 237.

9. Lewis, *Walking with the Wind,* 34–37; Anne Moody, *Coming of Age in Mississippi* (New York: Delta Trade Paperbacks, 2004), 32–35; and Melba Pattillo Beals, *Warriors Don't Cry* (New York: Simon Pulse, 2007), 3–11.

10. See Thomas J. Ward Jr., *Black Physicians in the Jim Crow South* (Fayetteville: University of Arkansas Press, 2003), 40–41, and James Summerville, *Educating Black Doctors: A History of Meharry Medical College* (Tuscaloosa: The University of Alabama Press, 1983), 86, 96–99.

11. Data from physician lists published annually in the *Transactions* of the Medical Association of the State of Alabama (MASA) show that Meharry graduates accounted for 60 percent of black doctors practicing in Alabama between 1895 and 1970. Those from Howard University College of Medicine in Washington, D.C., made up an additional 19 percent. Most of the rest were products of black medical schools that by Hereford's time had ceased to exist.

12. See the tables in "Medical Licensure Statistics for 1946," *Journal of the American Medical Association* 134 (17 May 1946): 255–69. See also table III in Helen Edith Walker, *The Negro in the Medical Profession* (Charlottesville: University of Virginia, 1949), 36–37.

13. See Reginald Horsman, *Josiah Nott of Mobile: Southerner, Physician, and Racial Theorist* (Baton Rouge: Louisiana State University Press, 1978), and Gary Michael Dorr, "Defective or Disabled?: Race, Medicine, and Eugenics in Progressive Era Virginia and Alabama," *Journal of the Gilded Age and Progressive Era* 5 (October 2006): 359–92.

14. For an example of one black doctor's efforts to gain admission to state medical societies, see Gilbert R. Mason M.D. with James Patterson Smith, *Beaches, Blood, and Ballots: A Black Doctor's Civil Rights Struggle* (Jackson: University Press of Mississippi, 2000), 37–41.

15. Figures extracted from census records by Todd L. Savitt show a total of 3,495 licensed black physicians practicing in the United States in 1920, of which just under half were located in the states of the former Confederacy. See "Entering a White Profession: Black Physicians in the New South, 1880–1920," *Bulletin of the History of Medicine* 61 (1987): 507–40.

16. See Edward H. Beardsley, *A History of Neglect: Health Care for Blacks and Mill Workers in the Twentieth Century South* (Knoxville: University of Tennessee Press, 1987).

17. In his study of the Medical Committee for Human Rights, created in 1964 by physicians and nurses from the North who wished to provide care for civil rights workers, John Dittmer notes that in Mississippi civil rights activists were unwelcome not only among white doctors but also among many of the older black physicians. See *The Good Doctors: The Medical Committee for Human Rights and the Struggle for Social Justice in Health Care* (New York: Bloomsbury Press, 2009), 43–47.

18. See John Dittmer, *Local People: The Struggle for Civil Rights in Mississippi* (Urbana: University of Illinois Press, 1995).

19. David Barton Smith, *Health Care Divided: Race and Healing a Nation* (Ann Arbor: University of Michigan Press, 1999), 96–121.

20. Janet B. Mitchell and Jerry Cromwell, "Large Medicaid Practices and Medicaid Mills," *Journal of the American Medical Association* 244 (28 November 1980): 2433–37, and Janet B. Mitchell, "Physician Participation in Medicaid Revisited," *Medical Care* 29 (July 1991): 645–53. For further information on the opposition of doctors and hospitals to Medicaid, see Jonathan Engel, *Poor People's Medicine: Medicaid and American Charity Care since 1965* (Durham: Duke University Press, 2006), 64–68.

21. *Journal of the National Medical Association* (January 1969): 40–43.

22. Karen Davis and Cathy Schoen, *Health and the War on Poverty: A Ten-Year Appraisal* (Washington, DC: Brookings Institution, 1978), 57–58, 90. See also Engel, *Poor People's Medicine,* 115–17, 148–51.

23. Smith, *Health Care Divided,* 148–53.

24. Examples are Ward, *Black Physicians in the Jim Crow South;* Mason with Smith, *Beaches, Blood, and Ballots;* Florence Ridlon, *A Black Physician's Struggle for Civil Rights: Edward C. Mazique, M.D.* (Albuquerque: University of New Mexico Press, 2005); and Douglas L. Conner M.D. with John F. Marszalek, *A Black Physician's Story: Bringing Hope in Mississippi* (Jackson: University Press of Mississippi, 1985).

CHAPTER 1

1. In the 1880 census for Madison County, Alabama, Matt Stewart (spelled with a "d" by the census taker) is listed as a nine-year-old boy, the son of Matt Steward, age 46, farmer, and Charlotte Steward, age 45, farm laborer. In 1910, the son is listed as a farmer, literate, and age 38, and married to Ollie, literate and age 30. The couple by then had been married for fifteen years and had a total of nine children. See Linda Hardiman Smith, *1880 Madison County Alabama Census* (Athens, AL: Limestone County Department of History and Archives, 1996), 34, and *1910 Madison County Alabama Census,* vol. 75, Enumeration District 134, sheet 8. In the 1910 census, Tom Johnson is listed as a black sharecropper, illiterate, and born in 1878. He and Annie by then had a total of six children. See *1910 Madison County Alabama Census,* vol. 74, Enumeration District 112, sheet 9.

2. In the *1880 Madison County Alabama Census,* Hereford's first name appears as "Sawnie," age 35, an illiterate black farmer married to Bettie Hereford, age 22, who "works on farm." Their children are listed as Georgia (George), age 7 (thus born in 1873), and daughter Odell (presumably Annie), age 4 (thus born in 1876). All are reported as having originated in Alabama. By the 1900 census, Hereford's name appears as "Soney" Hereford and by 1920 as "Sonnie" Hereford Sr., distinguishing him from his grandson, Sonnie Hereford Jr., born in 1896. See *1880 Madison County Alabama Census,* vol. 15, Enumeration District 201, sheet 5; *1900 Madison County Alabama Census,* vol. 38, Enumeration District 99, sheet 23, line 89; and *1920 Madison County Alabama Census,* vol. 60, Enumeration District 118, sheet 7.

3. James R. Grossman notes the difficulty of breaking free from debt peonage under the sharecropping system due to vagrancy laws and binding legal contracts that favored the landowner. The best time to move was thus between settlement time around

Christmas and early February, before new debts were incurred. See *Land of Hope: Chicago, Black Southerners, and the Great Migration* (Chicago: University of Chicago Press, 1989), 27.

4. What Hereford witnessed was the continuing exodus of blacks out of the South that had started around 1916. For information on Alabama migration, see Daniel M. Johnson and Rex R. Campbell, *Black Migration in America: A Social Demographic History* (Durham: Duke University Press, 1981), 74–77, 96, 116.

5. For a sketch of the families displaced, see the 2006 report of former Redstone Arsenal staff archaeologist Beverly S. Curry, *The People Who Lived on the Land That Is Now Redstone Arsenal: Pond Beat, Mullins Flat, Hickory Grove, the Union Hill Cumberland Presbyterian Church Area, and the Elko Area*, available in the Heritage Room of the Huntsville-Madison County Public Library.

6. In 1940, the median number of years of schooling for black children in the Deep South was five, compared to 8.5 for whites. See Patterson, *Brown v. Board of Education*, 9, table 6.6, and Anderson, *The Education of Blacks in the South*, 237.

7. Hereford's comments echo those of other young people growing up in the South, like Anne Moody in Centreville, Mississippi, who remembered that white businesses employed black men only as janitors and that jobs for black women were limited to cooking, housecleaning, and babysitting. See *Coming of Age in Mississippi*, 117.

8. The case involved a ten-year-old black child whose heart had stopped beating for two minutes while undergoing surgery at Huntsville Hospital. Drake, working with a white surgeon named Robert C. Bibb, did a quick incision in the child's chest and massaged his heart until his breathing became normal. Both Bibb and Drake received national attention, including a write-up in *Ebony* magazine titled "The Dead Boy Who Came Back to Life."

9. President Harry S Truman had ordered the desegregation of the armed forces in July 1948.

10. "My brother was able to pay the folks at Meharry exactly what he owed, and in a few days he left town for Aunt Susie's place—left town with just seventy-five cents in his pocket. That's all he had. Here was a boy who'd get out there and plow in the hot sun all day long and talk biology up and down the rows, and I can tell you that never at any time was there a poorer black kid who went off to make a doctor than was my brother." Thomas Edward Hereford, interview by Jack D. Ellis, Huntsville, Alabama, 23 June 2000.

CHAPTER 2

1. John Logan Cashin Jr., born in 1928, graduated from Meharry's School of Dentistry in 1952. With Hereford, he would later play a central role in Huntsville's civil rights movement. See the biography by his daughter Sheryll Cashin, *The Agitator's Daughter: A Memoir of Four Generations of One Extraordinary African American Family* (New York: Persus Books Group, 2008).

2. Born in 1902, Rolfe attended Florida A&M College and received his medical degree from Meharry in 1927. After postgraduate work in physiology at the University

of Chicago, he returned to Meharry, eventually becoming chairman of Physiology and Pharmacology and, in 1952, dean of the School of Medicine.

3. Sam Lillard Clark (1898–1960) earned his doctorate in medicine from Vanderbilt in 1930. He later revised and edited *The Anatomy of the Nervous System,* a standard textbook in the field first published in 1920.

4. Born in Iowa, Cazort received his doctorate from Meharry in 1947. After working as a research fellow at the National Institutes of Health, he joined the Meharry faculty in 1948.

5. Walker received his training at Meharry and was named chairman of the Department of Surgery there in 1944. Among his accomplishments was providing surgical services for the Taborian Hospital, located in the all-black town of Mound Bayou, Mississippi, which provided health care for the impoverished blacks of the Mississippi Delta. See Ward, *Black Physicians in the Jim Crow South,* 70–71, 244–48.

6. Born in 1919, Dorothy Lavinia Brown attended Bennett College in North Carolina and received her degree from Meharry in 1948. In 1959, she became the first black woman to be named a fellow of the American College of Surgeons.

7. While death rates from tuberculosis among blacks began to decline after 1900, they were still four times that of whites during the 1960s. According to Edward H. Beardsley, the disease killed three times the number of blacks as whites in North and South Carolina during the 1930s, a fact he ascribes to malnutrition, lack of medical care, and susceptibility to a particularly dangerous form known as miliary TB. See *A History of Neglect,* 13–14, and W. Michael Byrd and Linda A. Clayton, *An American Health Dilemma: Race, Medicine, and Health Care in the United States, 1900–2000* (New York: Routledge, 2002), 231–32.

8. A Fisk graduate, Crump received his degree from Meharry in 1941 and joined the Meharry faculty in 1947, becoming chairman three years later. He was among the first blacks to gain admission to the Nashville Academy of Medicine. Summerville, *Educating Black Doctors,* 122.

9. A rare exception to the neglect of therapeutic resources for black children during the polio epidemic was the Tuskegee Institute Infantile Paralysis Center of the John A. Andrew Memorial Hospital. See Edith Powell and John F. Hume, *A Black Oasis: Tuskegee Institute's Fight against Infantile Paralysis, 1941–1975* (White Plains, NY: March of Dimes Birth Defects Foundation, 2008).

10. In 1956, the all-black Donalson Hospital had fourteen beds, an operating room, X-ray, and labs. Its founder, Meharry graduate Latha M. Donalson (1900–1973), had opened an office in Fayetteville in the early 1930s and soon succeeded in creating the Lincoln County Negro Hospital, essentially one large room with three beds in a private residence. In 1939, he created a more modern hospital, which was destroyed by a tornado in February 1952. A third hospital was dedicated in January 1954. Information on Donalson is taken from assorted documents and newspaper clippings provided by his widow, Claudia Donalson, and from an interview conducted by Jack D. Ellis at Fayetteville on 31 July 1997.

11. According to the unsigned biographical portrait in the papers of Mrs. Donalson, the doctor actually arrived in Fayetteville with the following: "one A.B. degree from

Lincoln University; one M.D. degree from Meharry Medical College; one blue suit, purchased while at Lincoln; one pair of formerly sport shoes, then dyed black; one box of gauze; one box of adhesives; one bottle of liniment; one physician's bag; one tube of catgut; one artery clamp; one needle holder and no railroad fare."

12. Zephaniah Alexander Looby, born in 1899 in the British West Indies, was a Howard University graduate who held law degrees from Columbia and New York University. In addition to his law practice and duties as professor of jurisprudence at Meharry, he was active in Nashville politics and local civil rights causes. During the civil rights protests of 1960, a bomb destroyed his home near the Meharry campus.

13. In addition to Hubbard Hospital, Meharry graduates during Hereford's era traditionally served their internships at Homer G. Phillips (St. Louis); Kansas City General (Missouri); Freedmen's (Washington, D.C.); Harlem Hospital (New York); and Provident (Chicago and Baltimore). See "Howard and Meharry Internship Appointments, 1968–69," *Journal of the National Medical Association,* July 1968.

14. Chicago and its environs attracted great numbers of African Americans from Alabama. See Milton C. Sernett, *Bound for the Promised Land: African American Religion and the Great Migration* (Durham: Duke University Press, 1997), 154–79, and Grossman, *Land of Hope,* 148–49, which includes a map showing that in 1920 Alabama ranked second only to Mississippi as the state of birth for non-white residents of Illinois.

15. On 5 September 1956, Dr. George O. McCalep Sr. wrote to Local Board 137: "I [have] lived in Madison County twenty years and have a keen interest in the Social Welfare of the population of this county. On the bases [*sic*] of my personal observation and experience I sincerely believe that Dr. Hereford's Professional service is needed in Madison County more than any other time since I have lived in this area." Sonnie W. Hereford Papers, UAB Archives, The University of Alabama at Birmingham (hereafter cited as Hereford Papers), 1950s.

CHAPTER 3

1. Hereford's daybook, covering the period 8 October–31 December 1956, offers an example of how fast the practice of a black doctor could grow in areas deprived of practitioners. It totals seventy-three pages and provides information on numbers of patients, fees paid, balances, and daily totals. Only two patients are listed as having medical insurance. Hereford Papers, 1950s.

2. This incident still burned fresh in the mind of Dr. Drake's widow, Geneva Drake Whatley, during my interview with her forty-three years later.

And one evening—now all the doctors were not this way—but one night, the waiters came in and said, Okay, Doc, everything's cleared, so Harold went in and he sat down with . . . Bibb and [Frederick W.] Smith, because they helped him with his surgery. And there were two other doctors sitting at the table across from them, and when Harold sat down, one had a piece of pie, and they had two cups of coffee, and they got up and walked out. And that hurt Harold, Lord have mercy.

He came home and he told me about it. The next day he was making rounds in the Colored Wing, and he met Dr. Grote [Sr.], and Dr. Grote stopped and said, "Boy, um, um, what were you pulling last night?" And Harold didn't say anything. "Well, don't you pull that anymore." Well, I was upstairs making up the bed, and I heard the car come around the drive, and he come up the stairs, and he just fell into my arms, and he cried.

Geneva Drake Whatley, interview by Jack D. Ellis, Huntsville, Alabama, 26 July 1999.

3. Born in 1925, J. Ellis Sparks received his medical degree from The University of Alabama in 1949. He later became professor of internal medicine and then dean at the School of Primary Medical Care in Huntsville.

4. Geneva Drake Whatley, a 1944 nursing graduate of Meharry, went to work in the Colored Wing, or Annex, soon after her husband opened his practice. She lasted only two days: "Now the Annex, they had one room that was set up for surgery. So if there was an accident, *on this table* [she hits the table three times]; if there was a baby born, *on this table* . . . if there was a surgery, *on this table.* So I said, this can't be, because the man would come in, and he would mop, and he would go out. And I questioned it because the first night I was there, there was an accident, and then somebody had a baby, and the only thing we had done was just mopped the floor . . . just put some soap and water and wipe up the floor." Whatley interview.

5. As James Jones notes in *Bad Blood: The Tuskegee Syphilis Experiment,* new and expanded ed. (New York: The Free Press, 1993), 16–29, the attitude among white physicians that blacks were indifferent to their own medical welfare had a long history in Alabama. On the interplay of race, gender, and medical authority, see Susan L. Smith, *Sick and Tired of Being Sick and Tired: Black Women's Health Activism in America, 1890–1950* (Philadelphia: University of Pennsylvania Press, 1995), and Deborah Kuhn McGregor, *Sexual Surgery and the Origins of Gynecology: J. Marion Sims, His Hospital, and His Patients* (New York: Garland, 1989).

6. One letter to Hereford remarks: "I am paying on my past due bill. Thanks for much for your patient [*sic*] and understanding. You have been more than a doctor to me, over the years you have been a real friend. Sometimes when I was hurting so very bad only the help and understanding you gave me heal[ed] my body. I am going to continue to send this payment until my bill is payed [*sic*] in full." Hereford Papers, undated.

7. Hereford's records indicate that he was in attendance from noon until eight o'clock, and that payment in full (fifty dollars) was finally made in March 1981. Hereford Papers, 1950s.

8. Hereford's papers contain a breakdown of his medical expenses during his first months of practice, his largest expenditures being gasoline and automobile maintenance, consultations and professional services, nurse's salary, and medical and office supplies. His typed record of his gross annual income between 1957 and 1962 shows the following: 1957 ($20,621); 1958 ($28,691); 1959 ($28,222); 1960 ($27,404); 1961 ($26,455); 1962 ($31,707). Hereford Papers, 1950s. A survey of black physicians belonging to the National Medical Association that appeared in the January 1970 issue of the *Journal of the National Medical Association* showed that around 56 percent of black doctors living

in the South had gross annual incomes of under $30,000 a year. The heaviest groupings (around 43 percent) fell into the $20,000–40,000 range.

9. The diseases that Hereford encountered are reflected in numerous studies of black health in the United States and included heart disease, hypertension, pulmonary disorders, pneumonia, and diabetes, as well as high infant mortality rates. During the early 1960s, for example, the prevalence of heart disease among black males was 23.8 percent, as opposed to 11.5 for whites. For hypertension, rates were 26.7 versus 12.8. For comparisons on specific diseases, see the tables in Byrd and Clayton, *An American Health Dilemma,* 239, 361, 366–67, 370–71, and Smith, *Health Care Divided,* 210–12.

10. According to the *Huntsville Times* (11 May 1958), Georgia native Gay, a Tulane medical graduate who had served in the U.S. Army Medical Corps during World War II, was an "uncompromising stickler for the observance of sanitary regulations," disliked by café owners and trailer park proprietors alike.

11. Hiram B. Moore, born in 1914, was a 1944 Meharry graduate who practiced medicine for fifty-five years in South Pittsburgh, Tennessee, not far from the Alabama line.

12. Hereford preserved a small, two-volume "Bedside Birth Record Book" for the years 1956, 1957, 1958, and 1959. In his first full year of practice (1957), he did 51 home deliveries. Mothers' ages ranged from 15 to 43, the average being around 26. Of the 28 fathers' occupations noted, 7 were farmers and, except for a single technician at Redstone Arsenal, the rest were at the lowest levels of the city's economy—waiters, janitors, dish washers, truck drivers, street cleaners, tire repairmen, sanitation workers, and cotton seed mill laborers. Hereford Papers, 1950s.

13. See Margaret Charles Smith with Linda Janet Holmes, *Listen to Me Good: The Life Story of an Alabama Midwife* (Columbus: Ohio State University Press, 1996). Holmes notes that despite their long record of success, by 1981 over 150 black midwives had been forced to end their practices under a law approving only those certified by the American College of Nurse-Midwives.

14. See Hugh Pearson's *Under the Knife: How a Wealthy Negro Surgeon Wielded Power in the Jim Crow South* (New York: The Free Press, 2000), which deals with his great-uncle Dr. Joseph Griffin and his highly successful hospital in Bainbridge, Georgia, which provided abortions for blacks and whites.

15. William F. Jordan had received his degree from Jefferson Medical College in 1909. John Howard Lary Sr., a specialist in obstetrics-gynecology, received his doctorate from Tulane in 1935 and opened his practice in Huntsville in 1938. See *Who's Who in Alabama* (Birmingham, AL: Sayers Enterprises, 1972), 3:237.

16. Milton Eugene Whitley, born in 1923, was a 1951 graduate of The University of Alabama Medical School; Charles Selah, born in 1927, received his doctorate from Tulane in 1951; and Thomas Wright, born in 1925, received his from Vanderbilt in 1948.

17. A specialist in obstetrics-gynecology, William Brooks Cameron, born in 1928, received his medical degree from the University of Tennessee in 1952; Horace Bramm Jr., born in 1928, received his doctorate from Tennessee in 1951; Richard Edwin Rice, born in 1936, received his from Tulane in 1961; and Alfred P. Owen, born in 1919, received his doctorate from the Louisiana State University School of Medicine in 1947

and opened his obstetrics-gynecology practice in Huntsville in 1947. See Medical Association of the State of Alabama, *Transactions*, 1965, Madison County, pp. 29–30. See also *Who's Who in Alabama*, vol. 2, and obituary for Owen in the *Huntsville Times*, 16 March 2001.

18. Ephraim Elias Camp, born in 1909, received his medical degree from the University of Tennessee in 1936 and started a radiology practice in Huntsville in 1949.

19. Bibb was a Huntsville native and University of Alabama graduate who had studied medicine at Tulane. A veteran of the U.S. Medical Corps during World War II, he had returned to his hometown and spent forty-six years as a general practitioner. See his obituary in the *Huntsville Times*, 31 October 2000.

20. The beating of John Cashin Jr. is described in the biography by his daughter Sheryll Cashin, *Agitator's Daughter*, 115–16.

CHAPTER 4

1. Katherine Lester, wife of Huntsville pediatrician Richard L. Lester Jr., recalled that when she registered to vote after moving to Huntsville in 1958 she was asked by the registrar to name the colors of the American flag. A black man in line behind her was asked to recite the First Amendment to the U.S. Constitution. Dr. Richard L. Lester Jr., interview by Jack D. Ellis, 20 January 2000, Huntsville, Alabama.

2. A Mississippi native, Virgil M. Howie had moved to Huntsville in 1959 after medical training at Vanderbilt and service as an air force medical officer. The discussion group of which he was a part called itself the Human Relations Council and met in black churches and private homes. Evelyn Howie remembers that it usually had only twenty or so people in attendance. Besides the Cashins, Reverend Bell, and a few other black ministers, members included a small number of whites, such as a local Episcopal rector named Emile Joffrion and his wife, Martha. Dr. Virgil Howie, Evelyn Howie, and Dr. William Goodson, interview by Jack D. Ellis, Huntsville, Alabama, 24 September 1999.

3. John Dittmer's study of the civil rights movement in Mississippi notes the same pattern in communities across the state, where young people "on their own initiative confronted the forces of white supremacy publicly and dramatically." See *Local People*, 89.

4. The editorial congratulated the city on passing its first test in dealing with a movement that had long "plagued" the South and reminded readers that agitators loved violence and publicity. It also reassured them that only "a small fraction of our colored people" would want to go into places where they were not welcome. *Huntsville Times*, 4 January 1962.

5. Titled "It's Time to Call a Halt," the piece declared: "We cannot believe that anything like the majority of the responsible colored citizens here either endorse or support the tactics used. Such demonstrations do serve one purpose. They harm Huntsville's position in the highly competitive race for industrial and intellectual development." *Huntsville Times*, 9 January 1962.

6. An undated mimeographed list of bond signers in Hereford's papers shows that in addition to Hereford, Cashin, and Howie, the bulk of the signers came from

the ranks of black businessmen, including Charles Ray, Howard Barley, Dan Barley, J. H. Slaughter, Frank Jacobs, Nick Fitcheard, R. E. Nelms, Sydney Gurley Jr., Milton Bradley, Aaron Burns, Cary Hammonds, and Rev. Earl McDonald. Hereford Papers, 1960s. Evelyn Howie recalls that the need for people to sign bonds for the arrested students had been discussed in the Human Relations Council and that she herself signed over fifty of them because the house was in her name. Howie, Howie, and Goodson interview.

7. In 1999, Dr. Howie recalled that he had probably lost patients because of his support of the sit-in campaign in 1962, but he said that the fact that the city had only four pediatricians to serve a growing population was in his favor. Howie, Howie, and Goodson interview.

8. The full text of the statement from Huntsville Hospital said the following: "There is no definite evidence of injury detectable at this time: however, the presence of the powdery substance on the skin may obscure abnormal color change. Examination, though not positively excluding the possibility of a transient irritative injury, did exclude any serious injury." *Huntsville Times,* 15 January 1962.

9. The victim of the attack says that the three men were armed and had driven him to a remote area, where he was forced to undress and doused with a caustic substance. According to the emergency room physician, the victim had suffered "first degree and possibly some second degree burns, mainly on the delicate areas of the body." *Huntsville Times,* 24 January 1962.

10. In March 1960, student protesters in Nashville had succeeded in persuading Mayor Ben West to create a biracial committee to address the city's problems. Activists used the same tactic in other cities in 1962 and 1963, including Greenville, South Carolina; Fayetteville, North Carolina; Albany, Georgia; Baton Rouge, Louisiana; and Jackson, Mississippi.

11. Born in Greensboro, North Carolina, in 1927, Randolph T. Blackwell had been involved in civil rights since his student years at North Carolina A&T University during the late 1940s. A law graduate of Howard, he had joined the faculty at Alabama A&M in 1954. See the sketch in Andrew Young, *An Easy Burden: The Civil Rights Movement and the Transformation of America* (New York: HarperCollins, 1996), 279–80.

12. Born in 1928, James M. Lawson Jr. had grown up in Ohio and as a student at Baldwin-Wallace College in Berea had been drawn to nonviolent tactics as a method for social change. During the Korean War, he had served time in federal prison for refusing to cooperate with the draft. After his release, he worked as a Methodist missionary in India, where he continued studying the teachings of Mohandas Gandhi. Later, he studied theology at Oberlin College and then at Vanderbilt, which expelled him for his participation in the Nashville sit-in campaign of 1960. See Lewis, *Walking with the Wind,* 74–79, and Young, *An Easy Burden,* 126–27.

13. Like the hymns sung during Huntsville's mass meetings, the singing of spirituals by student protesters reflected the importance of music in the civil rights movement as a whole, from performers like Odetta to the SNCC Freedom Singers. In the Mississippi Delta, freedom songs drew on both gospel music and the Delta Blues tradition. See Dittmer, *Local People,* 77, 131–32.

14. A 1965 master's thesis by Theresa Powers Shields reported a total of 260 sit-ins with more than 400 people having participated, most of them students. Bond was usually set at $200–300. See "The Acquisition of Civil Rights in Huntsville Alabama from 1962–1965" (master's thesis, Division of Graduate Study, Alabama Agricultural and Mechanical College, 1965), 42–43.

15. On 28 January 1962 the *Huntsville Times* described (on page 2) a large downtown rally and sit-in protests in this way: "About 150 Negroes met on the north steps of the Madison County Courthouse Saturday and sang hymns and said prayers. The meeting lasted fifteen minutes. Throughout the day groups of Negroes took seats at several lunch counters. They were not served. There were no incidents or arrests."

16. In 1999, Charles Younger, Huntsville's city attorney in 1962, said, "We had the best information any community could have. We always knew what type of civil rights demonstration was going to happen before it happened." *Huntsville Times,* 4 December 1999.

17. Huntsville's black churches appear to have been more favorably disposed toward the civil rights movement than in places like Birmingham, where, according to Andrew Young, only fourteen of the city's four hundred black churches were willing to host mass rallies during King's campaign of 1963. In Mississippi, black ministers were largely absent from the ranks of movement leaders. Part of the reason, as John Dittmer explains, was a tradition of white empowerment of black leaders who cooperated with the power structure. See Young, *An Easy Burden,* 208–10, and Dittmer, *Local People,* 75–77.

18. Born in 1924, Vivian had been part of the protests against segregated lunch counters in Peoria, Illinois, in 1947. While a theology student in Nashville during the 1950s, he had studied Gandhi's ideas with James Lawson and helped organize the student sit-in campaign of 1960. Also active in the 1960 campaign was Kelly Miller Smith, a native of Mound Bayou, Mississippi, who had studied at Morehouse College before earning a divinity degree from Howard. In Nashville, he served as pastor of the First Colored Baptist Church, the city's oldest black church. See Lewis, *Walking with the Wind,* 73–74.

19. For an account of the jailing of Martha Hereford and Joan Cashin, see Cashin, *Agitator's Daughter,* 141–45.

20. In one letter sent out in March 1962, Hereford explains that

[w]e have engaged in "Sit-in" demonstrations for about eight weeks now and have had three acts of violence on the part of the other race. I suspect that you have heard little about this. This is my main reason for writing you. The newspaper refuses to print the whole truth and gives only a very small section on the second or third page to this movement. The city officials feel that they have kept this matter quiet, and they have. They know that if the news reaches the outside and especially Washington, there will be outside pressure. This is especially true in as much as this city is considered the "Space capital of the Universe." There are those of us who believe that a sudden influx of letters or phone calls from the outside by our friends will help to exert some pressure on the city officials.

Hereford Papers, 1960s.

CHAPTER 5

1. See the mimeographed report by school superintendent V. M. Burkett, "History of Civil Action Suits Regarding Desegregation of Huntsville City Schools," March 1975, Hereford Papers, 1970s.

2. In his summary of the goals of the committee, Hereford noted that the Supreme Court's decision of 1954 had ruled that school segregation was inherently unequal and that the separation of a black child created a feeling of inferiority that was unlikely ever to be undone. He argued that segregated schools could not train children for the jobs of the future because they lacked facilities. Hereford Papers, 1960s.

3. Melba Pattillo Beals has recalled a similar dwindling in the number of parents willing to challenge segregation at Little Rock's Central High School in 1957: the numbers went from sixteen to nine as the effects of intimidation began to take hold. See *Warriors Don't Cry: The Searing Memory of the Battle to Integrate Little Rock's Central High*, abr. ed. (New York: Simon Pulse, 1995), 25–27.

4. Born in Connecticut in 1921, Constance Baker Motley received her law degree from Columbia Law School in 1946 and became a law clerk at the NAACP's Legal Defense and Education Fund, whose chief counsel was Thurgood Marshall. She was involved in many of the most important civil rights cases in the South during the 1960s and was later named to the federal bench by President Lyndon B. Johnson. She was the first African American woman to hold such a position.

5. *Newsweek,* 23 September 1963. See also *Huntsville Times,* 3–10 September 1963.

6. On other efforts to integrate Alabama schools in September 1963, see Robert J. Norrell, *Reaping the Whirlwind: The Civil Rights Movement in Tuskegee* (New York: Alfred A. Knopf, 1985), 136–52; Glenn T. Eskew, *But for Birmingham: The Local and National Movements in the Civil Rights Struggle* (Chapel Hill: University of North Carolina Press, 1997), 316–24; and Taylor Branch, *Parting the Waters: America in the King Years, 1954–63* (New York: Simon and Schuster, 1988), 888–96.

7. These were among the goals mentioned in an undated memo prepared for the CSC by Hereford. Others included hiring blacks at Southern Bell and other stores and businesses; creating recreational facilities and a black community center; and integrating the YMCA. Hereford Papers, 1960s.

8. Theresa Powers Shields notes some of the ways in which a local group of thirty-two private industries called the Association of Huntsville Area Contractors, led by L. C. Mcmillan, worked to improve job opportunities for blacks. See "The Acquisition of Civil Rights in Huntsville Alabama from 1962–1965," 50–54.

9. For a discussion of physicians involved in the Selma to Montgomery march, see Dittmer, *The Good Doctors,* 87–96. The Medical Committee for Human Rights sent a total of six doctors and three nurses to assist the marchers, having failed to consult any of Alabama's black physicians.

10. Part of President Lyndon B. Johnson's War on Poverty, both programs were designed to assist low-income families—Head Start, to assist preschool children in the areas of health, nutrition, and counseling; and Upward Bound, to prepare high school

students for college through preparatory classes, tutoring, and math and science education.

11. While Hereford and the other parents named in the suit against the City Board of Education had won their case in 1963, the court issued a detailed plan for desegregation only in 1970, following years of appeals. By 2003, Huntsville remained one of 375 school systems nationwide still under court order. See *Huntsville Times*, 31 August 2003.

CHAPTER 6

1. A native of Mobile and a 1970 law graduate of The University of Alabama, Charles Allen Graddick had been elected attorney general in November 1978. He served in that position until 1987.

2. Hereford faced a total of forty-six counts—one for each patient cited in the indictment—for allegedly filing false claims to Medicaid, punishable under the Code of Alabama by a fine of $10,000 and one to five years in prison for each violation. See *Huntsville Times*, 17 August 1979.

3. The letter, dated 17 December 1981 and written by the manager of Utilization Review/Cost Containment at Blue Cross Blue Shield, indicates that the records provided by Hereford "verify that you or one of your associates rendered daily inpatient services to the Blue Shield subscribers we previously questioned." It instructed him to disregard an earlier request for reimbursement in the amount of $327.07. Hereford Papers, 1980s.

4. The petition got more than three thousand signatures. While acknowledging that the Medicaid fraud charges were serious, it stressed Hereford's importance to the black community: "I do not feel, if by chance found guilty, that Dr. Hereford should receive or even be considered for the maximum penalty of imprisonment or expulsion from the Medical Profession due to the years of his dedication to our community." Hereford Papers, 1980s.

5. On 2 August 1979, Alabama A&M president R. D. Morrison wrote of Hereford, "His professional service, to a large extent, has been with low-income Black clientele who often had very little, if any, funds with which to pay doctor bills." A lease manager for an automobile agency praised his medical services to young boxers on the Huntsville Golden Gloves Boxing team, for which he had never charged. An undated letter from a pharmaceutical representative called Hereford "one of the finest doctors I know" and added, "If for whatever reason Dr. Hereford loses his license, it will not only be a great personal injustice, but will be an enormous loss to the city of Huntsville." Hereford Papers, 1980s.

6. As part of the plea bargain, the remaining forty-four accounts in the original indictment were dropped. Hereford was to be placed on thirty-six months' probation and was ordered to pay $80,000 to Medicaid in restitution, with a deadline for payment of 5 August, six months following the guilty plea. *Huntsville Times*, 6 February 1980.

7. On 16 April 1980, the attorney for the Alabama State Board of Medical Exam-

iners presented a motion to the board that it hear a complaint on 21 May against Hereford regarding the Medicaid fraud conviction and that, following the hearing, the board revoke his license to practice or any other action deemed appropriate. Hereford Papers, 1980s.

8. The Committee for S. W. Hereford III M.D. was made up of thirty-two prominent figures from the black churches, the business community, and Oakwood College and Alabama A&M. Members included civil rights activist R. C. Adams; A&M professors Henry Bradford and Bessie W. Jones; and clergymen Charles F. Thomas and L. F. Lacy. Several black funeral homes, black fraternities and sororities, and at least half a dozen local white physicians also contributed money to Hereford's defense. Hereford Papers, 1980s.

9. A letter of 15 May 1981 from the Parole and Probation Office to the Alabama State Board of Medical Examiners stressed that though Hereford had fallen behind in his monthly payments, he had demonstrated a good attitude and was trying hard to meet his obligations. It noted that during the first quarter of 1981, he had reported an income of $23,312, with expenses of $21,845. A few days later, Hereford provided further specifics, noting that between 19 February and 19 May he had seen a total of 1,627 patients. About a quarter of these, he said, were Medicaid or Medicare patients. Hereford Papers, 1980s.

10. On 7 December 1988, Hereford wrote to the executive director of the Alabama State Board of Medical Examiners, pointing out that on pages 43–44 of the *Guide to Controlled Substances Regulations,* Lortab (along with such painkillers as Darvocet, Wygesic, Talwin, and others) was permitted in Schedule IV. Hereford Papers, 1980s.

11. The order to revoke Hereford's medical license came on 3 February 1993. From a review of twenty-two patient files, the commission had concluded that in the majority of those cases, "the sole treatment rendered was a prescription for controlled substances which have the potential for producing drug dependence" and that there had not been appropriate follow-up and monitoring of each patient. Hereford Papers, 1990s.

12. In a letter of 8 February 1993, the chairman of the Medical Licensure Commission wrote to Hereford that the commission "is not unsympathetic to your situation and we want you to know that we feel that it is possible for you to regain your license. However, we feel that extensive remedial training will be necessary." Hereford Papers, 1990s.

13. Letter of 17 May 1994 from James E. Chandler, professor and chief of medicine at The University of Alabama School of Medicine in Huntsville. Chandler noted that he had known Hereford for fifteen years, starting in the emergency room of Huntsville Hospital, and that while he did not know what had caused the revocation of his license, he had always provided care to a large number of black patients in the community: "I always felt that he was a good man and provided [an] extraordinary amount of time to our needy patients." Hereford Papers, 1990s.

14. "My father," Martha [Kita] Hereford told the commission,

has always been loving to our family, he cares about his community, and he was a wonderful physician. I am aware that he may not have always used the best judgment in his practice but I think you can agree with me when I say that none of us are perfect. . . . I can honestly say that I have seen my father suffer these last few years. I have watched as everything he and my mother worked to build has come crashing down. But do you know what else I have seen? I have seen a man who wanted to make amends so badly that he took as many of the assigned courses as possible, despite a lack of funds and physical ailments. I have seen a man who loves Medicine so much that he took on a biology teaching position and has worked hard to rebuild his sense of usefulness. But most of all, I have seen a man of whom I am still proud and whom I love very much.

Hereford Papers, 1990s

AFTERWORD

1. In May of the same year, Hereford was named guest of honor at the fiftieth reunion of his graduating class at Meharry. The *Huntsville Times* featured a front-page account, along with the now familiar photograph of Hereford and his son leaving the Fifth Avenue Elementary School in September 1963. *Huntsville Times,* 21 May 2005.

2. Dittmer, *The Good Doctors,* 133–37.

3. Huntsville's white physicians appear to have been well aware of repeated surgical malpractice in the city. "One of the reasons we got a pathologist," one later recalled, "is that we sent appendixes over to Memphis, and they'd put out a diagnosis that [it] wasn't appendicitis. We couldn't have control of bad surgery if we didn't have pathologists." Dr. William A. Kates Jr., interview by Jack D. Ellis, Huntsville, Alabama, 28 February 2001.

4. Byrd and Clayton, *An American Health Dilemma,* 320–21, 414–15.

5. Recalling his struggle to be admitted as the first black into the Jefferson County Medical Society in 1962, Dr. James T. Montgomery of Birmingham remembered its officers admonishing him to keep silent about his acceptance: "They didn't want other people to know. They were afraid not of the black people or of the white people. They were afraid of the conservative medical doctors. In my mind, the most conservative people in Alabama have been the lawyers, and the next most conservative have been the physicians . . . the group that thought you never should have opened the doors." James T. Montgomery, interview by Jack D. Ellis, Birmingham, Alabama, 28 October 1998.

6. "The time that frequently most black people could come to the doctor's office was after they had been to work that day, because they would need the transportation to get to and from work, and if they had a family member, they had to wait. The family member had of necessity to wait at home so they could pick him up and bring him back to the doctor. So, as a matter of fact, this meant that the doctor's office hours were very strange . . . all day, and then way into the night, quite often, eight, nine or ten o'clock at night." Dr. Dodson M. Curry, interview by Jack D. Ellis, Birmingham, Alabama, 21 July 1999.

7. Clement P. Cotter to Edward D. Boston, administrator, Huntsville Hospital, 1 October 1979. Hereford Papers, 1970s.

8. See the letters to the *Journal of the National Medical Association* 59 (September 1967) in response to a 31 March 1967 article appearing in *Time,* which had quoted excerpts from a recent article on black colleges by Harvard sociologists Christopher Jenks and David Riesman stating that Meharry and Howard were ranked among the worst medical schools in the county.

9. Henry N. Pontell, Paul Jesilow, Gilbert Geis, and Mary Jane O'Brien, "A Demographic Portrait of Physicians Sanctioned by the Federal Government for Fraud and Abuse against Medicare and Medicaid," *Medical Care* 23 (August 1985): 1028–31.

10. Dr. Rios also noted that the authors had made no effort to compare Medicaid fraud with that to private insurers. See *JAMA* 267 (15 April 1992): 2037, and 266 (18 December 1991): 3318–22.

11. See Andrew Julien and Jack Dolan, "Med Schools: Four That Flunk," and "Black Medical Schools Struggle to Compete," *Hartford Courant,* 29 and 30 June 2003.

12. See the comments of National Association of Medicine president Natalie Carroll and cardiologists Malcolm P. Taylor and B. Waine King in *ABC* [Association of Black Cardiologists] *Newsletter* 29 (Summer 2003).

13. Dodson M. Curry, a Meharry graduate who began practicing on Birmingham's Avenue North in 1950, cited the names of several Birmingham black doctors who had lost their licenses in the wake of drug investigations. He also related several instances in which he himself was visited by whites in search of pain relief and who he had reason to believe were actually agents from state drug enforcement authorities. Curry interview.

14. The 11 percent figure appears to be close to the mark, even though the numbers on which it is based include everyone who has had a license to practice in Alabama from 1993, when the database was created, to 2007. When the database was created, the Medical Association of the State of Alabama provided additional names going back to 1960, when many black doctors were still not members of the state association. My thanks to Mr. Ron Hunter of the Alabama Board of Medical Examiners for providing this information.

15. Public Action Reports of Alabama Board of Medical Examiners, *Newsletter* 19–22 (2005–7). Additional documentation on individual cases is provided online at http://www.albme.org.

16. Sidney Wolfe, Phyllis McCarthy, Alana Bame, and Benita Marcus Adler, *Questionable Doctors Disciplined by State and Federal Governments: Alabama, Georgia* (Washington, DC: Public Citizen Health Research Group, 2000), Al-1–48.

17. In several of the cases involving black doctors who eventually lost their licenses, the alleged offenses involved behavior that unquestionably rendered them unfit to practice. Examples included mental disorders, unexcused absences while on emergency room duty, credit card fraud, illegal use of a social security number, and sexual misconduct involving patients.

Bibliography

GENERAL STUDIES DEALING WITH AFRICAN AMERICAN HEALTH CARE AND THE HISTORY OF BLACK PHYSICIANS

The history of minorities in American medicine has been a subject of intensifying interest over the last few years. Among the best overall studies is that of W. Michael Byrd and Linda A. Clayton, *An American Health Dilemma: Race, Medicine, and Health Care in the United States, 1900–2000* (New York: Routledge, 2002), which includes chapters and tables on the inequalities in health and welfare between blacks and whites, and David Barton Smith, *Health Care Divided: Race and Healing a Nation* (Ann Arbor: University of Michigan Press, 1999).

A source of extraordinary richness is the *Journal of the National Medical Association,* founded in 1909. The publication features scientific articles as well as news on state and local affiliates, black medical and nursing schools, biographies, and obituaries. Volumes for the years 1909–2007, often difficult for scholars to locate in past years, are now available online at http://www.ncbi.nlm.nih.gov/pmc/journals/655/.

An excellent study of African American physicians is that of Thomas J. Ward Jr., *Black Physicians in the Jim Crow South* (Fayetteville: University of Arkansas Press, 2003), which focuses on New Orleans; Wilmington, North Carolina; Mound Bayou, Mississippi; Columbia, South Carolina; and Knoxville, Tennessee. A pioneer in African American medical history is Todd L. Savitt, who has authored or coedited numerous books in the field, starting with *Medicine and Slavery: The Diseases and Health Care of Blacks in Antebellum Virginia* (Urbana: University of Illinois Press, 1978). Savitt's "Entering a White Profession: Black Physicians in the New South, 1880–1920," *Bulletin of the History of Medicine* 61 (1987): 507–40, is one of numerous articles by him on topics ranging from black medical schools to the history of sickle-cell anemia.

Of special importance in depicting the link between health and social status is Edward H. Beardsley's *A History of Neglect: Health Care for Blacks and Mill Workers in the Twentieth-Century South* (Knoxville: University of Tennessee Press, 1987). Beardsley's "Making Separate, Equal: Black Physicians and the Problems of Medical Segregation in the Pre–World War II South," *Bulletin of the History of Medicine* 57 (Fall 1983): 382–96, is likewise useful.

Among the best autobiographies by black physicians are Florence Ridlon, *A Black Physician's Struggle for Civil Rights: Edward C. Mazique, M.D.* (Albuquerque: University of New Mexico Press, 2005); Gilbert R. Mason M.D. with James Patterson Smith, *Beaches, Blood, and Ballots: A Black Doctor's Civil Rights Struggle* (Jackson: University Press of Mississippi, 2000); and Douglas L. Conner M.D. with John F. Marszalek, *A Black Physician's Story: Bringing Hope in Mississippi* (Jackson: University Press of Mississippi, 1985).

ALABAMA MEDICAL HISTORY, BLACK HEALTH-CARE PRACTITIONERS

Though it includes little about Alabama's black populations, Howard L. Holley, *A History of Medicine in Alabama* (Birmingham: The University of Alabama School of Medicine, 1982), offers useful information on medical education, clinical developments, and state medical leaders. J. Mack Lofton Jr.'s *Healing Hands: An Alabama Medical Mosaic* (Tuscaloosa: The University of Alabama Press, 1995) features numerous oral histories of practitioners, including several black doctors.

Among the most important primary sources are the *Transactions* of the Medical Association of the State of Alabama, which provide articles and summaries of yearly activities, plus county membership rosters that include the names, dates of birth, medical schools attended, and specialties for each member. Black physicians are listed under the heading "non-member" with the designation "col." after the names. Because Meharry Medical College in Nashville trained the vast majority of black physicians practicing in Alabama, valuable insight can be found in James Summerville's *Educating Black Doctors: A History of Meharry Medical College* (Tuscaloosa: The University of Alabama Press, 1983).

The pseudoscientific racism that characterized much of Alabama's medical past is treated in several studies, including Reginald Horsman, *Josiah Nott of Mobile: Southerner, Physician, and Racial Theorist* (Baton Rouge: Louisiana State University Press, 1978); Deborah Kuhn McGregor, *Sexual Surgery and the Origins of Gynecology: J. Marion Sims, His Hospital, and His Patients* (New York: Garland, 1989); and Gary Michael Dorr, "Defective or Disabled?: Race, Medicine, and Eugenics in Progressive Era Virginia and Alabama," *Journal of the Gilded Age and Progressive Era* 5 (October 2006): 359–92.

For the Tuskegee syphilis experiment, see James H. Jones, *Bad Blood: The Tuskegee Syphilis Experiment,* new and expanded ed. (New York: The Free Press, 1993), as well as Susan M. Reverby, ed., *Tuskegee's Truths: Rethinking the Tuskegee Syphilis Study* (Chapel Hill: University of North Carolina Press, 2000) and *Examining Tuskegee: The Infamous Syphilis Study and Its Legacy* (Chapel Hill: University of North Carolina Press, 2009).

Additional information on Tuskegee's role in Alabama's medical history is found in Vanessa Northington Gamble, *Making a Place for Ourselves: The Black Hospital Movement, 1920–1945* (New York: Oxford University Press, 1995), which traces the early struggles for control of the Tuskegee Veterans Hospital. Susan L. Smith's *Sick and Tired of Being Sick and Tired: Black Women's Health Activism in America, 1890–1950* (Philadelphia: University of Pennsylvania Press, 1995) details Tuskegee's leadership in the black health movement of the early twentieth century. For further reading, see the excellent biography by Robert J. Norrell, *Up from History: The Life of Booker T. Washington* (Cambridge, MA: Harvard University Press, 2009).

For midwifery, see Margaret Charles Smith with Linda Janet Holmes, *Listen to Me Good: The Life Story of an Alabama Midwife* (Columbus: Ohio State University Press, 1996); Gertrude Jacinta Fraser, *African American Midwifery in the South: Dialogues of Birth, Race, and Memory* (Cambridge, MA: Harvard University Press, 1998); and Onnie Lee Logan as told to Katherine Clark, *Motherwit: An Alabama Midwife's Story* (New York: E. P. Dutton, 1989).

Where Alabama's black doctors are concerned, the oral histories that I conducted between 1997 and 2002 are being made available at the Medical Archives of The University of Alabama in Birmingham as transcriptions are completed. There are around fifty interviews (sixty-eight ninety-minute cassette tapes) with black practitioners or their surviving family members, including a dozen or so retired Meharry faculty, some of whom had Alabama roots.

In addition, A. J. Wright, associate professor and director of the Section on the History of Anesthesia in the Department of Anesthesiology Library at The University of Alabama at Birmingham, provides Web-based information on Alabama's black physicians before World War I. For an example, see http://sites.google.com/site/earlyblackdocsalabama/.

THE CIVIL RIGHTS MOVEMENT IN ALABAMA, MEMOIRS, ORAL HISTORIES

Events in Alabama figure largely in Taylor Branch's trilogy on America during the civil rights era. The books are *Parting the Waters: America in the King Years, 1954–63* (New York: Simon and Schuster, 1988); *Pillar of Fire: America in the King Years, 1963–65* (New York: Simon and Schuster, 1998); and *At*

Canaan's Edge: America in the King Years, 1965–68 (New York: Simon and Schuster, 2006).

Frye Gaillard's *Cradle of Freedom: Alabama and the Movement That Changed America* (Tuscaloosa: The University of Alabama Press, 2004) provides an overview of events, while other studies focus on particular cities or events. Examples are Robert J. Norrell, *Reaping the Whirlwind: The Civil Rights Movement in Tuskegee* (New York: Alfred A. Knopf, 1985); Glenn T. Eskew, *But for Birmingham: The Local and National Movements in the Civil Rights Struggle* (Chapel Hill: University of North Carolina Press, 1997); Andrew M. Manis, *A Fire You Can't Put Out: The Civil Rights Life of Birmingham's Reverend Fred Shuttlesworth* (Tuscaloosa: The University of Alabama Press, 1999); Charles E. Connerly, *"The Most Segregated City in America": City Planning and Civil Rights in Birmingham* (Charlottesville: University of Virginia Press, 2005); Fred Gray, *Bus Ride to Justice: Changing the System by the System* (Montgomery, AL: Black Belt Press, 1995); Charles W. Eagles, *Outside Agitator: Jon Daniels and the Civil Rights Movement in Alabama* (Chapel Hill: University of North Carolina Press, 1993); and Mary Stanton, *From Selma to Sorrow: The Life and Death of Viola Liuzzo* (Athens: University of Georgia Press, 1998).

Though its focus is neighboring Mississippi, John Dittmer's *Local People: The Struggle for Civil Rights in Mississippi* (Urbana: University of Illinois Press, 1995) describes many of the patterns of civil rights activities seen at the local level during the struggles in Alabama. On the state's political climate at that time, see Dan T. Carter, *The Politics of Rage: George Wallace, the Origins of the New Conservatism, and the Transformation of American Politics* (New York: Simon and Schuster, 1995).

A fascinating account of the era leading up to the civil rights movement can be found in John Egerton, *Speak Now Against the Day: The Generation before the Civil Rights Movement in the South* (New York: Alfred A. Knopf, 1994).

The civil rights movement has produced a rich variety of memoirs. Examples include John Lewis with Michael D'Orso, *Walking with the Wind: A Memoir of the Movement* (San Diego: Harcourt Brace and Company, 1998); Andrew Young, *An Easy Burden: The Civil Rights Movement and the Transformation of America* (New York: HarperCollins, 1996); and Anne Moody, *Coming of Age in Mississippi* (New York: Delta Trade Paperbacks, 2004).

Examples for Alabama include J. L. Chestnut Jr. and Julia Cass, *Black in Selma: The Uncommon Life of J. L. Chestnut, Jr.* (New York: Farrar, Straus and Giroux, 1990); Sheyann Webb and Rachel West Nelson, *Selma, Lord, Selma: Girlhood Memories of the Civil Rights Days* (Tuscaloosa: The University of Alabama Press, 1980); and Sheryll Cashin, *The Agitator's Daughter: A Memoir of Four Generations of One Extraordinary African-American Family* (New York: Persus Books Group, 2008).

The expanding field of civil rights oral history is one of the most encouraging steps toward documenting America's history of race relations, and several universities maintain Web sites that make interviews and transcriptions available. One example is the Civil Rights Documentation Project at the University of Southern Mississippi, where transcripts can be accessed at http://www.usm.edu/crdp/html/transcripts.shtml.

Index